Pass the 63 ™

A Training Guide for the NASAA Series 63 Exam

A comprehensive study guide for passing the
NASAA Series 63 "Uniform Securities Agent State Law Exam"

3rd Edition

by

Robert Walker

FIRST BOOKS ®

PORTLAND • OREGON
FIRSTBOOKS.COM

www.firstbooks.com

ISBN-13 978-0-912301-95-2
ISBN-10 0-912301-95-3

Publisher: First Books®

Printed in the U.S.A.
All paper is acid free and meets all ANSI standards for archival quality paper.

First Books is a signer of the Treatise on Responsible Paper Use, guided by the Green Press Initiative. Our printers have received certification through one or all of the following sustainable forest management organizations: the Forest Stewardship Council (FSC), the Sustainable Forestry Initiative (SFI) and the Program for the Endorsement of Forest Certification (PEFC). Certification through these organizations ensures that our company and our printers maintain a high standard of environmental responsibility by sourcing paper from sustainable forests and by providing long-term protection for the wildlife, plants and water quality within these forests and beyond.

Contents at a Glance

Detailed Table of Contents

The Big Picture

If you are studying for the Series 63 exam, you are attempting to register to sell securities or provide investment advice. That means you belong to the majority of professionals who play by the rules. For most people, ripping off investors is not part of the business plan. However, for a small but active minority, ripping off investors is the name of the game. How do they do it? Usually, they gain referrals from investors' friends, ministers, book club members, etc. The regulators call this "affinity fraud," because the scam artist likes to talk to investors who are referred by someone with whom they feel an "affinity" or connection. If Pastor Paulson introduces the nice, young man in the blue suit attending this Sunday's coffee hour, chances are the congregation will let the salesman into their home when he "follows up" on Monday. What happens next is often a long, drawn-out ordeal in which people who can least afford to lose money end up watching their life savings disappear. Virtually every state has sickening examples of senior citizens who turn over their savings to some scam artist, who tells them the money is going into a stock, bond, or mutual fund when, in fact, the money goes straight into the guy's bank account.

The state regulators have one mission—to provide necessary protection to investors. Notice how they do not have a second mission of making sure that agents, investment advisers, and broker-dealers are protected—you are not protected under your state's securities law as an agent, broker-dealer, or adviser. Only the investor is protected. You simply watch your p's and q's, file your required paperwork, pay your fees on time, and maybe—just maybe—you'll be *allowed* to sell securities or provide investment advice within a particular state.

Before your state *allows* you to sell securities or provide investment advice, they want you to prove that you have some knowledge of the industry. After passing your exams, you will submit a U-4 or a Form ADV, which will disclose your residential and employment history and any disciplinary or criminal problems in your past. If you were convicted of armed robbery four years ago, your chance of getting licensed as an investment adviser or securities agent is about as high as the chance of the Chicago

Cubs facing the Chicago White Sox in the World Series this year—could happen, but I wouldn't bet any actual money on it.

Speaking of Chicago, the office of the Illinois Securities Administrator is located at 69 West Washington Street, about a 20-minute El ride from my office. I often attend the public hearings held by the Illinois Securities Department when they're trying to officially determine that someone's license should be denied, suspended, or revoked after mistreating investors or filing false documents with the State. The hearings are held at a conference table in the Securities Administrator's office. The State hires an independent hearing officer, who is an attorney specializing in this area of the law. He doesn't wear a black robe or a powdered wig, and no one cries "Hear ye, hear ye" when he enters the room. Remember—it's not a court case. It's an Administrative hearing. The Securities Administrator sends one of their attorneys to the hearing, and the "respondent' to the allegations usually comes in with an attorney as well. The hearing officer listens to the State's arguments and also the arguments of the respondent's attorneys. He examines the evidence presented by both sides, listens to the testimony of witnesses on both sides of the issue, and then recommends appropriate enforcement action to the state.

Recently, I attended a hearing that arose after a very nice woman cut a large check to the wrong person. The Securities Administrator's office was represented by one of their enforcement attorneys. The investor who cut the large check was there to give her sworn testimony. The hearing officer was there. I was there. Regrettably, the only person who wasn't there was the guest of honor, the respondent.

Not a problem. The hearing officer determined that proper notice had been sent to the respondent, and that the hearing would go forward without him. So, the enforcement attorney for the State of Illinois Securities Department presented his case, complete with exhibits that included a copy of the check and a copy of the promissory note that was sold to the investor. The investor told the hearing officer her sad story, and after about 10 minutes, the hearing was over.

We're going to look at the official version momentarily, but since attorneys write in the same hard-to-read legalese used on the Series 63 exam, I'll give a brief summary first. This is what happened, as I understand it. An investor in her 50's was referred by a friend to a man who was apparently quite the real estate wheeler-dealer. The guy said he was in the business of buying and rehabbing properties and talked the investor into cutting a check for $50,000 in order to finance construction of a house. He "secured" the investment of $50,000 with a "promissory note" that promised to pay interest monthly at an annual rate of 20%. Unfortunately, the investor never received one interest payment on her money, and then couldn't seem to get back the money at all.

Not to worry. Even though she hadn't received any money, the guy told her she was listed as the owner on the house that was rehabbed with her $50,000. So, not surprisingly, she asked several times to see the thing. Unfortunately, the respondent repeatedly cancelled appointments and never actually showed her that an actual house was ever actually built with the money he took from her. In short, she cut this guy a check for $50,000, and that was the last she would ever see of that money.

The reason that the Securities Administrator had any authority over the real estate deal is that the respondent secured the loan with a "promissory note," which meets the definition of a *security*. And, with the word "promissory" right there in the name, the person who borrows money by issuing a "promissory note" *promises* to repay you. If he takes your money based on this promise, says nothing about a chance of default or risk, and then does *not* pay you, you have been defrauded. Securities fraud involves the wrongful taking of money or property through false pretenses when offering or selling securities. The Securities Administrator is primarily out to protect investors from fraudulent, deceptive offers and sales of securities, and this one provides a textbook example of exactly that.

Okay, so you have the background, but in order to prepare for the Series 63 you'll have to be able to translate legalese back to English. So, let's have you take a look at the actual notice of hearing in order to help you sharpen your skills. Don't be scared by the legalese. This book is written in Plain English, as you were told by your friend or your co-worker. But, we also have to show you the original legalistic version of various laws and securities regulations. Rest assured—we will always translate the legalese back into a language you are more familiar with—English.

STATE OF ILLINOIS
SECRETARY OF STATE
SECURITIES DEPARTMENT

_____)
)
IN THE MATTER OF: MORTGAGE SPECIALIST INC.>RILEY,)Case No.
MICHAEL J., PRESIDENT   )0700376
_____)
)

NOTICE OF HEARING

TO RESPONDENT: Michael J. Riley
3-a General Sheridan Ct.
Apple River, Illinois 61001

The Mortgage Specialists
1550 Spring Road #310
Oak Brook, IL 60523

Trust One Mortgage f/k/a The Mortgage Specialists
430 W. Erie St. Suite # 205
Chicago, Illinois 60610

You are hereby notified that pursuant to Section 11.F of the Illinois Securities Law of 1953 [815 ILCS 5] (the "Act") and 14 Ill. Adm. Code 130, Subpart K, a public hearing will be held at 69 West Washington Street, Suite 1220, Chicago, Illinois 60602, on the 25th day of January, 2008, at the hour of 10:00 a.m., or as soon as possible thereafter, before James L. Kopecky, Esq., or such other duly designated Hearing Officer of the Secretary of State.

Said hearing will be held to determine whether an Order shall be entered which would prohibit Michael J. Riley ("Respondent") from engaging in the business of selling or offering for sale securities in the State of Illinois, and/or granting such other relief as may be authorized under the Act including but not limited to the imposition of a monetary fine in the maximum amount pursuant to Section 11.E of the Act, payable within ten (10) business days of the entry of the Order.

The grounds for such proposed action are as follows:

1. That Michael J. Riley, ("Respondent") is an individual whose last known address is 3-a General Sheridan Ct., Apple River, Illinois 61001.

2. That The Mortgage Specialists ("Mortgage Specialists"), is a business entity with the last known address of 1550 Spring Road, #310, Oak Brook, Illinois 60523.

3. That Trust One Mortgage f/k/a The Mortgage Specialists ("Trust One") is a business entity with the last known address of 430 W. Erie St., Suite #205, Chicago, Illinois 60610.

4. That in or around March 2004, Respondent met with Illinois Investor at the office of The Mortgage Specialists. At the meeting Respondent represented to Illinois Investor that he was the President of The Mortgage Specialists. Respondent also told Illinois Investor that he was in the business of buying and rehabilitating homes for people in financial distress, and that Illinois Investor could make a profit by providing Respondent with a loan of $50,000 to purchase a property located in Diamond Lake, Illinois. The loan was to be secured by a promissory note.

5. That on or around March 30, 2004, Respondent traveled to Illinois Investor's home and collected a $50,000 check from Illinois Investor. Respondent told Illinois Investor to make the check payable

to Roscara Capital, Inc. ("Roscara"), stating that he was also the president of Roscara.

6.   That in exchange of the $50,000 check, Respondent secured the loan with a promissory note, which was signed by Respondent and Illinois Investor on March 30, 2004,

7.   That the promissory note states that Respondent promised to pay the principal of the loan plus interest to Illinois Investor by the "maturity date" of August 1, 2004. Respondent was to pay interest to Illinois Investor on a monthly basis at a yearly rate of 20% beginning April 1, 2004. Respondent was to make those payments every month until he had paid all of the principal and interest and any other charges that he owed under the note. The monthly payments were to be applied to interest before principal, and if he still owed amounts after the "maturity date", he would make monthly payments to Illinois Investor in the amount of $833.00.

Failure to Register

8.   That the activities set forth in paragraphs 4 through 6 above constitute the offer and sale of a note, and therefore a security as those terms are defined at Sec. 2.1, 2.5, and 2.5a of the Illinois Securities Law of 1953 (815 ILCS 5) (the "Act").

9.   That Section 5 of the Act states, inter alia, that all securities except those set forth under Section 2a of this Act, or those exempt under Section 3 of this Act, or those offered or sold in transactions exempt under Section 4 of this Act, or face amount certificate contracts required to

be registered under Section 6 of this Act, shall be registered as hereinafter in this section provided, prior to their offer or sale in this State.

10. That Respondent failed to file with the Secretary of State an application for registration of the security described above as required by the Act and that as a result the security was not registered pursuant to Section 5 of the Act prior to its offer and sale in the State of Illinois.

11. That Section 12.A of the Act provides it shall be a violation of the provisions of this Act for any person to offer or sell any security except in accordance with the provisions of this Act.

12. That Section 12.D of the Act provides, *inter alia,* that it shall be a violation of the provisions of this Act for any person to fail to file with the Secretary of State any application, report or document required to be filed under the provisions of this Act or any rule or regulation made by the Secretary of State pursuant to this Act or to fail to comply with the terms of any order of the Secretary of State issued pursuant to Section 11 hereof.

Fraud or Deceit/Misrepresentations or Ommissions

13. That Illinois Investor has not received the principal Respondent promised to pay on the note, nor has Illinois Investor received any of the promised interest payments Respondent was to begin paying on April 1, 2004, nor was she advised of any risk to repayment of principal or payment of interest. In addition, Respondent has persistently failed and refused to show Illinois

Investor the property located in Diamond Lake, Illinois, despite numerous requests made by Illinois Investor to see it.

14. That Section 12.F of the Act provides that it shall be a violation of the provisions of this Act for any person to engage in any transaction, practice or course of business in connection with the sale or purchase of securities which works or tends to work a fraud or deceit upon the purchaser or seller thereof.

15. That Section 12.G of the Act provides that it shall be a violation of the provisions of this Act for any person to obtain money or property through the sale of securities by means of any untrue statement of a material fact or any omission to state a material fact necessary in order to make the statements made, in the light of the circumstances under which they were made, not misleading.

16. That by virtue of the foregoing, Respondent has violated Sections 12.A, D, F, and G of the Act.

17. That Section 11.E(2) of the Act provides, *inter alia,* if the Secretary of State shall find that any person has violated sub-section A, D, F, or G of Section 12 of this Act, the Secretary of State may by written order permanently prohibit or suspend the person from offering or selling any securities, any mineral investment contract, or any mineral deferred delivery contract in this state, provided that any person who is the subject of an order of permanent prohibition may petition the Secretary of State for a hearing to present evidence of rehabilitation or change in

circumstances justifying the amendment or termination of the order or permanent prohibition.

18. That by virtue of the foregoing violations of sub-sections 12.A, D, F, and G, Respondent is subject to an order of permanent prohibition from offering or selling any securities in the this state pursuant to Section 11.F(2) of the Act.

19. That Section 11.E(4) of the Act provides, inter alia, that in addition to any other sanction or remedy contained in this subsection E, the Secretary of State, after finding that any provision of this Act has been violated, may impose a fine as provided by rule, regulation or order not to exceed $10,000, for each violation of this Act, may issue an order of public censure against the violator, and may charge as costs of investigation all reasonable expenses, including attorney's fees and witness fees.

20. That by virtue of the foregoing, Respondent is subject to a fine, censure and costs of investigation pursuant to Section 11.E(4) of the Act.

You are further notified that you are required pursuant to Section 130.1104 of the Rules and Regulations (14 Ill. Adm. Code 130) (the "Rules"), to file an answer to the allegations outlined above within thirty (30) days of the receipt of this notice. A failure to file an answer within the prescribed time shall be construed as an admission of the allegations contained in the Notice of Hearing.

Furthermore, you may be represented by legal counsel; may present evidence; may crossexamine witnesses and otherwise participate. A failure to so appear shall constitute default, unless any Respondent has upon due notice moved for and obtained a continuance.

A copy of the Rules, promulgated under the Act and pertaining to Hearings held by the Office of the Secretary of State, Securities Department, is included with this Notice.

Delivery of notice to the designated representative of any Respondent constitutes service upon such Respondent.

Dated: This 7th day of December 2007.

JESSE WHITE
Secretary of State
State of Illinois

So, now what is this investor supposed to do about her $50,000? She can use the findings of the Securities Administrator to sue the guy, but if he's the sort who won't show up at his own hearing, he's not likely to show up in civil court, and he's not likely to pay the default judgment that the court would probably order him to pay.

What about the guy who took her money? How come he isn't in jail? First, the securities Administrator is not a criminal prosecutor—they're just the officials who can require agents, broker-dealers, investment advisers, and investment adviser representatives to be registered and to follow the rules. If the activities are criminal in nature, the securities Administrator can refer the case to a criminal prosecutor and see if the attorney general's or district attorney's office wants to sweat somebody over $50,000. Turns out, it wasn't enough money to get the criminal prosecutor's attention in this instance. If that sounds shocking, remember that this is Chicago we're talking about—the criminal prosecutors of Cook County are already busy enough prosecuting violent crime without devoting a lot of resources to a case like this. Then again, a few months ago I saw that the District Attorney in Montgomery, Alabama, was going after a husband and wife who sold promissory notes totaling just $45,000. The DA in Montgomery is going after them on multiple counts of securities fraud, all of which are felonies. So, the guy who skipped his own hearing got lucky, but if you plan on committing criminal violations of state securities law, you'd better watch where you do it. Sometimes you get lucky; sometimes you get a pair of prison scrubs and three squares a day.

I wish this were an isolated case, but actually this sort of thing happens in all the states with alarming regularity. Usually it goes like this: some unregistered person sells an unregistered security under false pretenses. Maybe the thing is presented as a "safe, secure investment" or one that's "guaranteed to make you a millionaire as soon as the company goes public." Either way, the stock or bond isn't worth the paper it's printed on. But by the time the investor finds out the true nature of her investment, the scoundrel who sold it has already made off with the money.

If the woman who lost $50,000 on a phantom house happened to be your mother, how would you feel? Would you want to maybe talk to the guy who took the money? Maybe, take some sort of, you know, action against him? That's pretty much how the state securities regulators feel, and if they catch anybody misleading people when offering/selling securities, they can take away their license. If you get in trouble with the Tennessee regulators, you're out of luck with the other states, too. If you got kicked out of Tennessee and tried to set up shop in Michigan, Michigan would use the revocation of your Tennessee license as a reason to deny you a Michigan license.

But how would the state be able to come down on somebody for offering and selling securities fraudulently unless they, first, defined exactly what they mean by the following terms:

- Offer
- Sale
- Security
- Fraud

Since those definitions are crucial to securities regulations, your Series 63 exam will require you to define such terms yourself. And, as frustrating as the process can be, it is not an exercise in futility. At another hearing I attended recently—one in which the respondent actually showed up—the attorney representing the guy in hot water continued to argue that the investment that his client had offered and sold did not even meet the definition of a "security," and, therefore his client did not, in fact, commit securities fraud and did not, in fact, have to register the investment in the first place. He actually had no luck whatsoever in convincing the hearing officer of this line of reasoning, but what are you going to do? A client pays you to provide some sort of defense; you work with whatever you have.

So, when the regulators try to come down on someone for offering and/or selling securities fraudulently, they have to carefully define all their terms. Did it really meet the definition of an "offer" or a "sale"? Was it a "security?" If not, the respondent and the investment are outside the scope of the securities Administrator's authority.

Investing in securities and helping investors can be extremely exciting and rewarding activities. Reading a bunch of dry rules and definitions surrounding the securities industry is nowhere near as exciting. Similarly, playing or watching baseball can be exciting. Reading the rules and definitions—not so much. Most readers are probably familiar with the game of baseball and many have played it either recreationally or competitively. At the very least, most readers are confident that they know what a "strike" is. Let's see if your definition matches up with the official definition in the Major League Baseball rulebook:

> A STRIKE is a legal pitch when so called by the umpire, which--
>
> (a) Is struck at by the batter and is missed;
>
> (b) Is not struck at, if any part of the ball passes through any part of the strike zone;
>
> (c) Is fouled by the batter when he has less than two strikes;
>
> (d) Is bunted foul;
>
> (e) Touches the batter as he strikes at it;
>
> (f) Touches the batter in flight in the strike zone; or
>
> (g) Becomes a foul tip.

In order to learn the baseball rulebook, you would have to learn the mind-numbing definitions of terms such as "strike," "strike zone," "batter's box," etc. In order to pass the Series 63, you'll have to learn the mind-numbing definitions of terms such as "offer," "sale," and "security." Definitions are hugely important to securities regulation and to the Series 63 exam. The most basic definition in securities law is the definition of "securities fraud," which the Uniform Securities Act defines like so:

> It is unlawful for any person, in connection with the offer, sale, or purchase of any security, directly or indirectly, to employ any device scheme or artifice to defraud. To make any untrue statement of material fact or to omit to state a material fact necessary in order to make the statements made not misleading. To

> engage in any act, practice, or course of business which operates or would operate as a fraud or deceit upon any person.

Notice how the law doesn't get picky here—the definition of "fraud" uses the phrase "<u>any person</u> in connection with the offer, sale, or purchase of <u>any security</u>." We'll see later that many securities don't have to be registered because of what they are or the way they're being sold. A security excused from registration is an "exempt security," but that has nothing to do with whether a "fraud" has taken place. The definition of fraud includes "<u>any</u> security." It could be something as high-risk as a penny stock, or as rock-solid as a Treasury bond. Since either one is a "security," it would be a fraud to sell it deceptively.

So the "offer" is the attempt to sell. The sale happens when a security is disposed of or transferred to another party in exchange for value—usually money.

But, what is a security?

Often the regulators are trying to pop somebody for selling something they're convinced is a security, while the other side's attorneys are equally convinced the thing is not, in fact, a security. It's like a baseball manager arguing with an umpire that the last pitch did not, in fact, meet the definition of a "strike," except that no one ever kicks dirt at an Administrative hearing, of course. An "investment contract" is an example of a security, and the US Supreme Court defined an "investment contract" through the Howey Decision. The Howey Decision said that an "investment contract"—which is a security—is "an investment of money in a common enterprise whereby the investor's fortunes are entwined with other investors and/or the promoter, and the investor hopes to benefit solely through the efforts of others."

Let's say an Iowa farmer needs to raise $500,000 to expand his soy bean and hog farming operation. He prints up 20 official-looking certificates at Kinko's. Each piece of paper is offered for $25,000 and gives the investor a 2% ownership stake in the farming operation. That's an investment of money in a common enterprise whereby each investor's fortunes are bound together with other investors and the promoter, and whereby the investor hopes to benefit solely through the efforts of others—the farmer. The investors sure as heck aren't getting up at 5 o'clock on a cold, February morning in Iowa to feed the friggin' livestock, right? They're just investors, and what they bought was an "investment contract," which is one example of a "security" as listed in the Uniform Securities Act and the Federal Securities Act of 1933. So, if the farmer gives them all offering documents with inflated profits or forgets to mention the tractors he's been sort of hiding in ole' Bud Biddington's barn in case the repo man shows up again, he has probably committed securities fraud. And, before he even *offers* these investment contracts, he needs to get them registered with the state, who will want to see the advertising, the prospectus, the underwriter agreements, etc.

But, not every investment of money meets the definition of a "security." The following investments are *not* securities:

- Fixed annuities
- Whole life, term life, universal life insurance
- Commodities futures contracts

If those aren't *securities*, who regulates them to make sure investors don't get burned? Luckily, we already have insurance regulators for the insurance products and commodities regulators for the commodities futures. The securities regulators only regulate *securities*.

So, the most important concept in state securities regulations is that if the thing fits the definition of a "security," and this security is "offered" and/or "sold" through any deceptive or manipulative device, that constitutes a "fraud," and the states simply will not tolerate it. In order to protect investors, the regulators make agents, broker-dealers, investment advisers, investment adviser representatives, and securities issuers fill out registration statements and pay fees before anybody does anything. Knowing who's offering and selling securities allows the regulators to keep tabs on things in order to "provide necessary protection to investors in keeping with the public interest." Some people entering the business take offense at the exam requirements, the annoying registration applications, the licensing fees, etc. And, they get mighty ticked to see how somebody just trying to make a living in the securities business could end up losing her license just because a few clients claim they were misled into losing money. One of the attorneys at the Administrator's office in Chicago explained it perfectly the other day when she said, "What a lot of people in the business don't understand is that they are not equal to the investor. Only the investor is protected under state securities law—if someone is harming or is likely to harm investors, we try to get them out of the business a soon as possible."

If you think about it, that makes perfect sense. Selling securities isn't in the Bill of Rights. It's not a right at all—it's a privilege. You have to earn that privilege by passing some difficult exams and getting registered. Then, you have to keep earning it every day by treating customers fairly and doing your job as diligently as you possibly can.

Some of this stuff might sound a bit fancy when you first read it, but it really all boils down to a simple concept. Regulators *hate* deception in the securities industry. Making you study for some exam called the Series 63 is their way of impressing upon you the importance of ethical sales practices before turning you loose with a license, a cell phone, and God knows what kind of intentions.

Let's get into some heavy details now, but no matter how difficult things get, just remember that it all really boils down to providing necessary protection to investors.

Ready?

Let's get started, anyway.

The Administrator

(6 of 60 questions on the exam)

THE NEED FOR UNIFORMITY

If every state has its own securities Administrator and its own securities law, how is it possible for broker-dealers and investment advisers to operate in different states without descending into chaos? Luckily, the securities laws among the states are fairly uniform, since they all use the same model called the "Uniform Securities Act." The Uniform Securities Act starts out by announcing its purpose:

> ```
> Relating to securities; prohibiting fraudulent prac-
> tices in relation thereto; requiring the registration
> of broker-dealers, agents, investment advisers, and
> securities; and making uniform the law with reference
> thereto.
> ```

The state regulators want to make the securities laws uniform from state to state, and they want to prevent fraudulent offers and sales of securities in order to protect their investors from getting ripped off by scam artists. To do that, they require persons in the securities industry and the securities themselves to be registered. The states end up altering things, but, overall, the various state securities laws are very similar or "uniform." The Uniform Securities Act makes that possible.

THE ADMINISTRATOR

The Uniform Securities Act calls the official in charge of securities regulation in a state the [Administrator] and puts the term in brackets, encouraging each state to insert the appropriate title (Commission, Secretary, Commissioner, Department of Securities, etc.). In the "real world," the Administrator might be referred to as the

"Bureau of Securities," or the "Illinois Securities Department." In the test world, we refer to that state-level office, whatever it's actually called, as "the Administrator." A Series 63 exam question might proclaim that "the Administrator is the official or agency empowered by state law to regulate the securities industry in that state." Under the Uniform Securities Act, in order to "provide necessary protection to investors," the Administrator can:

- Issue rules and orders
- Investigate violations of the securities law, both in and outside the state
- Require a written response to findings of fact
- Issue subpoenas to compel attendance and/or production of documents
- Issue and apply to a court to enforce subpoenas at the request of the Administrator of another state
- Administer oaths and affirmations
- Take evidence
- Publish results of investigations and hearings
- Cooperate with other regulators

Let's start by understanding the difference between "rules" and "orders." Rules apply system-wide. Those who violate the rules end up having *orders* issued against them. The Administrator writes rules that spell out registration requirements for investment advisers, for example. In my state an investment adviser is required to complete and submit Form ADV and pay a registration fee of $400 before operating as an investment adviser. That's the *rule*. So, if I decide to skip the hassle of registering and paying the $400 fee but go ahead and start managing client portfolios anyway, I would be violating the rules by operating as an unregistered investment adviser. To get my attention, the Administrator would probably issue an <u>order</u> called a "cease & desist." It would come to my office by registered mail, and after I had signed for and read the thing, it would, in fact, get my attention. I would comply with the cease & desist, and if I convinced the Administrator that I suddenly understood how important it was for me to refrain from any further violations and to never, ever try to operate without being registered, they would probably let me start all over and get myself properly registered. But I certainly wouldn't want to see any future registered mail from the Illinois Securities Administrator, whose patience would have already been tried by my maverick approach to a highly regulated industry.

As our bulleted list indicates, the Administrator can investigate both in and outside the state in order to provide necessary protection to investors. You mess with just *one* Alabama investor, and the Alabama Securities Administrator has the authority to make life really difficult for you, no matter where you're located. Maybe you think, "Big deal, so I lose my license in Alabama—I can still sell securities in the other 49 states."

Wrong. If your license is suspended or revoked by the State of Alabama, for example, *all* other states can use that as a reason to deny, suspend, or revoke your license in their states.

Also, the exam might ask about the Administrator of one state issuing a subpoena or applying to a court to enforce it at the request of another state Administrator. This can happen as long as the alleged misdeed would be a violation of securities law in the Administrator's state, whether the activity occurred there or not. Believe it or not, that is probably the answer to a Series 63 question right there, which shows how hard many of the questions hit at the exam center.

Still got your attention?

Excellent.

With so much power at their disposal, it's probably easier to talk about what the Administrator *can't* do. The Administrator cannot:

- Issue judicial injunctions
- Make arrests
- Sentence violators to prison

Why not? Because the Administrator is not a court of law. They can petition a court to issue a judicial injunction or have somebody fined and thrown in jail for fraud. But they have to ask first, and they have to convince the court to do what they ask. In other words, while an unruly agent can definitely have a court injunction slapped on him or get himself thrown in jail, it's not the Administrator who just snaps his fingers and makes it happen. It takes a court to issue an injunction or hand down a prison sentence, not just an Administrative order. Often, people won't cooperate with the Administrator's subpoena to appear at a hearing or turn over books and records. When that happens, the Administrator can apply to a court of law, asking the judge to issue an order to cooperate. Disobeying the Administrator's authority is called "contumacy," while disobeying a court order is a bigger deal called "contempt of court," which can lead to fines and even jail.

It might help to understand that the state securities Administrator has similarities with the federal Securities and Exchange Commission. As we see with just a few clicks at the SEC's excellent website www.sec.gov :

> The Commission's (SEC's) enforcement staff conducts
> investigations into possible violations of the federal

securities laws, and prosecutes the Commission's civil suits in the federal courts as well as its <u>administrative</u> proceedings.

In civil suits, the Commission *seeks* <u>injunctions, which are orders that prohibit future violations; a person who violates an injunction is subject to fines or imprisonment for contempt</u>.

The Commission can bring a variety of <u>administrative</u> proceedings, which are heard by administrative law judges and the Commission itself. With respect to regulated entities (e.g., brokers, dealers and investment advisers) and their employees, the Commission may institute administrative proceedings to revoke or suspend registration, or to impose bars or suspensions from employment.

So, the SEC is the federal securities regulator. The Administrator is the state securities regulator. In either case, they're a staff of attorneys who may *seek* court injunctions and who may hold administrative hearings to deny, suspend, or revoke licenses. But neither office is a criminal prosecutor or a police force. They are, literally, *administrative* authorities. Like the administrative authorities at a strict high school, the securities administrators can make life very difficult for those who ignore their authority by violating their rules.

ADMINISTRATIVE ORDERS

When the Administrator finds out that somebody is taking advantage of investors, they can issue an order to deny, suspend or revoke that somebody's license. But, usually, they give the respondents the reasons for taking such drastic action. If it's an order to deny, suspend or revoke a license, the Administrator will provide the affected parties with:

- Prior notice
- Opportunity for a hearing
- Written findings of fact, conclusions of law

We examined a notice of hearing in which the respondent was provided with exactly those bullet points above. It was a *notice* of a *hearing,* and it provided both the findings of fact and the conclusions of law. The Administrator is usually nice enough to provide the three bullet points above even before issuing a "cease and desist" order, but they don't have to in that case there. As the Uniform Securities Act states, "Whenever it appears to the [Administrator] that any person has engaged or is about to engage in any act or practice constituting a violation of any provision of this act or any rule or order hereunder, he may in his discretion bring either or both of the following remedies." Those remedies are:

- Issue a cease and desist order, with or without a prior hearing against the persons engaged in the prohibited activities, directing them to cease and desist from further illegal activity

- Bring an action in court to enjoin the acts or practices to enforce compliance. Upon a proper showing a permanent or temporary injunction shall be granted and a receiver may be appointed for the defendant or the defendant's assets. In addition, upon a proper showing by the [Administrator] the court may enter an order of rescission, restitution or disgorgement directed to any person who has engaged in any act constituting a violation of any provision of this act or any rule or order hereunder

So, even though the Administrator cannot snap his fingers and force people to comply with his orders or subpoenas, he can either bring action in the appropriate court himself or refer it to the attorney general's office. If the state convinces the court to issue an injunction or restraining order forcing someone to comply with securities regulations, that someone would be in contempt of court if he blew off the court order. Contempt of court would lead to some very serious problems for the people ignoring the court's authority. The extremely long second bullet point also mentions that the courts can order the seller of the security to repurchase the security (rescission), return any ill-gotten profits (disgorgement) and/or pay restitution to the people who were harmed by the violations of the securities law. So when the exam points out that the Administrator can't *issue* injunctions, it is just splitting hairs—they can't *issue* an injunction, but they could convince a court to issue one. Similarly, the Administrator can't sentence violators to prison, but they could turn the case over to criminal prosecutors, who are pretty good at convincing courts to sentence people to prison. Read carefully and avoid jumping to conclusions as you read through the material and later as you work through the practice questions.

So, there are plenty of emergency cease and desist orders issued because what's happening or what's about to happen is so out of control, the Administrator needs to take action right now. But your exam may ask you to say that before issuing a "stop" order (deny, suspend, revoke), the Administrator will provide "prior notice, opportunity for a hearing, and written findings of fact/conclusions of law."

If the agent has his hearing and loses, he can file an appeal of the Administrator's order in a court of law if he does so within 60 days. That's a testable point, by the way, like everything else I'm telling you.

Why would the Administrator want to issue a deny/suspend/revoke order against an agent, broker-dealer, investment adviser, or investment adviser representative? First, the order has to be "in the public interest, providing necessary protection to investors," and, then, somebody:

- Has filed a false or misleading application
- Has willfully violated or willfully failed to comply with any provision of this act, or any provision of the Securities Act of 1933, the Securities Exchange Act of 1934, the Investment Advisers Act of 1940, the Investment Company Act of 1940, or the Commodity Exchange Act
- Has been convicted, within the past ten years, of any misdemeanor involving a security or any aspect of the securities business, or any felony
- Is permanently or temporarily enjoined by any court of competent jurisdiction from engaging in or continuing any conduct or practice involving any aspect of the securities business
- Is the subject of an order of the Administrator denying, suspending, or revoking registration as a broker-dealer, agent, or investment adviser
- Is the subject of an adjudication or determination within the past 10 years by a securities or commodities agency or administrator of another state or a court of competent jurisdiction that the person has willfully violated the Securities Act of 1933, the Securities Exchange Act of 1934, the Investment Advisers Act of 1940, the Investment Company Act of 1940 or the Commodity Exchange Act, or the securities or commodities law of any other state;
- Has engaged in dishonest or unethical practices in the securities business
- Is insolvent; but the [Administrator] may not enter an order against a broker-dealer or investment adviser under this clause without a finding of insolvency as to the broker-dealer or investment adviser;
- Has willfully violated the law of a foreign jurisdiction governing or regulating any aspect of the business of securities or banking or, within the past five years, has been the subject of an action of a securities regulator of a foreign jurisdiction denying, revoking or suspending the right to engage in the business of securities as a broker-dealer, agent or investment adviser or is the subject of an action of any securities exchange or self-regulatory

organization operating under the authority of the securities regulator of a
foreign jurisdiction suspending or expelling such person from membership
in such exchange or self-regulatory organization

- Is not qualified on the basis of such factors as training, experience, and
  knowledge of the securities business
- Has failed reasonably to supervise his agents or employees if he is a broker-
  dealer, or his adviser representatives or employees if he is an investment
  adviser to assure their compliance with this act
- Has failed to pay the proper filing fee; but the [Administrator] may enter
  only a denial order under this clause, and (he) shall vacate any such order
  when the deficiency has been corrected

That might look like an intimidating list, but, really, it comes down to a few
important concepts. Obviously, if somebody conceals a disciplinary problem on Form
U-4 or Form ADV, when the regulators find out about the omission later, the license
will be revoked in most cases. If any other regulator already has a problem with the
applicant, the Administrator has a problem with the applicant. Or, if a registered
agent got in trouble with another regulator, that would be a reason to suspend or
revoke his securities license. Notice how trouble with any sort of financial industry
regulator (including banking, commodities, and foreign jurisdictions), or a court
injunction that is either permanent or still in effect is going to make it v-e-r-y difficult
for the applicant to get registered. Also, if the Administrator earlier denied or revoked
a license and now that person is re-applying, the state doesn't have to re-establish
the ground which led to the earlier denial or revocation order. *But,* if it was just a
suspension that has expired—that is not a reason to use against the person. If a firm
isn't supervising a bunch of rowdy, out-of-control agents, the Administrator can take
away or deny the firm's license. Not surprisingly, if somebody is a convicted felon,
or convicted of "money crimes" such as forgery, check kiting, embezzlement, fraud,
retail theft, theft of services…the state doesn't have to give him a license, and they
can take the one they foolishly granted him right back. After letting him tell his side
of the story, of course, and letting him spend a fortune in legal fees. If the broker-
dealer's or adviser's balance sheet is clearly about to implode, the state can shut
them down in order to protect investors, just as bank regulators shut down troubled
banks. The state would have to order a formal finding of insolvency in the case of a
firm. But, that also implies that if an agent of a broker-dealer or an investment adviser
representative is on shaky financial ground, no such formality would be required. So,
hypothetically, if the agent's bills are piling up, the state could protect investors by

taking the deadbeat dude out of the business before he starts churning, executing unauthorized transactions, making little private offerings of unregistered securities under the table, misappropriating customer funds, etc.

Now, bullet points are great, but to pass the Series 63 you will need an understanding of concepts and an ability to apply them in very challenging ways. So, we can't just fire off a bunch of bullets and walk away. Let's take a look at a few real-world examples, and let's start with the first one, filing a false or misleading document with the Administrator. You know that little U-4 that you have either filled out or are about to?

Turns out, that thing is like, a big deal.

STATE OF ILLINOIS
SECRETARY OF STATE
SECURITIES DEPARTMENT

_____)

IN THE MATTER OF: Stephanie Elliott) FILE NO. 0600009

_____)

CONSENT ORDER OF REVOCATION

TO THE RESPONDENT: Stephanie M. Elliott
(CRD#: 5025464)
4027 15th Street
Moline, Illinois 61265

C/o Metlife Securities, Inc.
200 Park Avenue
New York, New York 10166

William Gerald Chick Esq.
Law Office of William Gerald
Chick
423 Seventeenth Street, Suite 200
P.O. Box 3337
Rock Island, Illinois 61204-3337

WHEREAS, Respondent on the 2nd day of November 2006 executed a certain Stipulation to Enter Consent Order of Revocation (the "Stipulation"), which hereby is incorporated by reference herein.

WHEREAS, by means of the Stipulation, Respondent has admitted to the jurisdiction of the Secretary of State and service of the Second Amended Notice of Hearing of the Secretary of State, Securities Department dated October 11, 2006 in this proceeding (the "Notice") and Respondent has consented to the entry of this Consent Order of Revocation ("Consent Order").

WHEREAS, by means of the Stipulation, the Respondent acknowledged, without admitting or denying the truth thereof, that the following allegations contained in the Second Amended Notice of Hearing shall be adopted as the Secretary of State's Findings of Fact:

1. That on November 14, 2005, Metlife Securities, Inc., a registered dealer, filed a U-4 Form application dated November 7, 2005 (the "U-4 Form") for the registration of the Respondent as a salesperson in the State of Illinois pursuant to Section 8 of the Act.

2. That the Respondent became registered as a salesperson in the State of Illinois on November 18, 2005.

3. That the U-4 Form referred to in paragraph one (1) above, was electronically filed by means of WEB-CRD and contained the typewritten name of the Respondent on the signature line.

4. That Questions 14.B(1)(a) and 14.B(1)(b) of the U-4 Form ask, in pertinent part, if an applicant has been convicted of or pled guilty to a misdemeanor involving wrongful taking of property B(1)(a) or has been charged with a misdemeanor involving wrongful taking of property B(1)(b).

5. That November 7, 2005 U-Form (response to questions 14.B(1)(a) and 14.B(1)(b) contains material misrepresentations in that the Respondent failed to disclose that she was found guilty of, "Embezzlement of monies belonging to a credit union", in violation of Title 18 U.S.C.A., Section 657, a misdemeanor, on October 28, 1988. The matter was styled "United States of America v. Stephanie M. Elliott", Case Number 88-40022-0 filed in the

United States District Court, central District of Illinois on September 7, 1988.

6.   That on December 14, 2005 the Respondent filed an amendment to her previous U-4 Form disclosing that she had been charged with and convicted of a misdemeanor of embezzlement of monies belonging to a credit union.

7.   That Section 12.E(1) of the Act provides, _inter alia_, that it shall be a violation of the provisions of this Act for any person to make or cause to be made, in any application, report or document filed under this Act or any rule or regulation made by the Secretary of State pursuant to this Act, any statement which was false or misleading with respect to any material fact.

8.   That Section 8.E(1)(g) of the Act provides, _inter alia_, that subject to the provisions of subsection F of Section 11 of this Act, the registration of a dealer, limited Canadian dealer, salesperson, investment advisor, or investment advisor representative may be denied, suspended or revoked if the Secretary of State finds that the dealer, limited Canadian dealer, salesperson, investment advisor, or investment advisor representative or any principal officer, director, partner, member, trustee, manager or any person who performs a similar function of the dealer, limited Canadian dealer, or investment adviser has violated any of the provisions of this Act.

9,   That Section 8.E(1)(h) of the Act provides, _inter alia_, that the registration of a salesperson may be revoked if the Secretary of State finds that such salesperson made any material misrepresentation to the Secretary of State in connection with any information deemed necessary by the Secretary of State to determine a salesperson's repute or qualification

WHEREAS, by means of the Stipulation Respondent has acknowledged, without admitting or denying the averments, that the following shall be adopted as the Secretary of State's Conclusions of Law:

(1)   The Respondent has committed a violation of Section 12.E(1) of the Act;

(2)   The Respondent's registration as a salesperson in the State of Illinois is subject to revocation pursuant to Sections 8.E(1)(g) and 8.E(1)(h)of the Act;

WHEREAS, by means of the Stipulation Respondent has acknowledged and agreed that Stephanie Elliott's salesperson registration in The State of Illinois shall be REVOKED.

WHEREAS, the Secretary of State, by and through his duly authorized representative, has determined that the matter related to the aforesaid formal hearing may be dismissed without further proceedings.

NOW THEREFORE IT SHALL BE AND IS HEREBY ORDERED THAT:

1.   Respondent, Stephanie Elliott's registration as a salesperson in the State of Illinois is REVOKED.

2.   The Second Amended Notice of Hearing dated October 11, 2006 is dismissed.

ENTERED: This 8th day of ~~~~~~ 2006.

JESSE WHITE
Secretary of State
State of Illinois

Some readers might be thinking, but it happened 17 years earlier! I thought the regulators only go back 10 years? They do. But, that's not how Form U-4 reads. Form U-4 phrases the question like this:

Have you EVER been convicted of or pled guilty or nolo contendere ("no contest") in a domestic, foreign or military court to a misdemeanor involving: investments or an investment-related business or any fraud, false statements or omissions, <u>wrongful taking of property</u>, bribery, perjury, forgery, counterfeiting, extortion, or a conspiracy to commit any of these offenses?

What's really sad here is that if the applicant had answered, "Yes" to that question and then filled out a DRP (disclosure reporting page), the Administrator would probably have granted her a license. Most of us have done some pretty crazy things in the past, and the securities regulators know this. Heck, most of them did some pretty crazy things back when they were young, too. If it happened one time, and the individual clearly learned from the mistake, and the individual is being perfectly honest about the whole thing, why not let her into the business as a securities agent? But, if she's still lying about things on an official document filed with the Administrator, forget it.

Let's see what other types of examples I can scrounge together from my fine state. Oh, here's one. Remember that bullet point that read "has engaged in dishonest or unethical practices in the securities business"? See if you can relate that to the following order of revocation.

STATE OF ILLINOIS
SECRETARY OF STATE
SECURITIES DEPARTMENT

```
_____ )
IN THE MATTER OF: DEANE JOSEPH PANTALEO ) FILE NO.
_____ ) 0700036
```

ORDER OF REVOCATION

TO THE RESPONDENT: Deane Joseph Pantaleo
                    (CRD#: 4336722)
                    2004 Black Swan Court
                    Darien, Illinois 60561

WHEREAS, the above-captioned matter came on to be heard on May 17, 2007, pursuant to the Notice of Hearing dated April 6, 2007, FILED BY Petitioner Secretary of State, and the record of the matter under the Illinois Securities Law of 1953 [815 ILCS 5] (the "Act") has been reviewed by the Secretary of State or his duly authorized representative.

WHEREAS, the rulings of the Hearing Officer on the admission of evidence and all motions are deemed to be proper and are hereby concurred with by the Secretary of State.

WHEREAS, the proposed Findings of Fact, Conclusions of Law and Recommendations of the Hearing Officer, George Y. Berbas, Esq., in the above-captioned matter have been read and examined.

WHEREAS, the following proposed Findings of Fact of the Hearing Officer are hereby adopted as the Findings of Fact of the Secretary of State:

1.   The Department served Respondent with the amended

Notice of Hearing on April 6, 2007 ("Notice of Hearing").

2.   Respondent failed to appear either by himself or through his attorney at the hearing on May 17, 2007, and also failed to respond or otherwise answer to the allegations in the complaint.

3.   Due notice having been given to the Respondent, and Respondent having failed to appear, the Department was allowed to proceed to a Default Hearing.

4.   Mr. Pantaleo was registered with the Secretary of State as a salesperson in the State of Illinois pursuant to Section 8 of the Act, until July 7, 2005.

5.   On November 13, 2006, NASD entered a Letter of Acceptance, Waiver and Consent (AWC) submitted by the Respondent regarding File No. 20050022039-01 which sanctioned the Respondent as follows:

   a.   The Respondent was suspended from association with any member of NASD fro a period of two years; and

   b.   fined $20,000 .

   c.   Moreover the AWC found:

      i.   On June30, 2005, the Respondent sat for the series 7 (general securities representative) examination at a testing center in Chicago, Illinois. Prior to taking the examination, the Respondent was required to abide by certain NASD Rules of Conduct relating to the examination, and entitled "NASD

Rules of Conduct- Prohibition of Study Materials or Assistance." One of the Rules was that the Respondent must not receive (except from the center staff) any form of assistance during the examination/training or restroom breaks, Another Rule was that during the restroom breaks, the Respondent, "must not leave the premises and may only go to the restroom."

ii. During the examination, the Respondent requested permission to take a restroom break. After taking the restroom break, instead of returning to he testing area, the Respondent left the building where the examination was being conducted, and went to his vehicle, he obtained a book entitled "General Securities Representative Exam License Manuel 16th Edition." After obtaining this book, the Respondent returned to the building where the examination was being conducted. Examination staff found the Respondent in a hallway, immediately after he reentered the building, carrying the book entitled "General Securities Representative Exam License Manuel 16th Edition." After the examination staff questioned the Respondent, the examination staff took the book entitled "General Securities Representative Exam License Manuel 16th Edition."

iii. Such acts, practice and conduct set forth above constitute separate and distinct violations of NASD Conduct Rule 2110 by the Respondent.

WHEREAS, in addition to the findings of fact

by the hearing officer and adapted by the Illinois Secretary of State, the Illinois Secretary of State makes a supplemental finding of fact that the respondent registered as an investment advisor representative in the State of Illinois pursuant to Section 8 of the Act until July 7, 2005.

WHEREAS, the following proposed Conclusions of Law made by the Hearing Officer are correct and are hereby adopted as the Conclusions of Law of the Secretary of State:

1.   The Department properly served the Notice of Hearing on Respondent on April 6, 2007.

2.   The Secretary of State has jurisdiction over the subject matter hereof pursuant to the Act.

3.   Respondent failed to answer or otherwise appear at the hearing in accordance with Section 130.1104, therefore,

   a.   The allegations contained in the Notice of Hearing and complaint are deemed admitted;

   b.   Respondent waived his right to a hearing;

   c.   Respondent is subject to an order of Default.

4.   On November 13, 2006, NASD entered a decision regarding Complaint # 20050022039-01, which barred Respondent from association in any capacity with any member of the NASD. Section 8.E(1)(j) of the Illinois Securities Law provides, that the registration of a salesperson may be revoked if the Secretary of State finds that such salesperson has been suspended by any self-regulatory organization registered under the Federal 1934 Act or the Federal 1974 Act arising from any fraudulent

or deceptive act or a practice in violation of any rule, regulation, or standard duly promulgated by the self-regulatory organization.

5. Section 8.E(3) of the Act provides that withdrawal of an application for registration or withdrawal from registration of a salesperson, becomes effective 30 days after receipt of an application to withdraw or within such shorter period of time as the Secretary of Sate may determine. If no proceeding is pending or instituted and withdrawal automatically becomes effective, the Secretary of State may nevertheless institute a revocation or suspension proceeding within two years after withdrawal became effective and enter a revocation or suspension order as of the last date on which regulation was effective.

6. The Department proved the allegations contained in the complaint in the Default prove-up hearing on May 17, 2007.

WHEREAS, the Hearing Officer recommended that the Secretary of State should REVOKE the Respondent Deane Joseph Pantaleo's registration as a salesperson in the State of Illinois, and the Secretary of State adopts in it's entirety the Recommendation made by the Hearing Officer, and modifies it in accord with the additional conclusions of law.

NOW THEREFORE, IT SHALL BE AND IS HEREBY ORDERED:

1. The Department's request for a Default Judgment against the Respondent is granted.

2. Respondent's registration as an investment advisor and a salesperson in the State of Illinois is revoked effective July 7, 2005.

3.   This matter is concluded without further proceedings.

DATED: ENTERED This 9th day of July 2007.

>   JESSE WHITE
>   Secretary of State
>   State of Illinois

NOTICE: Failure to comply with the terms of this Order shall be a violation of the Section 12.D of the Act. Any person or entity who fails to comply with the terms of this Order of the Secretary of State, having knowledge of the existence of the Order, shall be guilty of a Class 4 Felony.

This is a final order subject to administrative review pursuant to the Administrative Review Law, { 735 ILCS 5/3-101 et seq.} and the Rules and Regulations of the Illinois Securities Act, { 14 Ill. Admin. Code Ch. I, Section 130.1123}. Any action for Judicial Review must be commenced within thirty-five (35) days from the date a copy of this Order is served upon the party seeking review.

Apparently, when the NASD (now FINRA) says that members and their associated persons must "maintain high standards of commercial honor," they do not include "cheating on your Series 7 exam" within that definition. As we mentioned, if your SRO kicks you out, they then notify the state, who, in turn, kicks you out. And, if you fail to cooperate or attend your own hearing, the Administrator issues a default order, meaning that your failure to appear is considered an admission of everything they're saying. Thank you—next?

Finally, let's explain what is meant by the bullet point, "has willfully violated or willfully failed to comply with any provision of this act." A "willful violation" is exactly what it sounds like—the Administrator, for example, held a hearing and ended up revoking your license as an investment adviser, requiring you to wait five years before even *trying* to apply for *any* type of securities registration. Unfortunately, you decide to ignore their authority (contumacy) and keep on advising investors for compensation, anyway.

You would not believe how cranky the securities regulators get over a willful violation like that! Many readers are parents. If you tell your five-year-old not to ride his bicycle across the busy street, but you see him just a-pedalin' across that dangerous street anyway, how do you feel about that "willful violation"?

How does the Administrator know that you "willfully" violated or "willfully" failed to comply with securities regulations? Everything they send you is delivered by registered mail. Your signature is on the consent order to suspend or revoke your license. That's plenty of proof that you knew you weren't supposed to do something but kept doing it anyway. As it says at the bottom of the last order of revocation we looked at, "Any person or entity who fails to comply with the terms of this Order of the [Administrator], having knowledge of the existence of this Order, shall be guilty of a Class 4 felony." Now, the Uniform Securities Act can't use the term "Class 4 felony" for Illinois or "Class C felony" for Alabama. Remember, it's just a model securities act. The model criminal penalties for willful violations of the Uniform Securities Act are 3 years imprisonment, a $5,000 fine, or both per violation. And, believe it or not, that's pretty close to what the actual state securities laws would authorize, regardless of what they're called in a particular state.

So, when we look at "business practices," the lengthiest section on your exam, we'll try to list all the things you shouldn't do there in extreme detail. But, frankly, the state regulators don't feel you should need a comprehensive list—you should just consider your clients' needs carefully and treat them honestly and fairly. Either that, or they can schedule a hearing at your earliest convenience.

Now, if the exam is in a bad mood, you may be required to know that the Administrator can actually take two specific actions even without being nice enough to first give you notice and an opportunity for a hearing. The "cease & desist" order can be issued without prior notice, because sometimes the thing that somebody is doing or is planning to do is so outrageous that the state has to at least try to stop him in his tracks. Yes, the Administrator can issue a "cease & desist" even *before* somebody has violated the Act.

Also, the Administrator can "summarily suspend a registration pending final determination" of the matter. That means that until the hearing has been held and the decision has been reached, your license is "summarily suspended." Obviously, there must be some serious violations or serious deficiencies in a firm's net capital…some special circumstances are making it necessary to summarily suspend a registration.

But, if you read enough enforcement orders, you'll see that special circumstances unfold more often than one might imagine.

So, the Administrator can never issue a punitive order without prior notice, opportunity for a hearing, and written findings of fact, conclusions of law.

Except in the two cases when he can: cease & desist, summary suspension.

Non-punitive Orders

Cease & desist, denial, suspension, and revocation orders stem from violations of securities regulations. The exam might refer to them as "punitive" orders, and "punitive" is based on the same word that "punishment" is based on. On the other hand, there are two orders that are non-punitive, as well: withdrawal and cancellation. A non-punitive order has nothing to do with punishment. If the firm or agent decides they no longer want or need a license in, say, the State of Rhode Island, they can withdraw rather than pay a renewal fee. A broker-dealer registers with Form BD; they would withdraw by filing Form BD-W. An investment adviser registers with a Form ADV. Not surprisingly, they withdraw by filing Form ADV-W. The withdrawal becomes effective thirty days or sooner. Of course, if they think they can withdraw to avoid disciplinary action, I've got news for them. The Administrator can actually initiate a suspension or revocation proceeding for up to one year if he finds out that there was actually a reason they were in such a hurry to leave the state. And, as we said, that strike against them can cause problems with all the other states.

But a withdrawal in and of itself has nothing to do with punishment. The applicant or the registrant simply says thanks—but no thanks. As long as they haven't done anything wrong, the Administrator simply accepts the withdrawal.

A cancellation order is issued because the party dies, goes out of business, is declared mentally incompetent, or simply can't be located. Canceled. The person, apparently, no longer needs the license, so it's canceled.

CRIMINAL PENALTIES

Your exam may ask what the criminal penalties are for "willful violations" of the Uniform Securities Act. As we mentioned, the criminal penalties are three years in prison, a $5,000 fine, or both, per violation. The Uniform Securities Act does split hairs here—although the criminal penalties for willful violations are three years in prison, a $5,000 fine, or both, if we're talking about the filing of information with the Administrator, it would have to be shown that the person knowingly filed false information. In other words, you'd hate to put someone in prison over a typo. In practicality, the

Administrator would simply revoke the license of an agent who signed a false U-4 or an adviser who filed a bogus Form ADV. No need to put those folks in prison in most cases. Then again, if a criminal prosecutor wanted to try to prove the false filing of information was done knowingly and caused great harm somehow, they could have a crack at it. Again, it's not the Administrator who hands down the sentence—that takes a court of law and at least one prosecuting attorney. But, really, the exam is splitting hairs. Can you be sentenced to prison for a willful violation of the securities law? Yes. Is it the Administrator who made the arrest or imposed the sentence?

No.

Also, the criminal courts have to come after you within five years of the alleged misdeed. Otherwise, the statute of limitations runs out in your favor. Not that you're ever going to work in the securities industry again, but at least you won't be spending any time in prison, which is something. So, in case the exam asks a few memorization-based questions, the statute of limitations for criminal action is five years. Why the exam would want you to know that you're free and clear after the fifth year, I have no idea. Chances are, it wouldn't.

Normally, you would think that ignorance of the law is no excuse. However, under the Uniform Securities Act, if the party can prove that they had no way of knowing that what they did was a violation, they can't be thrown in jail. The burden of proof here would be on the one claiming ignorance.

We're talking about the criminal penalties under the *Uniform Securities Act*. There are other state and federal laws that somebody can be tried under. As the Uniform Securities Act makes clear:

> Nothing in this act limits the power of the state to punish any person for any conduct which constitutes a crime by statute or at common law.

And, even though it's not the Administrator sweating somebody in criminal court, the following passage makes it very clear that this fact would not prevent securities violators from being prosecuted:

> The Administrator may refer such evidence as is available concerning violations of this act or of any rule or order hereunder to the attorney general or the proper district attorney, who may institute the appropriate criminal proceedings under this act.

CIVIL LIABILITIES

Nothing scares me more than prison, but the civil liabilities under the Uniform Securities Act are rather disturbing, as well. If your little concert T-shirt business sold an investor some unregistered "preferred stock," what would happen if her $50,000 investment became worthless? She could sue to make you return her $50,000 plus interest, plus court costs/attorneys' fees.

The answer to a test question on civil liabilities might include:

- Price paid for the security (or investment advice)
- Plus interest
- Plus court costs, including reasonable attorneys' fees
- Minus any income received on the security

That last item is a little jarring, but if you sold the security in violation of the act, you can still deduct any dividend or interest payment the security provided. But, let's be real—the security usually didn't provide any income. Notice that we're not talking about "pain and suffering" here. Just give the investor her money back, plus interest, basically. Let's be sure we understand that if somebody sells you a security in violation of the act, and you lose $50,000, you can only recover that $50,000, plus the rate of interest used by the courts in such matters, plus the costs you paid for your attorney and the court filing. The fact that the situation led to a sleep disorder, which led to a serious drug dependency that forced you into a 90-day stay at a detox center in Beverly Hills or Maui…sorry, the courts aren't listening to any of that.

If it's discovered that the security was sold unlawfully, the buyer can sue if he initiates action within two years. Your exam might say that the statute of limitations for civil action is "two years from discovery or three years from the event, whichever comes first." That means that if you've known about it for more than two years, it's too late to sue. And, if it happened more than three years ago, it's too late to sue, in any case.

Sometimes the seller realizes that the security sold was unregistered. If so, he screwed up, but he can make the buyer a formal offer of rescission in which he offers to buy back the security plus interest. The buyer now has 30 days to either accept or reject the offer. If they reject the offer or fail to accept it within 30 days, their right to recover is lost.

Let's take a quick look at the real world here and see how the State of New Jersey provides an easy-to-use form letter for offers of rescission.

Form of Rescission Offer
[Letterhead of Issuer]

[Name of Security Holder]
[Address of Security Holder]
[City, State, Zip Code]

Dear [ ]:

On [date of purchase], [# of shares] shares of [type of security i.e. common, preferred, debentures] of [name of issuer] at a price of [$] were sold to you.

The sale of these securities did not comply with the New Jersey Uniform Securities Law (1997). Therefore, [name of issuer] hereby offers to rescind this sale and to refund to you the entire purchase price paid together with interest at the rate of [This rate is to be determined by using the rate established for interest on judgments for the same period by the Rules Governing the Courts of the State of New Jersey at the time the offer was made.] [ ]% per year from the date of payment, less the amount of any income received on the security.

Should you decide to accept this offer of rescission, return the above described securities to this office, together with a written notice of your acceptance, and the purchase price plus interest will be refunded to you.

This offer is good for thirty (30) days after you receive this letter. If you fail to accept it within that period, your right to recover under the New Jersey Uniform Securities Law (1997) will be lost.

Very truly yours,

[Officer of Issuer]
[Title]
[Name of Issuer]

Rescission and civil liability are usually associated with the unlawful sale of a security, but they also cover investment advice given in violation of the Uniform Securities Act. An investment adviser who breaches his fiduciary duty to clients can definitely end up being sued, which is partly why I prefer to write books instead. I could register as an investment adviser since I've passed the Series 65, but if my advisory clients all lost 40% when the Dow plummets unexpectedly, did I just fail to honor my fiduciary obligation? Maybe, maybe not. Trouble is, some clients might want a civil court to make that determination and perhaps force me to return all the money they lost, plus interest.

Another concept that could show up on the exam is that even though the person who defrauded investors has died, his estate can be sued by those affected. Similarly, if the investor who was ripped off has passed away, the heirs could still file suit on the seller to try to recover the price paid, plus interest, etc. The Uniform Securities Act says:

> Every cause of action under this statute survives the death of any person who might have been a plaintiff or defendant.

FINAL CONCERNS

Let's wrap up this section, which accounts for 6 of your 60 questions on the Series 63 exam. First, remember that it would be a violation for anyone to suggest that the Administrator "approved" them or has passed out an opinion that what they're offering is a good investment opportunity. But, let's enjoy it in the original legalese first:

> Sec. 405. [UNLAWFUL REPRESENTATIONS CONCERNING REGISTRATION OR EXEMPTION.] (a) Neither (1) the fact that an application for registration or notice filing under Part II or a registration statement or notice filing under Part III has been filed nor (2) the fact that a person or security is effectively registered constitutes a finding by the [Administrator] that any document filed under this act is true, complete, and not misleading. Neither any such fact nor the fact that an exemption or exception is available for a security or a transaction means that the [Administrator] has passed in any way upon the merits or qualifications

```
of, or recommended or given approval to, any person,
security, or transaction.

(b) It is unlawful to make, or cause to be made, to
any prospective purchaser, customer, or client any
representation inconsistent with subsection (a).
```

Of course, I would not even subject you to such painful legalese were I not so certain that you will encounter said legalese on your Series 63 exam. What is the above section of the Uniform Securities Act actually saying? Basically, this: if an agent tells investors that she was recently endorsed or approved by the Administrator, she would be violating the Act. If a religious organization offers $50 million of debt securities that are exempt from registration requirements, the offering circular to investors will explicitly state that while the securities don't have to be registered with the Administrator, that fact does not imply that the Administrator has passed out an opinion as to the merits or safety of the investment. If the offering circular said something crazy like the following, the issuers and underwriters would be violating this provision of the Uniform Securities Act: *the securities regulators of this state do not require registration of this offering, after deeming the offering to be of higher quality than other investment products typically offered in the state.* Again, no statement like that would ever be put on an offering document for securities unless the issuer and underwriters simply didn't know any better or actually wanted to get into all kinds of legal trouble.

The section that follows what we just copied and pasted above describes how the Act will be administered. The Administrator—which means the office itself and any of the officers and employees of the office—are prohibited from using any information gathered through their position to their personal benefit. I guess that means that if I'm an employee of the Securities Administrator and I know that a major broker-dealer is about to get into all kinds of trouble, I can't sell their stock short just before the action becomes public knowledge. That's just one thing that comes to mind. I also probably shouldn't visit that broker-dealer and offer to make the whole thing go away in exchange for $50,000 cash money. The information gathered by the Administrator is not to be disclosed to others or even among employees beyond what is necessary to do their job. That means that if an agent is being investigated over allegations that customer accounts are being churned, then certain relevant information will be shared among certain employees and supervisors of the Administrator. That doesn't mean that everyone in the office needs to have access to all information. If it's public information, fine. But if it's confidential, the Administrator has to respect that. Also, the Administrator and its officers and employees have to respond to subpoenas and other legal demands for information.

Registration of Persons

(18 of 60 questions on the exam)

How do you feel knowing that the driver in the lane next to you is not actually licensed or insured? Does that make you feel safe? An unlicensed broker-dealer, agent, or investment adviser is like an unlicensed, uninsured driver. They're all potentially dangerous. They have not paid licensing fees into the system, which isn't fair to everybody else. They have not proven basic competency, nor secured any form of insurance to cover any damages they might cause. Even if they're good people, they're a menace to society. So, just as with unlicensed, uninsured motorists, the states would prefer to keep these persons off the road before they cause any injuries.

By requiring a license application such as a U-4 the states can keep convicted felons and persons with misdemeanor convictions for theft, extortion, bribery, forgery, etc., out of the business. How? As we'll see, if you disclose a felony conviction from, say, three years ago, there is little chance of getting your license granted by the state. But, if you fail to disclose the unfortunate fact and they find out anyway—which they always seem to do—it's much worse. Filing false documents with the Administrator, as we saw, is about as bad as it gets. So, just making people register provides some protection to investors.

The professionals required to register can be firms or individuals. Either way they are "persons." A person may *include* an individual, but the definition of "person" is not limited to that. Microsoft is a person. The Estate of Jonathon T. Smith is a person. Since the definition of "person" includes corporations, partnerships, etc., when the regulators want to refer to an individual, they usually call him a "natural person." When they use the word "person" or "any person," they're referring to any individual, partnership, corporation, estate, trust, etc. These are all "legal persons" or "legal entities."

The list of who *is* a person is too long to complete, but I can tell you who is *not* a person. A person is not:
- Dead
- Declared mentally incompetent by a court of law

- A minor child

So, if they're not dead, declared mentally incompetent, or a minor child, they are a legal person. As a former English teacher, I can assure you that the phrase "they are a legal person" is not a grammatical error. It's just freaking weird. Are you a person? If you're reading this book you are—dead people aren't reading this book. Eleven-year-old children aren't reading this book. And if you've been declared mentally incompetent by a court of law, you aren't now on page 44 still hanging with this discussion of securities law.

Let's think of it this way: Elvis Presley is not a person. Why not? The King is dead, people; get over it. So, Elvis Presley is not a legal person; however, the Estate of Elvis Presley *is* a person. The estate is an entity with a taxpayer ID number (FEIN), investment accounts, and god knows how much income from Graceland, movie and TV rights, recording royalties, merchandising, etc.

A "legal person" such as an estate, trust, or corporation is simply a legal entity able to enter into contracts, open investment accounts, etc. When your grandmother passes away, she is no longer a legal person. But, if her will named you the executor of her estate, you will need to open a bank account in the name of the estate. Maybe the name would be something like The Estate of Maude P. Meriwether, Deceased. Maybe your name would follow: "Jeremiah Meriwether, Executor." Whatever the exact title might be, the estate will receive a taxpayer ID number, just as a corporation would, and will be a "legal person." You will transfer checking and savings account balances into this "person's" new account. When you sell the house, you will put the proceeds into this account owned by a legal person known as an estate. If somebody sues the estate and wins a judgment of, say, $3 million, they cannot go after the personal assets of you and your sisters and brothers. If the assets of the estate are valued at only, say, $80,000, that's all the plaintiff is going to be able to collect. Why? Because the Estate of Maude P. Meriwether, Deceased, is a separate legal entity from you and your siblings. Does that mean that a plaintiff could win a judgment that wipes out all the stocks, bonds, and real estate you thought you were going to inherit? Absolutely. Can they take money out of *your* pocket or force *you* to sell stocks or real estate? No. The estate is a legal person. You and your siblings are completely separate legal persons from that estate.

So, when you see that a broker-dealer is defined as a "person," do not assume that a broker-dealer is some guy named Ralph. Not that it *couldn't* be some guy named Ralph, but think of a broker-dealer as a firm. All the big Wall Street firms are broker-dealers, for example: Morgan Stanley, Merrill Lynch, Goldman Sachs, and so on. In a test question, you would answer that a broker-dealer *could* be an individual, also known as a "natural person." But, to help you grasp the concepts, I recommend picturing the big firms mentioned above or any other large broker-dealer that you are familiar with. A broker-dealer is a firm that underwrites securities on the primary market and/or helps people trade them on the secondary market. The agents are the individuals like you hired by the broker-dealer.

BROKER-DEALER VS. INVESTMENT ADVISER

THE SELL SIDE

Let's start by separating two different business models within the securities industry. A "broker-dealer" makes money through transactions in securities. When they bring an issuer's stock onto the primary market through an IPO, they get paid a percentage of the public offering price (POP) that investors pay. When they sell an investor a mutual fund A-share, they get paid a percentage of the POP once again. When the client holds individual stocks and bonds, the broker-dealer gets paid to help the client buy those securities. So, think of broker-dealers and their agents as sitting on the "sell side" of the table, across from the investor. The broker-dealer and agent have to dig into the investor's financial situation to make sure that their recommendations are suitable, but they only get paid if and when an investor runs a transaction through them. They aren't spending the investors' money on their behalf—they're trying to sell them an investment or investment product that seems to be suitable for their objectives. Broker-dealers are in the transaction business, trying to sell somebody something.

The Uniform Securities Act defines a broker-dealer as:

> any person engaged in the business of effecting trans-
> actions in securities for the account of others or for
> its own account.

The companies who sponsor mutual funds are broker-dealers who belong to an SRO called FINRA (formerly NASD). The companies who *manage* the mutual fund portfolios in exchange for a percentage of the assets are *not* broker-dealers and do *not* belong to FINRA or any other SRO. The folks who manage mutual funds for a percentage of assets are investment advisers. To use a real-world example, American Funds Distributors sponsors or distributes American Funds, not surprisingly. They make money when investors buy the funds through the front- or back-end sales charges. Like all broker-dealers, they make money *because* somebody just bought or sold a security. Capital Research and Management Company is the investment adviser to the American Funds—they choose when to buy and sell the stocks and bonds inside the Growth Fund of America, or Bond Fund of America, etc. They make more money when the assets of the fund grow and less money when the assets of the fund shrink. But that's a different business model. Instead of sitting on the "sell side" of the table trying to interest an investor in purchasing a product that comes with a brochure called a "prospectus," investment advisers sit on the "buy side" of the table, spending the investor's money on his or her behalf.

THE BUY SIDE

Unlike a broker-dealer, an "investment adviser" does not make money *because* somebody is buying or selling securities. You might be startled to read that an investment adviser is compensated for *advising investors*. They are either charging investors to tell them what to do, or they actually use their written authority from the client to invest the client's money in the best interests of the client.

Whoa—hold on a minute. You mean that some investors actually give their written authorization to let some firm called an "investment adviser" start buying and selling securities in the investors' accounts as the *firm* sees fit?

Sure. In fact, it seems to be the way the industry is headed. Think about it—when a broker-dealer is "advising" you to buy a security, it doesn't matter financially whether the stock goes up, down, or sideways after you buy it—they get paid if you buy the security, and they don't get paid if you don't. After a while a big light bulb might go off above your head. Gee, my stockbroker really might just be trying to sell me something here. Even if most agents/stockbrokers are honest, there will always be that percentage that wants to churn accounts and sell totally inappropriate investment products to people who shouldn't touch them with a ten-foot pole. I'll never forget the man in a seminar in St. Louis a few years ago who exercised a bunch of options during the tech bubble and made a profit of $3.2 million. Of course, you have to invest that kind of money when you're 35 years old with a wife and two kids, and, luckily, he met up with a stockbroker who figured out a way to quickly turn the $3.2 million into $40,000.

No, that's not a typo. Like the young man in this true story, we wish we could add at least two zeroes to that figure, but the agent, who got paid when he *sold* the mutual fund shares, unfortunately had no ethics and no financial incentive to monitor the value of the account after putting the victim—I mean investor—into some aggressive and expensive mutual funds. On the other hand, if the stockbroker had been acting instead as an *investment adviser* earning a percentage of assets, he would have seen his own billings drop right along with the account and would have had an incentive to protect the principal. Unfortunately, he had no financial incentive to even look at the account after getting paid a long time ago when he made the sale.

That's not to say that stockbrokers are bad and investment advisers are good. The point is, when you tie the guy's compensation to the value of your account, it no longer matters whether he's a "good guy," really. In fact, the greedier he is for management fees, the more incentive he has to keep the account value on a steady upward climb. If he starts churning the account, he'll feel the pain if the trades go south, whereas a "stockbroker" churning an account gets paid the same commissions again, and again, and again.

An adviser doesn't sell securities to investors. An investment adviser gets paid for providing the service of advising people on securities investments. If I draw up a detailed financial plan for you and charge you $3,000, I get compensated for investment *advice*. If I tell you to buy five stocks and you decide not to, oh well—I'm getting compensated just for *advising* you. More likely, I'm your portfolio manager billing you 1% of assets annually, .25% every quarter. As your account value rises, so does my 1%; as your account value falls…well, since my compensation is tied to your account value, I try not to let that happen too much.

The Uniform Securities Act defines an investment adviser as:

> …any person who, for compensation, engages in the business of advising others, either directly or

> through publications or writings, as to the value of
> securities or as to the advisability of investing in,
> purchasing, or selling securities, or who, for compen-
> sation and as part of a regular business, issues or
> promulgates analyses or reports concerning securities.
> "Investment adviser" also includes financial planners
> and other persons who, as an integral component of other
> financially related services, provide the foregoing
> investment advisory services to others for compensation
> and as part of a business or who hold themselves out as
> providing the foregoing investment advisory services
> to others for compensation

What the law is saying is that if you get compensated for advising others on securities, you are acting as an investment adviser. What if somebody is advising people
on fixed annuities? Those aren't securities, so he probably wouldn't fit the definition
of an "investment adviser." If he did something stupid, he'd probably be busted under
insurance laws. And, let's face it, if the dude can't sell something as safe and simple
as a fixed annuity without deceiving people, it might be time for a career change.

AGENTS AND INVESTMENT ADVISER REPRESENTATIVES

The Uniform Securities Act defines an agent as follows:

> Agent means any individual other than a broker-dealer
> who represents a broker-dealer or issuer in effecting
> or attempting to effect transactions in securities.

Keep in mind that a broker-dealer is, by definition, *not* an agent and vice versa.
One is the firm, the other is the individual who represents the firm. On your Series
63, if the question is saying something like, "Which of the following are securities
agents," you would skip over any choice that started with "a broker-dealer who..."
Broker-dealers aren't agents, and agents aren't broker-dealers. Also, an investment
adviser is not an investment adviser representative. As with the broker-dealer and
agent, one is the firm, one represents the firm.

The Uniform Securities Act defines an investment adviser representative as, "any
partner, officer, director of, or other individual employed by or associated with, an
investment adviser that is registered or required to be registered under this act, or

who has a place of business located in this state and is employed by or associated with a federal covered adviser," and who:

- makes any recommendations or otherwise renders advice regarding securities
- manages accounts or portfolios of clients,
- determines which recommendation or advice regarding securities should be given,
- solicits, offers or negotiates for the sale of or sells investment advisory services
- supervises employees who perform any of the above.

Not all employees of the adviser have to register, of course. The employees of an investment adviser who perform clerical or "ministerial" work do not have to register. In other words, the maintenance guy for an investment adviser does not have to pass the Series 65 and 63 any more than the maintenance guy at the hospital has to be an M.D. We're not letting the janitors administer EKG's or 401(k)'s, so let's keep it real here. But, as always, don't look for the easy, black-and-white answer. Is a receptionist for an investment adviser considered an investment adviser representative? Probably not. But, if the test question implies that she's soliciting clients and receiving some form of compensation, or she is telling clients what to do with their money, now she has crossed the line and will have to pass some rather difficult securities license exams and pay a bunch of testing and registration fees. Not that she would get much sympathy from anyone reading this book, but you get the idea.

I would expect your exam to address a rather vexing problem for securities Administrators. That is the problem of insurance agents referring their clients to an investment adviser in exchange for a share of the adviser's management fee. Doesn't that fit pretty neatly into the bullet list above? Selling the services of an investment adviser for compensation—that's an investment adviser representative, right? So, what should the insurance agent do if he wants to keep getting paid for these referrals?

Exactly right—make sure nobody finds out. Or, do the smart thing and register as an investment adviser representative of that adviser. Many people in the real world gasp at such news, but, if you think about it, all that generally entails is passing the Series 65 or 66 & 7 exams, filling out the U-4 to associate with the adviser, and paying the licensing fee. It's a business—you need a license. That's how the regulators see it. And, it's pretty hard to disagree. I don't want an unlicensed dentist administering anesthetic to my daughter. I don't want an unlicensed investment adviser administering the lump sum payment my mom just got from her teacher's retirement pension.

Another likely question will bring up the tricky situation of an unregistered person helping a registered agent as an assistant. What can the unregistered assistant do and not do? Well, he or she definitely cannot solicit purchase or sale orders and cannot accept unsolicited orders for securities, either. He or she cannot share in the agent's commissions. Could the assistant talk to clients? Sure. The assistant could give the client information about her account, or read off stock and bond quotes, or fax important documents for the client's signature. Just make sure in the test question (and in the real world) that the unregistered person and the agent are not sharing commissions or pushing the edge of the envelope so that the unregistered assistant is really acting as an unregistered securities agent.

REGISTRATION REQUIREMENTS

As the Uniform Securities Act says, "It is unlawful for any person to transact business in this state as a broker-dealer or agent unless he is registered under this act." Pretty straightforward—if the state finds out that you're transacting business as a broker-dealer or agent without being registered, they will take action against you. Since these under-the-table operators would generally be a rather stubborn and defiant group, the Administrator will often tell the attorney general to get a court to slap an injunction on the unregistered persons because it is a very big deal when people are operating under the regulatory radar screen—that's where money is usually lost faster than anyplace outside of Las Vegas. Shut it down before they destroy anybody else's life savings.

The next few sentences of the Uniform Securities Act provide material for all kinds of Series 63 questions:

```
It is unlawful for any broker-dealer or issuer to
employ an agent unless the agent is registered. The
registration of an agent is not effective during any
period when he is not associated with a particular
broker-dealer registered under this act or a particular
issuer. When an agent begins or terminates a connection
with a broker-dealer or issuer, the agent as well as
the broker-dealer or issuer shall promptly notify the
[Administrator].
```

The first sentence is not surprising—a broker-dealer would get in big trouble for employing an agent who wasn't registered. But, notice that the law also inserts the word "issuer" in there, too. We're so used to thinking of an "issuer" as a large, legitimate corporation such as GE, Microsoft, or Coca-Cola, that we don't often think of issuers as employing securities agents. I mean, when they do an offering of stock or bonds, wouldn't they go through a big underwriting firm such as Goldman Sachs or Merrill Lynch, who have their own small army of securities agents working the phones?

Probably. But we're talking about "issuers" at the smaller, much more dangerous level. Remember that the guy who took the $50,000 from the Illinois investor was the "issuer" of that promissory note. Kind of a different situation, right? Some small company wants to offer preferred stock or promissory notes to the Average Joe and JoAnn investor. Okay, first let's have them register the securities. And, let's make sure that if the company is hiring individuals to solicit investors in exchange for compensation that they register those individuals as agents of the issuer. Why? Well, maybe we'll find some interesting things on their U-4. See, we get nervous when "agents" were recently referred to as "parolees" or "defendants." Any convictions or charges of embezzlement, extortion, forgery, fraud, etc., and the state will likely deny the registration or revoke the one they accidentally granted in the first place. So, if an issuer of securities is going to compensate people for selling those securities, those individuals almost always have to register as agents. The Administrator is out to protect investors. Nothing poses a bigger threat to investors than a smooth-talking convicted felon being compensated with a percentage of several millions of dollars. So, the state insists that these agents be registered as agents of the issuer. And, the states always insist that agents of broker-dealers get themselves registered. In either case, the agent and the broker-dealer/issuer fill out a Form U-4. And, we've already seen that Form U-4 asks many probing questions about your employment history (10 years), residential history (5 years), and any criminal charges/guilty pleas/no contest pleas/convictions (ever).

A common Series 63 question asks what needs to happen when an agent terminates employment with one broker-dealer or issuer and signs up with another broker-dealer or issuer. Answer: both broker-dealers/issuers and the agent must notify the Administrator promptly. In practical terms, that means that the one firm completes the U-5 to terminate the agent's employment, and the other firm completes the U-4 to hire the agent. The Administrator wants "persons" to register and they insist that they keep all their registration information current. The Administrator will do unannounced inspections from time to time, and if they come in for an inspection and find a hair & nail salon at the address they have for a broker-dealer, that's a problem. The address or name of the firm could change, and if so, the broker-dealer or adviser needs to update that information. Broker-dealers and many advisers have to meet minimum net capital requirements. If their balance sheet suddenly slips below the minimum net worth, they have to inform the Administrator promptly, which means by close of business on the next business day. If the firm fails to inform the Administrator that their net capital is not currently being met, they are in huge trouble when the Administrator eventually finds out. And, like many Moms that I know, the Administrator always finds out. Always.

Investment advisers also have to be registered, and they have to let the state know about the investment adviser representatives employed by the firm. The firm registers with Form ADV, and they have to promptly update it if a major change occurs. They file a U-4 for each of their investment adviser representatives and a U-5 if they terminate an IAR.

REGISTRATION PROCEDURE

The Uniform Securities Act gives the Administrator the power to issue the rules spelling out the registration requirements for a broker-dealer, agent, investment adviser, and investment adviser representative. The Act says:

> The application shall contain whatever information the Administrator by rule requires concerning such matters as:
>
>> Applicant's form and place of organization
>>
>> Applicant's proposed method of doing business
>>
>> Qualifications and business history of the applicant
>>
>> For broker-dealers and investment advisers—qualifications and business history of any partner, officer, or director
>>
>> Any injunction or administrative order or conviction of a misdemeanor involving a security or any aspect of the securities business, and any conviction of a felony
>>
>> Applicant's financial condition and history

Even if that seems like dense legalese, all it's really saying is that before you start doing business in the securities industry within a state, you need to apply for a license, on which you tell the state about your background and how you propose to do business. Is the broker-dealer a partnership or a corporation? If a corporation, where is it incorporated and can we please see a copy of the articles of incorporation and the bylaws? Does a court or another state Administrator sort of have a problem with you? Are you financially sound, or teetering on the verge of bankruptcy?

That sort of thing.

After you register, assuming the state sees no problem with the information provided, your license will be granted no later than noon of the 30th day after filing. Of course, if you did indicate that another state Administrator or the Commodities Futures Trading Commission sort of had a problem with you not too long ago, it's probably going to take more than 30 days to grant your registration if, against all odds, they decide to grant one at all. If while reviewing your application they see that you indicated an arbitration award you had to pay to a client in New Jersey, they may need you to file an amendment to your application, which could slow things down a bit.

So, your registration will be granted by noon of the 30th day, unless it isn't.

Remember that a broker-dealer registers with Form BD and registers their agents and principals with a Form U-4. When a principal or agent leaves the firm, the broker-dealer files a U-5. With any luck, they don't have to indicate "terminated for cause" and can just indicate that the individual quit or got a better job. An investment adviser registers with Form ADV and files a U-4 for all of their investment adviser representatives. And, we also saw that an issuer will often have to file a Form U-4 to register a securities agent, as well.

The Uniform Securities Act also states that when filing your initial application as a broker-dealer, agent, adviser, or adviser representative, you need to attach a form called a "consent to service of process." This thing gives the Administrator the authority to receive "service of process" in any non-criminal suit against the applicant. In other words, should another state need to serve papers on an out-of-control investment adviser, they don't have to chase them around and around. Instead, they can just serve the papers on the Administrator, and now the clock starts ticking. The applicant already signed their "consent to service of process," right? So, now the out-of-control adviser can hide and duck phone calls all he wants; since he's been "served," the plaintiff or a securities regulator can get a default judgment against him. See? These regulators think of everything—they're lawyers for crying out loud. By the way, you can see one of these consent to service of process forms at www.nasaa.org, currently under, first, "industry and regulatory resources," then "uniform forms." The first is a rollover, and then the other links pop up. Or, maybe the webmaster will use a different interface by the time you read this book. But they won't eliminate the uniform forms, and they are definitely worth looking at when studying for any NASAA exam (Form BD, ADV, U-4, Securities Registration).

The Uniform Securities Act states that, "Every applicant for initial or renewal registration shall pay a filing fee of $___ in the case of a broker-dealer, $___ in the case of an agent, and $___ in the case of an investment adviser." The individual states seem to really like the idea of these application and renewal fees, and especially seem to enjoy the way the dollar amounts were all left blank. I noticed the other day that in the real world (not the exam) it costs $300 to register as an investment adviser in Massachusetts, $400 in Illinois, and just $100 in Indiana. Of course, these fees could change tomorrow, so they're only given as an indication of how the Uniform Securities Act guides the real world of state securities regulation. The Model Act stipulates that the Administrator has the authority to establish registration and renewal fees, so the state regulators do so, just as they do for driver's and vehicle owner licenses. The Model Act leaves the amounts blank because it's being passed in the 1950's, when $1 could probably feed an entire family at some new-fangled burger joint called McDonald's. And the states have the authority to charge what they see fit, so the amounts are left blank, and in the real world the states fill them in and raise them as necessary and appropriate in keeping with the public interest.

And *you* thought the Series 63 was going to be boring. Hah!

NET CAPITAL REQUIREMENTS

When a broker-dealer or investment adviser registers or renews their license, the Administrator has the authority to require a minimum net capital. Notice how it doesn't say the Administrator *has* to require a minimum net capital. But, trust me, they will. Depending on their activities, the Administrator can rule that the broker-dealer's or investment adviser's balance sheet must show a net worth of at least *this* amount. NASAA's Model Rules have informed the state Administrator's rules so that it is now standard that an investment adviser with custody of client assets must have a minimum net worth of $35,000; an adviser with discretion but not custody must have minimum net worth of $10,000; and an adviser who accepts upfront payments of over $500 six or more months in advance must always have positive net worth. In the real world the states are going to want to see audited balance sheets if the adviser has custody or accepts the prepayment as indicated. That's why many advisers avoid having custody or accepting such prepayment. The state securities Administrator is also limited by the Securities Exchange Act of 1934 when establishing net capital for broker-dealers and the Investment Advisers Act of 1940 when establishing net capital for investment advisers. The state cannot require a higher standard for broker-dealers than what is required under the Securities Exchange Act of 1934. The Investment Advisers Act of 1940 states that if an adviser with an office in State A is meeting that state's minimum net capital requirement, the other states where the firm does business cannot require a higher requirement. As long as the firm is properly registered in the other state and is, in fact, meeting that state's net capital requirement, that's enough. For federal covered advisers and for broker-dealers, remember that the Administrator cannot impose requirements for books & records, net capital, or margin in excess of SEC requirements.

Perhaps you've noticed that carpet cleaners, electricians, and plumbers announce that they are "bonded" if they want to ease the fears of their prospects and customers. I mean, what if this nice-looking 21-year-old guy in the kelly green uniform brings in his carpet cleaning equipment and accidentally destroys $75,000 worth of carpeting or knocks over a Ming vase worth millions? Is he going to, like, cut the customer a check? No. That's why he needs to be bonded and insured. Of course, electricians can do a lot more damage than carpet cleaners, so most villages would not issue a building permit for an electrician to perform services without him providing proof that he's bonded/insured.

Similarly, the Administrator may require registered broker-dealers, agents, and those investment advisers with custody of or discretion over client assets to post surety bonds. These bonds cover the cost of possible legal action arising from violations of the Uniform Securities Act. We've seen that investors harmed by the purchase or sale of a security, or some really bad investment advice, can sue. That's why the Uniform Securities Act stipulates that "Every bond shall provide for suit thereon by any person who has a cause of action under section 410." By the way, you can download a PDF of the Uniform Securities Act (57 pages) at the NASAA website. Might be fun to see everything in the original legalese. Or not. Either way, instead of securing a bond, the firm or agent could make a deposit of cash or securities. While the Administrator can determine which type of securities may be deposited, the exam might point out that he cannot insist on cash. Also, if the broker-dealer's or investment adviser's net capital exceeds the specified minimum amounts, bonds will not be required. So, basically, if bad things could happen to customer accounts, the Administrator wants the person to be on solid financial footing, or they'll either post a bond or make a deposit of securities or cash.

The exam might also point out that the Administrator has the authority to require the applicant to place an announcement of the application in one or more specified newspapers published in the state. As you may be starting to notice, there is almost no end to all the things the exam might bring up.

RECORD-KEEPING REQUIREMENTS

The Uniform Securities Act, in Section 203's "Post-Registration Provisions" says:

> Every registered broker-dealer and investment adviser shall make and keep such accounts, correspondence, memoranda, papers, books, and other records as the Administrator by rule prescribes. All records required shall be preserved for three years unless the Administrator by rule prescribes otherwise for particular types of records.

Broker-dealers keep records such as originals of client correspondence, written customer complaints, cold calling scripts, and other sales literature (market letters, research reports, circulars, flyers, etc.), advertising, which includes kiosk presentations, websites, billboards, radio, television, and print advertising, etc. The Administrator not only wants those documents preserved; he may want to have a look at them someday. He might even have to subpoena those documents right out of somebody's defiant hands. If you poke around the state regulatory websites long enough you'll probably find instances where some hard-nosed broker-dealer or investment adviser told the state they couldn't see client emails or account statements that were "protected by attorney-client privilege." And, once they've finished wiping the tears of laughter away, the Administrator and his staff will then prepare a notice of an opportunity for a hearing to announce their intent to revoke the license for willfully failing to comply with the Act.

Broker-dealers and investment advisers have to file financial reports as required by the Administrator (balance sheets, trial balance sheets, etc.). The Uniform Securities Act states that "if the information contained in *any* document filed with the Administrator becomes inaccurate or incomplete in any material respect, the registrant shall promptly file a correcting amendment."

Remember that broker-dealers and some advisers maintain custody or possession/ control of client securities and cash. See, when I log in to my online brokerage account this morning, I see an entry under "balances" called "cash." "Cash - $1,235.67" it says this morning—what does that mean? Does it mean they have $1,235.67 sealed in an envelope with the name "Walker" across it? No. Similar to a bank, they *owe* me that amount and must pay it if I request a check for that amount. But how do I know they're good for it?

That's the question that piques the Administrator's curiosity, as well. How do we know these broker-dealers are good for all this "cash" and all these securities they're supposedly holding as trustees for the investors? What if a broker-dealer maintaining custody of $500 million of client cash goes belly-up? Hopefully, they were covered by SIPC and, hopefully, there was no more than $100,000 of "cash" in any one account. But, it's a real concern for state regulators and investors, so if the broker-dealer's net capital is not being met, the state shuts them down.

We mentioned that the Administrator has the authority to inspect books and records whenever there is good reason to do so. The Uniform Securities Act makes this point with the following passage:

> All the records referred to are subject at any time or from time to time to such reasonable periodic, special, or other examinations by representatives of the Administrator, within or without the state, as the Administrator deems necessary or appropriate in the public interest or for the protection of investors.

Broker-dealers keep most of their records for three years, two years on-site. Investment advisers preserve copies of their required books and records for five years. A Series 63 question might ask you what happens if an investment adviser goes out of business. Do they still have to keep copies of the required books and records?

Yes. They have to notify the state of the location of the books and records and bear the expense of keeping them nice and safe for the next five years. What sort of "books and records" have to be kept? Actually, you wouldn't believe how long the list is. Advisers and broker-dealers have to keep records of all advertising, client communications, financial statements of the firm, all client transactions and transactions for the firm's account, etc. These records can be maintained electronically provided that the electronic records are kept according to the following procedures:
- Maintain and preserve the records, so as to reasonably safeguard them from loss, alteration, or destruction
- Limit access to the records to properly authorized personnel and the Administrator (including its examiners and other representatives)
- Reasonably ensure that any reproduction of a non-electronic original record on electronic storage media is complete, true, and legible when retrieved

Another likely question is what would happen if an investment adviser has its principal place of business in State A and also has a place of business in State B. Does it have to meet the books and records and net capital requirements of both states?

No. As long as they are properly licensed and in compliance with the requirements of their "home state," the adviser is not subject to State B's requirements here.

Not only must persons in the securities industry file an initial registration, but also they must renew their license every year. When do registrations of persons expire? On December 31st, unless properly renewed. How do you renew your license? By paying the required fee. Now, this will almost certainly generate a test question and, for some reason, students seem to find it much harder than it really is. The question will say something like, "Jill Janson just passed her securities license exams and is applying as an investment adviser on November 17th of this year. Will Jill pay a registration fee for all of this year, for next year only, or will she pay a pro-rated registration fee covering only the remainder of this calendar year?"

Many people seem to think Jill should and will only have to pay a pro-rated amount representing the remainder of this year. Wrong. She'll pay this year's fee now if she wants to register now, and if she wants to renew for next year, she'll pay that fee by December 31st. What if she doesn't want to pay this year's fee? That's okay, too, but she'd better not try to set up shop under the radar screen. If you're thinking the system would be improved if Jill only had to pay for the remainder of this year, does that mean that the registration fee would drop a little bit each day of the year? If there are 111 days left in the year, you pay $73.67, while last week's suckers were paying a full $75.11? Wouldn't that encourage people to keep putting off the whole registration process and maybe just work with a few clients under the table until next year?

No. You pay your registration fee when you register. And, if you want to stay in the business, you pay your renewal fee by December 31st. If not, your license expires.

So, the Uniform Securities Act and the Series 63 exam want you to understand that broker-dealers, agents, investment advisers, and investment adviser representatives need to apply for a license, need to renew that license every year, and need to keep whatever records the Administrator requires. The Administrator has the power to take a look at the required records whenever it's in the public interest or provides necessary protection to investors. And, if you try to prevent him from inspecting the required records, you just violated the Act right there and will soon be signing for some registered mail.

MORE SPECIFICS ON REGISTRATION

You may see a test question about a broker-dealer registering also as an investment adviser. First, know that this is *very* common. Many firms are *both* broker-dealers and advisers. The exam requirements are different and the business models/forms of compensation are different, but, still, many firms perform both activities. The exam may point out something from the Uniform Securities Act, which states:

> When the Administrator finds that an applicant for initial or renewal registration as a broker-dealer is not qualified as an investment adviser, he may by order condition the applicant's registration as a broker-dealer upon his *not* transacting business in this state as an investment adviser.

What the law is saying is this: if you're a broker-dealer who also wants to be an investment adviser, the state may say, "No. You can be a broker-dealer *as long as* you don't try to stretch and hurt yourself acting as an investment adviser, which you, apparently, have no business trying to do." In other words, they don't lose their broker-dealer license just because they also wanted to transact business as an adviser. They simply have to promise not to act as an adviser if they want to keep their broker-dealer license.

The Uniform Securities Act also states:

> The Administrator may not enter an order solely on the basis of lack of experience if the applicant or registrant is qualified by training, knowledge, or both.

We actually indicated that in our bullet point list covering reasons for Administrative orders, but it's a good idea to point it out again. If you don't have any experience yet, but you do have training and knowledge—as evidenced by passing a bunch of tough exams and being supervised by a broker-dealer—they have to give you a chance to get some experience. Otherwise, you'd be stuck in a weird catch-22, with the state telling you that you can only get some experience as an agent if you already have experience as an agent.

The Uniform Securities Act also points out that when the Administrator is determining the qualifications of broker-dealers and investment advisers, they can base their decision *only* on the firm and the agents themselves...not on the receptionist or the file clerk, for example. Or on the limited partners who simply invested in the firm and have nothing to do with its day-to-day operations.

Also, when a firm or individual files their application, as long as they properly disclose every material fact, the Administrator has 90 days after the effective date of the registration to initiate a proceeding. If the Administrator has known about a fact disclosed to him on the application or any amendments for more than 90 days, it's too late to then get all hostile and send you a notice that the state intends to deny your license. Why the test wants you to know the limits of the Administrator's authority, I have no idea. It's NASAA's world. We merely live in it.

If you get a test question about the registration of a successor firm, first of all, your luck is running dangerously low—please call someone to pick you up from the testing center and make sure all your insurance premiums are paid up, just in case. Secondly, remember this passage from the Uniform Securities Act:

```
A registered broker-dealer or investment adviser may
file an application for registration of a successor,
whether or not the successor is then in existence,
for the unexpired portion of the year. There shall be
no filing fee.
```

In other words, if Able-Brooks Broker Dealers, LLC, is going to become Able-Brooks, Inc., in early spring, they can go ahead and register the new entity, which can use the rest of the year's registration without paying a fee.

If any of the bigwigs at the broker-dealer are also agents, the process of registering the broker-dealer makes it unnecessary for those bigwigs to also register as agents. As the Uniform Securities Act puts it: "Registration of a broker-dealer automatically constitutes registration of any agent who is a partner, officer, or director, or a person occupying a similar status or performing similar functions." And, as usual, the Act says pretty much the same thing about investment advisers, but let's not cheat you out of a chance to see it in its original legalese: "Registration of an investment adviser automatically constitutes registration of any investment adviser representative who is a partner, officer, or director, or a person occupying a similar status or performing similar functions. "

Why the test digs that deep into the nuances of registration of persons…no idea. But be prepared for just about anything on the Series 63.

Business Practices

(21 of 60 questions on the exam)

More than one of every three questions on your Series 63 exam will be concerned with business practices in the securities industry.

FRAUD

Part 1 of the Uniform Securities Act is entitled, "Fraud and Other Prohibited Practices." Fraud is a big deal, and preventing fraud is the main purpose of "blue sky" or state securities law. As the title of Part 1 indicates, fraud is prohibited. But the exam might force you to distinguish fraud from other violations that are simply prohibited. If a broker-dealer is charging excessive markups when dealing securities, that's a prohibited practice that could get their license denied, suspended, or revoked. On the other hand, if the broker-dealer sends trade confirmations indicating that the municipal bonds were marked up by $1 per bond, when the markup was, in fact, $12.50 per bond, now *that* is fraud.

Fraud involves lies, deceits, and omissions of important facts. If there is criminal intent and the amount of money is high enough, the Administrator can refer it to the attorney general or district attorney, who might file criminal charges and try to put the person in jail plus fines. If the activity is occurring in more than one state, the Administrator can refer it to the US Attorney's office and let the better-funded feds take it from there. Securities fraud involves using deception, misstatements, and omissions in connection with the offer, sale, or purchase of any security, or in connection with the investment advisory side of the business. If an agent, broker-dealer, investment adviser, or adviser representative deceives an investor by lying or leaving out important information, the Administrator will suspend or revoke the license. The following press release from the Illinois "Administrator," which is the Securities Department under the Secretary of State's Office, provides a good example of fraud. Notice how the investigation started with the "Administrator," but since it involved large amounts of money and interstate commerce, the Administrator handed it off to the feds.

JESSE WHITE ANNOUNCES FATHER AND DAUGHTER GUILTY OF DEFRAUDING MORE THAN 100 INVESTORS OF OVER $4 MILLION IN OIL AND GAS INVESTMENT SCAM

A father and daughter pled guilty to a fraudulent oil and gas investment scheme in which over 100 people lost more than $4 million.

Carl E. Royse, of Fairfield, Illinois, and his daughter Jeanette Riley, of Olney, Illinois, as well as their company Hughes Energy, Inc., pled guilty in federal court to charges of conspiracy to engage in fraudulent interstate transactions and in the sale of unregistered securities. Both face up to five years in prison, mandatory restitution of $4 million and fines up to $8 million. The corporation faces fines up to an $8 million.

"Here is a case where the promoters used the Internet and sales representatives to gain the trust of investors with false promises of new methods of recovering oil." White said. "With the price of gas on the rise, con-artists are preying on people's fears to lure them into risky investments promising low risk and high rewards." White encourages investors to investigate whether a company is registered and the salespeople are licensed before making an investment."

As part of a federal plea agreement with the U.S. Attorney's Office of the Southern District of Illinois, the two admitted that from approximately July 2003 until June of 2007, they fraudulently offered and sold fractional interests in well projects to investors nationwide. They operated a Ponzi scheme, using new investor funds to pay off old investors. Royse and Riley misled investors on what they could expect from the investments. The funds were not used for drilling the particular promised well projects, they instead used the funds to make payoffs to complaining investors and to make what was represented to oil investors to be oil production payments. Sentencing is scheduled for October 20, 2008.

The case was the result of an investigation conducted by the Postal Inspection Service and White's Illinois Securities Department. The case is being prosecuted by U.S. Attorney's Office for the Southern District of Illinois.

Investors who believe that they have been a victim of securities fraud should contact Secretary White's Illinois Securities Department at 1-800-628-7937.

So, fraud is a big deal. Federal and state securities laws prohibit the use of deception and manipulation in connection with the offer, sale, or purchase of any security. So, if the investment fits the definition of a "security," and the security is being offered or sold, it is unlawful to "employ any device, scheme, or artifice to defraud any person." And, in connection with an offer, sale, or purchase of *any* security, it would be unlawful to make any misstatement of a material fact or to omit any material fact.

Let's make sure you understand that it's not just what you say, but also what you *didn't* say that can get you in trouble. If you print up a prospectus showing investors your company's medical equipment that has generated profits but you leave out the fact that it is also the subject of several major product liability lawsuits, that would be an omission of a material fact. You would be attempting to take the investor's hard-earned money under false pretenses.

Do you have to tell investors *all* facts in relation to a security? If you're pitching 1,000 shares of GE, do you have to tell them that the average height of the GE executive has increased by .38 inches per decade, now topping 5-feet, 9 and 3/4 inches? What if you tell them that GE is planning to paint their boardroom red but somebody determines the paint color is, in fact, mauve; can investors come after you for omissions or misstatements of material facts?

No—that information was im-material, or irrelevant to the investor's decision. So, don't let the exam steal a cheap point from you by tricking you into thinking you have to state "all facts" about a security. Just make sure you state all *material* facts, meaning the facts that are relevant to the investor's decision. Investors are entitled to full disclosure of all the risks—if you mislead them about the risks involved or the amount of money being charged, you are defrauding them, taking their money or property under false pretenses.

What if an investor tells her agent to purchase "government bonds" to meet her objective of "capital preservation and conservative income" and that agent purchases "government bonds" issued by Nicaragua and Honduras? Was the investor mistreated? Absolutely. She needed US Government bonds, which are guaranteed by an issuer with perfect credit scores. What she got, instead, were shaky bonds that could easily default and cause her to lose the entire principal that she is trying to preserve. Is the agent subject to criminal charges? No. And since he didn't mean any harm, the Administrator isn't going to take away his license, right?

Wrong. To protect investors, the state would suspend or revoke that agent's license. His actions weren't criminal, but the "act, practice, or course of business operated or *would* operate as a fraud or deceit upon any person" because of his incompetence. They don't let dentists continue to conduct business once their incompetence is revealed. If your child were harmed by an overdose of anesthetic while having a tooth pulled, would you really care what the dentist "meant" or "intended" to do? The dentist probably had no intent to harm anyone, but you and the state would still want him shut down immediately before anyone else suffers from his apparent incompetence. The state administrative licensing authorities have to protect residents from dangerous doctors, dentists, securities agents, and investment advisers. It's not really a matter of what the person "meant" to do—that's a matter for criminal courts. The Administrator is simply out to protect investors. If an individual or business entity poses a threat to investors, it would be "in the public interest" in that it "provides necessary protection to investors" to stop that threat. Surprisingly, the state securities Administrator is often very nice about taking away somebody's license. They aren't the prosecutors shown in TV legal dramas trying to rip the respondent a new one in some humiliating, tearful verbal smack-down. Often the state just sort of says, "Look, no hard feelings, Sweetie. You just need to find a new career, okay? Good luck now and thanks for coming in this morning. Buh-bye."

So whether the person intended to deceive somebody or not, when an investor is given false information or is not given important facts necessary to make an informed decision, that operates as a fraud on the investor. The question of whether the person *intended* to deceive would only matter in a criminal case. That's why the Uniform Securities Act points out that if someone can prove he/they had no knowledge of a particular rule or order and could not have reasonably known it was, like, a bad idea, he/they cannot be *imprisoned*. But, to protect investors, the Administrator can take away licenses. If an agent doesn't know what the heck he's doing, he is engaging in a course of business that would operate as a fraud on any person. In fact, pretty soon, he won't be operating.

OTHER PROHIBITED PRACTICES

UNSUITABLE RECOMMENDATIONS

So, fraud is a prohibited practice and can easily be prosecuted as a criminal violation, plus all the civil liability to people who were harmed by the deception. However, not every violation of securities law has to do with fraud. The following "prohibited practices" do not always contain an element of fraud/deceit, but if you engage in any of these prohibited practices, your license could end up being denied, suspended, or revoked by the Administrator. And, your SRO will likely fine you and suspend or bar you, depending on the severity of the violation. In fact, it usually goes the other way—FINRA disciplines an agent or broker-dealer and is then kind enough to provide prompt notification to the state securities Administrator. Now, the state has a reason to suspend or revoke the license after notice and opportunity for a hearing, etc.

Perhaps the main job of a securities representative is to make suitable recommendations to investors. The only way to know what's suitable for an investor is to get some important background information. What is their net worth? What is their annual income? What other investments do they already have? What are their investment objectives? What's their time horizon, risk tolerance, etc.? If your investor has no financial ability to withstand a loss of principal or needs to make sure a certain amount of money will be available when he purchases a home some time this year, put that money in the money market. No, he won't get rich in the money market, but he also won't lose the principal, and you won't lose your license. Municipal bonds are for high-tax-bracket investors, so if you recommend them before you know your client's tax situation, that's a bad idea. It would also be a bad idea to recommend municipal bonds for 401(k) or Traditional IRA plans. Muni's pay interest that is tax-free at the federal (and maybe the state/local) level. If you put those things in a 401(k), all the interest earned would end up getting taxed at ordinary income rates, which would be silly. Deferred annuities involve steep surrender charges, maybe for 10, 15 years, or more. So, if you're trying to put senior citizens into these investments, you're probably violating suitability requirements, since they may need to withdraw money to cover a medical emergency. If they get hit with a 10% surrender charge after being told they "could not possibly lose money," or after being told nothing about the surrender charge, the regulators will get mighty ticked. It happens to be an issue of extreme concern currently, in fact, and no matter what your *opinion* might be of deferred annuities, I would expect a regulatory exam to take a very skeptical if not hostile view toward the pairing of senior investors and deferred annuities. And, please remember, if you sell deferred annuities for a living, you might accidentally think I have an opinion about them—I do not. I'm not doing opinions in this book. I'm just trying to help you pass a tricky, annoying exam called the Series 63.

But we have a lot more to talk about than suitability, so let's keep moving.

CHURNING

If a broker-dealer or agent is pressuring customers into trading more than they're comfortable trading in order to pocket commissions, *that* is churning. For most customers frequent trading is by definition unsuitable. Even if an individual could somehow time the market, the short-term capital gains taxes, commissions, and other transaction costs would eat into any profits. When the agent is pressuring customers to trade, he is putting their money at risk while shielding himself from any financial risk; in fact, he makes the same commission whether the investor wins, loses, or draws. Some investors will trade more frequently than others, so the "character of the account" is what determines how frequently trades should be encouraged. Regulators talk about "turnover rates" when they find evidence of churning. There is no perfect number, but I have seen some regulators write that "a turnover rate of six or higher" is generally considered excessive. A turnover rate of six would be found in an account with an average balance of, say, $25,000 but with total trading of $150,000 for the year. That would be like purchasing $25,000 of stock in January, selling it in March, buying it back in May, selling it in July, buying it back in September, and selling it again in November.

So, there is no magic number, but you can see that it's hard to justify frequent trading. I would expect the exam to try to snare you with a false answer choice such as, "as long as the client's account achieves a profit, the agent is not in violation." Watch out for that. Someone who had not studied enough would easily buy into that—come on, as long as the guy is making money, what's he got to complain about? Oh no, no, no. If an agent makes an unsuitable recommendation, her license could be suspended or revoked even if the client ended up profiting. You told an 81-year-old widow to sell 1,000 shares of Google short and ended up netting her a profit of $10,000? I'm sure the client is pleased, but if FINRA found out about it, your license would likely be suspended, and then FINRA would let your state Administrator know about the little mishap. That's the kind of thing that makes a good and likely Series 63 question—they love to write questions in which two answers seem as if they could be defended equally well. Is it fair? No idea. You simply have to miss 18 or fewer questions on this test. You can do that, whether it's fair, accurate, or whatever. This is a test. This is only a test.

UNAUTHORIZED TRANSACTIONS

When a registered representative or "securities agent" takes a trade ticket up to the wire room, the folks there assume it's because the customer just called in an order to buy or sell stock. Sometimes they assume too much. Sometimes the registered representative simply decided to enter "a couple of small trades" in the accounts of a few customers who never seem to notice anything about their accounts, anyway.

We're talking about a very serious violation called executing an "unauthorized transaction." And, it's also fraudulent. Why? You're spending the client's money and trying to conceal that fact from the client so that you can earn a commission. So remember to *never* enter a customer order that no customer ever ordered. And, if you direct the trade confirmations to your own PO box to keep the customer in the dark, you are never going to work in the securities industry again, although running for Congress would obviously still be an option.

MISREPRESENTING THE STATUS OF CUSTOMER ACCOUNTS

If an agent wanted to execute a series of unauthorized transactions, how would he do it? He'd probably indicate "unsolicited" on each trade ticket and pretend that the client had called him to place each order. But won't the client get the trade confirmations? Not if the agent indicates a bogus mailing address or uses his *own* mailing address to keep the customer in the dark. He might have the actual account statements sent to the false mailing address, or if he has the audacity, he might even create his own version of the truth and send his clients bogus account statements. Just in case you hadn't already assumed so, an agent who executes trades in a customer account without the customer's knowledge and then sends bogus account statements to the customer through the US mail to hide the activity is *never going to work in the securities industry again.*

ACCEPTING ORDERS FROM AN UNAUTHORIZED THIRD PARTY

One of your best customers is too busy to call you, so he has his wife give you a ring. Buy 10,000 shares of Google at $415.95, she says.

What do you do?

You don't execute the order, that's for sure. Not until you get it from your client. For an individual account, you only accept orders from that individual. If that individual gives trading authorization to another individual—i.e., his wife—and you have that on file with their signatures, then it's okay to accept the order. But a third party without authorization can't tell you what to do for your client's account. Another third party who would have authorization would be a trustee in a trust account or an investment adviser entering trades on behalf of his advisory clients. But in all cases, the agent and broker-dealer only accept orders from other people if there is something in writing on file. Another name for trading authorization is "power of attorney." Full power of attorney lets the other party tell you to not just sell securities, but to send a check to the account owner. Limited power of attorney only allows the party to tell you what to buy or sell.

UNAUTHORIZED BORROWING OF CLIENT FUNDS/SECURITIES

Chances are you have enough sense to resist the temptation of calling up all your investors and asking them to, like, spot you a thousand bucks until payday. Unfortunately, many reps do not have that good sense, so the regulators want you to know it's a really bad idea to ask for, let alone accept, a loan from a client.

Of course, if your client is a lending institution (bank, thrift, S&L, credit union), no problem. They make loans for a living. And, if your client is an immediate family member or someone you have a business relationship with, that's different. Still, you need to let your firm know what you're doing. They'll follow the FINRA rule on customer borrowing/lending activities, and you'll avoid getting yourself in trouble.

Since an investment adviser is a "fiduciary," they really wouldn't be able to borrow money from a client and also put the needs of that client ahead of their own. So, I don't see how they're going to be able to do it and still pass the smell test. I mean, an adviser is a business or a business person. He/she/they like to borrow money at the same interest rate we all do—zero percent. *Okay, Granny, we'll give you 2% interest if you front us a hundred grand for 90 days.* Wait a minute now—maybe T-bills are paying 4%. Is the adviser pretending that their credit score is higher than the United States Government's? Aren't they clearly taking advantage of the investor, putting their own selfish needs ahead of hers? They should be sticking her $100,000 into a safer security, or if they're going to put her into unrated junk bonds, at least give Granny the risk premium she's entitled to. And, advisers should not be acting as issuers of securities. "Advising" an investor to put money into your advisory business is totally unethical—there's no way you can put the investor's needs ahead of your own when you're trying to get as much capital for your business as you possibly can at the best possible terms. Can you objectively compare the investment risks of your firm versus all the other investment opportunities he could be putting his money into? Is there a secondary market if he wants to liquidate this so-called "preferred stock" you're offering? The regulators hate it when advisers engage in "self-dealing," which means to use the relationship with the client to an unfair advantage.

COMMINGLING

Borrowing and commingling both involve the fatal mistake of forgetting the subtle yet important difference between your money and the *investor's* money. In fact, what the heck would *your* money *ever* be doing mixed in there with client funds? Several of the orders I've read at the various state Administrative websites recently involve agents having clients cut checks in their name and then depositing the money into the agents' own bank or trading accounts. That would be known as commingling or, technically, as "a really bad idea." So, in case you actually had to be reminded, don't be driving around with your client's cash and securities in your glove box. And, if you sell her one of Fidelity's mutual funds, I'm thinking the check they write should be payable to Fidelity rather than to you or to "cash."

Just a suggestion.

The NASAA website at www.nasaa.org has an "Investment Fraud Awareness Quiz." One of the questions is, "Ways to protect yourself from investment fraud include…" with choice "D" being "Never write the check for an investment in the name of your salesperson."

Sounds like good advice to me. So, if the agent in the exam question is having customers write checks in his name or depositing their funds into his own account, that is a violation known as commingling.

Broker-dealers hold customer securities in safekeeping, usually in "street name." All the securities I own are titled in the name of the broker-dealer carrying my account. This is partly why "books and records" are such a big deal. The regulators don't want to come in for an examination and discover that there is no way to tell which securities belong to the firm and which to the customer accounts. Regulators want broker-dealers to list each security that they hold, and they want a clear record of which account holds how many shares of the bazillion shares of GE, Wal-Mart, etc. that the firm is sitting on. If you get a question about a broker-dealer who is getting sloppy and mixing up the firm's own trading account with the securities they hold for customers, remember that this is a serious violation known as commingling.

MISAPPROPRIATING CLIENT FUNDS

It seems natural to follow up "commingling" with "misappropriating client funds" because seldom do you see one without the other. Once the investor's money gets all mixed up in there with the agent's money, and then the market starts tanking, and the bogus account statements don't work any more…well, you can see where this is headed. Misappropriating client funds could easily rise far above any trouble the agent might have under the Uniform Securities Act, too. Again, the district attorney or attorney general might be talking about mail and wire fraud charges, larceny, theft by deception, etc. So, remember that it's a really bad idea to mix client funds with your own, and an even worse idea to start spending client funds or lending their securities without their knowledge and consent.

SHARING IN THE PROFITS/LOSSES OF CLIENTS

Some people in the securities industry will actually offer to go halfsies with their investors. "Look, this is such a sure thing that I'm willing to match you dollar-for-dollar. That's right, you put in ten grand, and I'll put in ten grand. If we make money, we split the gain, and if we lose money we split the loss."

Excuse me?

You can't go partners on the trade with your client. Your client has an account. You have a recommendation for the client's account that they may or may not choose to take.

That's it.

Now, if you were talking about a family member or a really good friend or business partner, your firm *might* let you set up a joint account with your client. But, as the exam will ask, you need "the customer's written consent and the firm's written consent." And, good luck getting your firm's written consent.

REFUSING TO FOLLOW A CUSTOMER'S LEGITIMATE INSTRUCTIONS

Now, obviously, if your customer tells you to invest $1,000 today and turn it into $10,000, you don't have to follow that instruction. But, you might be shocked to see how many agents will completely blow off legitimate customer requests. If your customer doesn't want to hold her 1,000 shares of GE anymore and wants you to sell them—sell them. If the customer wants your firm to cut her a check for $5,000 when she has at least that much cash in the account, cut the check. It's her money.

IMPROPERLY USING THE WORD "GUARANTEE"

"Joe—buddy, I understand your hesitation. But, if you buy 1,000 shares of EMC, I *guarantee* you'll make money. Huh? No, you can't possibly lose on this one, Joe-buddy."

You could talk that way to your clients if A) you wanted the Administrator to take away your license or B) you were reasonably sure they would never find out. But the regulators hate phrases such as "can't possibly lose on this investment." As we indicated, a security always involves some chance that the principal could fluctuate if not evaporate, which is, of course, what makes investing in securities so much fun in the first place. The "Investment Fraud Awareness Quiz" mentioned above starts out with a question asking, "Which of the following phrases should raise concern about an investment?" The choices are:

- High rate of return
- Risk-free
- Your investment is guaranteed against loss
- All of the above

The answer is "all of the above," because, unfortunately, NASAA makes their investor quizzes much easier than the Series 63.

Investing in stock carries all kinds of risks, even if it's a solid company. My buddy lost about $40,000 investing in Microsoft for crying out loud, so don't try telling him he "can't lose" by investing in stock, even in a solid blue chip stock like MSFT. If you tell somebody their money is guaranteed when, in fact, it isn't, you have defrauded the investor. Again, even though the confused securities agent meant the investor no harm, he told her he bought her a "secure, government bond" that was guaranteed as to interest and principal, implying that it was a US Treasury Note, Bond, or STRIP, maybe.

No, the money was at extreme risk. I mean, hedge funds can buy unrated government bonds issued by shaky issuers, but if a little old lady thinks she's getting a US Government guarantee against default when she isn't, she has been defrauded. She might end up losing *all* of her principal even as she's thinking that *all* of her principal is guaranteed by the United States Treasury.

Now, the word "guarantee" *can* be used, but you'd better use it carefully. A US Treasury bond, note, bill, etc. would definitely be guaranteed as to interest and principal. But, if interest rates rise, the market value will drop, so investors could lose money on Treasury securities if they sell them after interest rates have risen. Give investors all material facts, right?

Some corporate bonds are "guaranteed," usually by the parent company. If one of GE's subsidiaries issues a "guaranteed" bond, investors know that if the issuer can't pay the interest and/or principal, GE will step up to the plate. What if GE also goes bankrupt before the bonds mature?

Hate it when that happens. So, the agent would need to be clear as to exactly what the word "guarantee" means and does not mean. If you saw a question on your exam that asked something like, "If an investor notices that a security has been guaranteed, he should conclude…," please don't tell the test the investor should conclude "there is no chance of sustaining a loss." Tell the test, instead, that he "should conclude that interest, principal, or dividends will be paid by a third party if the issuer defaults." The "payment of capital gains" would make a good fourth choice on a test question. No, the guarantee would only be as to the payment of interest, principal, or dividends.

MISUSING THE WORDS "CERTIFIED" OR "APPROVED"

When you pass your license exams and register with the state, the state will—we hope—grant you a license. At no time, however, will the state "certify" or "approve" you. No offense here; we're not saying they disapprove of you. They simply make no value judgments about your abilities compared to anyone else's. Agents, broker-dealers, investment advisers, and investment adviser representatives are registered with the regulators, not certified or approved.

If you get your "CFP," you will be certified by a professional organization, but still not by the regulators. So, if you told an investor that you had recently been "approved" by the state to offer securities recommendations, you may end up signing for some registered mail from the state. Sometimes regulators like to use the phrase "passed upon," as in "no regulator has passed upon this offer of securities." That's just a legalistic way of saying that the regulators have not passed out an opinion on the quality of the investment, or the adequacy or truthfulness of the disclosure document. So, if a security or an investment adviser has been registered with the Administrator, all this means is that the proper registration procedure has been followed. In no way, shape, or form has the security or the investment adviser been given a seal of approval from the state. To imply otherwise would be a sure way of getting into trouble with the securities Administrator.

MISUSING CERTIFICATIONS

One of the hottest regulatory topics currently is the way certain sales people have conferred upon themselves impressive-sounding credentials of dubious worth. My own favorite is the "certified financial gerontologist" that some people are using at free lunch seminars to imply that they are specially qualified to offer investments to senior citizens. NASAA has already issued a model rule and many states have already adopted guidelines for using certifications, especially those with the word "senior" in them or anything targeted at elderly investors. Before printing a credential on your business card, check with compliance or your state's guidelines.

Let's take a look at the main part of the new NASAA model rule:

```
The use of a senior specific certification or desig-
nation by any person in connection with the offer,
sale, or purchase of securities, or the provision
of advice as to the value of or the advisability
of investing in, purchasing, or selling securities,
either directly or indirectly or through publications
or writings, or by issuing or promulgating analyses
or reports relating to securities, that indicates or
implies that the user has special certification or
training in advising or servicing senior citizens or
retirees, in such a way as to mislead any person shall
```

be a dishonest and unethical practice in the securities business. The prohibited use of such certifications or professional designation includes, but is not limited to, the following:

- use of a certification or professional designation by a person who has not actually earned or is otherwise ineligible to use such certification or designation
- use of a nonexistent or self-conferred certification or professional designation
- use of a certification or professional designation that indicates or implies a level of occupational qualifications obtained through education, training, or experience that the person using the certification or professional designation does not have
- use of a certification or professional designation that was obtained from a designating or certifying organization that:

> is primarily engaged in the business of instruction in sales and/or marketing

> does not have reasonable standards or procedures for assuring the competency of its designees or certificants

> does not have reasonable standards or procedures for monitoring and disciplining its designees or certificants for improper or unethical conduct

> does not have reasonable continuing education requirements for its designees or certificants in order to maintain the designation or certificate

Which organizations *can* grant certifications that don't end up getting the "certifcant" in hot water? The model rule lists the following: The American National Standards Institute, The National Commission for Certifying Agencies, or an organization on the US Department of Education's list called "Accrediting Agencies Recognized for Title IV Purposes."

So, if a CFP has earned her CFP, she can definitely use that certification. But, if somebody just printed "CFP" on her business cards without actually going through the program, that would be unethical and prohibited. Or, if somebody makes up a title that no one else actually recognizes. Or if he just sort of orders a certificate from a sales and marketing organization that does no background checks and has no real standards for issuing certificates beyond making sure the check clears. The regulators are on the lookout for people trying to mislead investors, especially senior investors. Be careful on the exam and in the real world about using the word "senior" in any credential.

FAILURE TO BRING WRITTEN COMPLAINTS TO YOUR EMPLOYER'S ATTENTION

If a customer sends her securities agent a written complaint, it's always tempting for the agent to accidentally drop the complaint in the shredder. Unfortunately, the agent's principal has to respond to this written complaint, keep a record of the complaint in a special file, etc. Also unfortunately, the complaints are updated on the agent's U-4 and are, therefore, available to customers and prospects at www.finra.org under "broker check." I'm guessing that can't possibly help a sales person's close ratio, so it is tempting to conceal the written complaint from your principal. However, it's a serious violation, especially if you get caught.

INSIDER INFORMATION

If your sister's company were about to be purchased by American Express, chances are when the announcement comes out, American Express's stock will drop a little bit, and her company's stock will probably shoot up. Therefore, if the announcement won't come out until next Thursday, you could probably make a lot of money for your customers by telling them to buy puts on AXP and calls on your sister's company.

You could probably also lose your license. Both the person passing around the inside information and the one trading on it violate insider trading rules. The SEC handles most cases in civil court, where they ask the court to penalize the insider trader three times the amount of the benefit. Some cases are handed off to the US Attorney's office for criminal prosecution, and people have ended up in prison for insider trading.

Remember that CEOs, CFOs, and members of the board of directors are watched very closely to make sure they aren't dumping shares ahead of bad news, or trying to quietly pick up shares before announcing good news, but anyone with privileged, non-public information is treated potentially as an insider under insider trading rules. If your buddy was a sales rep who knew that a large public company was about to lose their three biggest customers, you and he could not buy puts on the stock, then go into several investment chat rooms spreading the bad news, profiting when the company announces that they've had to revise earnings estimates downwards by 50% for the year.

How would they ever catch anybody?

The SEC pays *bounties* to people who drop a dime on an insider trader. As you can see at their website, the SEC is authorized to do a little revenue share with people whose tips lead to big civil penalties against insider traders. And, the fact is, if he's the sort who likes to cheat, there's a decent chance he has a few enemies who would love to do their civic duty while also earning, say, 10% of a $3 million civil monetary penalty.

If you get a question about an agent or adviser who has spoken with a fiduciary of a public company, such as the CFO or a board member, and knows that the company is about to be acquired by a larger competitor, which will likely send the price of the stock up when it's announced, that information cannot be used or passed around. So, the exam will probably ask what you would do if you had this sort of privileged, non-public information yourself. Would you use it to solicit orders for customers whom you'd like to make rich in a hurry? Of course not, but what if a customer just happened to call in and give you an unsolicited order to purchase that company's stock—would you have to refuse the order based on what you know? No. As long as the customer just happens to want to buy the stock, execute the order as instructed. But, if you buy shares or tell other people to hurry up and buy before the announcement comes out, that will likely be the end of a career.

For a test question asking which of the following four examples represent insider trading violations, look for a case where the information is known only by a select few and is being used or passed around before it becomes public. Once the information is released to the media, SEC, etc., then it's too late to worry about "insider trading." The information, by definition, now gives you no advantage. Insider information is only profitable if you know something the rest of the market doesn't know yet.

SOLICITING ORDERS FOR UNREGISTERED, NON-EXEMPT SECURITIES

We haven't gotten very deep into the concept of exempt and non-exempt securities, but for now, just break down the words. The word "exempt" means "excused from registration." So, if a security is "non-exempt" it is "not excused from registration." Therefore, soliciting orders for a security that should be registered but isn't would be a bad idea. That first notice of hearing we looked at was an example of a non-exempt security, the promissory note, being offered and sold without being properly registered.

Offering/selling unregistered, non-exempt securities is a major, major violation. It usually means that a scam artist offers some type of promissory note or so-called "preferred stock" that is supposedly guaranteed to pay huge rates of return. Why investors would believe that a company could afford to pay 10% interest per *month* or would have to pay that rate if their finances were as solid as they claim, I have no idea, but finding gullible investors is not difficult. If the seller has no ethical compass, it's easy to take the investor's money and disappear before the investor realizes the thing he bought isn't worth the paper it's printed on. If the seller had to actually register the security, he would not be able sell it under the table. In fact, the so-called "issuer" might not even have enough money in the bank to pay the registration fee, regardless of what they tell and show investors. The state regulators want to see the financial statements of the company, and they want to see all the disclosure they plan to provide to investors. Once the Administrator sees that the company has exactly $14 in the bank and intends to sell "guaranteed subordinated notes," things are going to come to a screeching halt. But this will only happen if and when these non-exempt securities are *registered*.

OUTSIDE BUSINESS ACTIVITIES

An agent of a broker-dealer must notify the broker-dealer of *any* outside activity for which he earns compensation. Industry rules require the agent to notify the firm in writing before taking any sort of part-time job, speaking engagement, what have you. While the rules don't quite say that the firm needs to grant written permission, they do make it clear that the firm can deny the agent's outside activity, supervise it, or limit it. We're not just talking about activities connected to the investment business— we're talking about *any* outside activity for which the agent receives compensation.

SELLING AWAY OR PRIVATE SECURITIES TRANSACTIONS

An agent is a registered representative of a broker-dealer. The broker-dealer has to supervise the sales activities of all agents. Therefore, if an agent offers any security outside the firm's knowledge and control, that agent has committed a violation called "selling away," which is short for "selling away from the firm." Maybe the agent likes to sell a family of mutual funds that his firm doesn't offer through his buddy's broker-dealer. Unfortunately, when his employer finds out, the agent is going to get in trouble with FINRA and will almost certainly be fired. Some agents think they can call their customers and offer them opportunities to invest in some condominium rehab project they're cooking up with an old college roommate—whatever. Agents simply cannot offer investment opportunities outside the scope of their employment at the broker-dealer. If the agent wants to offer any sort of investment to clients that the firm doesn't generally sponsor, he would have to get the firm's written approval, provide them with all kinds of disclosure documents, and the firm would have to supervise the sales activities and record them on their regular books and records. Which is why the firm is going to say, "No way." If the agent goes ahead and does it, anyway, we're talking about "selling away," a major violation.

ARBITRAGE—NOT A VIOLATION

Before computer trading, arbitrageurs exploited the slight difference in price for the same stock trading on various exchanges, selling GE for $20 on the NYSE, for example, and quietly buying it on the Philadelphia or Midwest exchange for $19.82. Hedge funds today might exploit the difference in price between a convertible bond and the underlying stock that occurs due to market inefficiencies and other factors way beyond the scope of this exam. So, in case the exam tries to pull a fast one on you, please know that arbitrage is often presented as a false choice in a Series 63 question. It might be made to look like a violation, but it is not.

ORDER TICKETS AND TRADE CONFIRMATIONS

Agents, also called registered representatives, take orders from customers to purchase and sell securities. Whether the order is entered electronically or through a paper form, the exam will refer to the form as an "order ticket" or "trade ticket" and may expect you to know what is and is not included on this form.

- First, you can take a look at an order ticket at www.passthe63.com/extra
- Second, remember that the essential information includes: buy or sell, stock symbol, agent's ID #, customer account #, market/limit/stop order, trade and settlement date, whether solicited—unsolicited—discretionary
- Third, remember that the order tickets must be approved by a principal
- Fourth, notice that the agent's commission is not indicated on an order or trade ticket…that important detail would go on the order or trade *confirmation*, which, unlike the trade ticket, is sent to the customer

To see a sample of a trade confirmation, go to the same link above, www.passthe63.

com/extra. A trade confirmation simply confirms a trade. When you buy brushes, drop cloths, and paint at the home improvement store, you get a receipt listing all the items, prices, taxes, etc., involved with that transaction. When you buy or sell securities through a registered representative, you receive a more complicated receipt called an order or trade confirmation. The confirmation has the customer's account number, the transaction number, the registered rep's code or number, the activity, the security, the number of units, the principal amount, the commission, the trade and settlement dates, and a description of the transaction. The trade confirmation is due no later than settlement. For common stock, as well as for corporate and municipal bonds, settlement occurs on the third business day after the trade. So if the trade is executed on Monday, settlement takes place on Thursday, unless Thursday is a holiday. If the transaction occurs on a Wednesday, it settles on Monday. Options and Treasury securities settle on the next business day. "T + 3" is an abbreviation for "regular way settlement" of common stock, corporate bonds, and municipal bonds. "T + 1" is an abbreviation for "regular way settlement" for listed options and Treasury securities trading on the secondary market.

Remember that the order ticket is an internal document at the firm, while the trade confirmation is a document that is delivered to the customer, with copies, of course, maintained by the broker-dealer. Falsifying order tickets or trade confirmations would lead to very serious regulatory actions. If a registered representative is trying to execute unauthorized transactions, one way he would do that is to falsify the trade ticket, marking it "unsolicited" and pretending that the customer had called in the order. To keep the customer in the dark, maybe the registered representative provides the firm with a bogus mailing address for the customer, which is really a PO box owned by the registered rep. NYSE regulators recently censured and barred a registered representative who misrepresented the source of a client's funds when entering an application to purchase a variable annuity for the client. Had the agent indicated that the money came from talking the 84-year-old investor into cashing in a fully paid life insurance policy, the purchase order would have been rejected by the firm. So, the agent tried to conceal that important information from his compliance department, which is always a bad idea. Oh well, he has a year off now in which to consider that mistake and tweak his whole approach to the financial services industry.

BUSINESS PRACTICES FOR INVESTMENT ADVISERS, IARS

The Uniform Securities Act reminds investment advisers not to "employ any device, scheme, or artifice to defraud the other person," or "engage in any act, practice, or course of business which operates or would operate as a fraud or deceit upon the other person" when rendering investment advice. And then the Act adds:

> In the solicitation of advisory clients, it is unlawful for any person to make any untrue statement of a material fact, or omit to state a material fact necessary in order to make the statements made, in light of the circumstances under which they are made, not misleading.

In other words, the Uniform Securities Act not only prohibits deception when providing investment advice, but also when soliciting advisory clients.

CONTRACTS, COMPENSATION

Investment advisory contracts need to spell out the terms of the "deal" between the advisor and the client: the services provided, fees charged, method for calculating the fee, does the adviser have discretion, etc. The Uniform Securities Act requires that at least three items are spelled out between the adviser and their client:

- the investment adviser shall not be compensated on the basis of a share of capital gains or capital appreciation
- no assignment of the contract may be made by the investment adviser without the consent of the other party to the contract
- the investment adviser, if organized as a part-nership, shall notify the other party to the contract of any change in the membership of the partnership within a reasonable time after the change.

Let's start with compensation. Investment advisers either charge an hourly rate to give financial planning advice, or they manage a client's portfolio in exchange for a percentage of the assets. Maybe they charge 1%. That's a great incentive for the adviser, right? One percent of $150,000 is nice, but one percent of $200,000 is even nicer. So, the percentage stays flat and the adviser's compensation only grows if the customer's assets grow.

Sounds like a great way to compensate an investment adviser, right? Absolutely. In fact, the Uniform Securities Act immediately clarifies the first bullet point by stating, "Subparagraph (c)(1) does not prohibit an investment advisory contract which provides for compensation based upon the total value of a fund averaged over a definite period, or as of definite dates or taken as of a definite date. "

Okay, maybe "clarifies" was pushing it. The Uniform Securities Act is saying that the adviser can charge a percentage of the client's account value taken as of the last day, or first day, maybe, of each financial quarter. What the adviser can't do is take half of the capital gains that he makes trading the client's account. See, some advisers would rather just take a share of the gains or appreciation on particular *stocks*. Every time the adviser buys a stock at 10 and sells at 18, he gets 20% of that $8-per-share capital gain. Take a $1 million account and spread it evenly among 10 stocks. This one stock turned $100,000 into $180,000, and the adviser gets his customary one-fifth, or $16,000. What about the rest of the stocks?

Who cares, right? The client had a big gain, and the adviser wants his cut. Those other stocks simply didn't work out the way he figured—sorry about that.

See how quickly an unsophisticated investor could think he was making money while the overall value of the account was dropping? He now has $64,000 cash money in his hand because of this one lucky stock pick, but, overall, his account is down drastically. The other $900,000 invested among the other 9 stocks is actually down 57.5%. In other words, he's sitting on $382,500 of stock after walking away with $164,000. His $1 million is now worth $546,500, but the adviser walked away with $16,000 for being such a hero?

And, if a client were to pay the adviser with a share of capital gains or appreciation, the adviser would be given a major incentive to avoid dependable, blue chip stocks in favor of high-risk securities. Wal-Mart (WMT) is a solid company, but there's no conceivable way the stock could triple this year. All those crazy penny stocks out there—why not buy 100 of them and play craps with the client's money?

That's why advisers shall not be compensated "on the basis of a share of capital gains upon or capital appreciation of the funds or any portion of the funds of the client." Portfolio managers are compensated as a percentage of assets over a specified time period. Financial planners and consultants bill their clients a flat or hourly rate—a financial planner doesn't charge $250 per hour plus 20% of any appreciation on any of the mutual funds she recommends. If I'm charging you 1% of assets to manage your portfolio, we'll probably take the account value at the end of each financial quarter and charge you .25% of that. Not 1% a year plus 20% of any upside.

Remember that investment advisers can never be compensated as a share of capital gains or capital appreciation.

Except when they can.

These regulations are designed to provide <u>necessary</u> protection to investors. Some investors don't need so much protection. The regulators are like parents, with their children being the investors in their state. If you're a parent, you will come after *anybody* who messes with your kids. But you have to provide more protection to your two-year-old than you do your 12-year-old. You can't let your two-year-old out of your sight for more than a few seconds, while the 12-year-old has the freedom to walk to school, ride her bike to a friend's house, and possibly go away to music or tennis camp for weeks at a time.

For securities regulators, the average investor is the two-year-old who needs lots of protection. But sophisticated investors are like the 12-year-old, who can be trusted not to get into somebody's car pursuant to an offer of candy. Because sophisticated investors understand the higher risks involved and because they have a lot more money to throw on the fire if they do get burned, the regulators will allow advisers to share in capital gains/appreciation and charge performance bonuses. If your adviser is paid a bonus for matching or beating the S&P 500, what happens in a year in which the adviser loses 30% of your account value when the S&P dropped 33%?

You owe him a bonus.

For losing 30% of your account value?

Absolutely—he blew the index away by three percentage points. So, we can imagine how the average-Joe investor might not take kindly to paying extra money when his account is down by almost a third its value. But, for the following sophisticated investors, advisers can charge performance bonuses versus a particular index:

- Registered Investment Companies (mutual funds, annuities)
- Private Investment Companies (only take money from qualified purchasers)
- Qualified Purchasers (corporations with $25 million, family-owned corporations with $5 million, individuals with $5 million)
- Partnerships where all investors are accredited (hedge funds)
- Individuals with either $1.5 million net worth or $750,000 in assets under management with the firm
- Any director or officer of the advisory firm, or any individual working in the investment operations (the IARs, not the secretary or receptionist)

That weeds out the average investor, right? The adviser taking on the individual has to believe that the individual understands that by paying the adviser for matching or beating some index, the adviser may take on extra risk. And the adviser has to factor in the whole portfolio—one good stock pick isn't going to cut it, not if the assets overall have lost value. If the exam mentions a "fulcrum fee," this is basically what we're talking about here. A fulcrum fee has to reduce the adviser's compensation for underperformance by as much as it would raise it for performance so that the metaphorical see-saw would rise and fall equally. Even though hedge fund managers typically take the first 20% of any capital gains, on top of their 1–2% annual management fees, investment advisers don't share capital gains or charge performance bonuses unless the investors are sophisticated. Hedge funds are made up of accredited investors, and they play hardball—not tee ball. So, again, when all the participants are "sophisticated," they get to play hardball. But, if the investors are Little Leaguers, the adviser cannot be compensated with a performance bonus or share of capital gains/appreciation.

The next bullet point states that an adviser cannot assign a client's contract to another party unless and until the client gives her consent. The advisory contract has to state that no assignment of contract is allowed, and I've seen advisers get in trouble for failing to include that clause in their contracts, even though no assignment of contract ever actually occurred. So, if another entity buys your wealth management firm, they would need to execute new contracts with clients—those contracts don't automatically get "assigned" to the new firm. Not sure the exam digs this deep, but the Uniform Securities Act does clarify what it means by "assignment" by stating: Assignment, "as used in subparagraph (c)(2), includes any direct or indirect transfer or hypothecation of an investment advisory contract by the assignor or of a controlling block of the assignor's outstanding voting securities by a security holder of the assignor."

Ouch. Why do I do this for a living again?

Anyway, the third bullet point is saying that if the firm is a partnership, any time any partner is admitted, withdraws, or dies, clients need to be informed. If the change in partnership structure has to do only with a minority interest, no assignment of contract has occurred. In other words, they simply sold a couple of interests representing, say, a 20% ownership stake—the firm has not changed drastically enough for us to consider that to be assigning the client's contract to a new entity. But, if the change of control involved more than a minority interest, then the new entity would have to get clients to sign new contracts. And, yes, the exam might actually go that far.

So, the adviser cannot transfer clients' contracts without their consent, and if the adviser transfers a controlling block of voting securities in their firm, they have, by definition, become a different entity. Advisory clients would have to sign new contracts in that case.

CONFLICTS OF INTEREST

Investment advisers are defined as "fiduciaries," which means they have to put the needs of the client first at all times. Remember that advisers aren't selling securities to clients—they are investing the client's money. The *client's* money. So, if a recommendation or transaction could pit the adviser's interests against the interests of the client, or if the adviser's interests suddenly get placed into the mix when, really, it should all be about the client, we have a potential "conflict of interest." *All* potential conflicts of interest must be disclosed to the client ahead of time. Potential conflicts of interest include:

Acting as Principal

Investment advisers with discretion buy securities in client accounts and sell securities out of client accounts. What if it turned out they were actually selling clients *their* securities? As a seller they want to get the highest price possible for their security, but as a buyer, you want to get the lowest price possible. Or, when you're selling securities, they're the buyer on the other side—are they *really* giving you the best available price for your securities? Since they're supposed to put your needs first, we now have a conflict of interest, right? That's why the adviser would have to disclose the fact that he/they will act as a principal in the transaction and get your written consent by "completion of the transaction," or "settlement/clearance" of the transaction. To act as a principal means the adviser will either buy the security for inventory from the customer or sell it out of inventory to the customer. It's okay to do it, as long as the potential conflict of interest is disclosed and the customer's written consent is given before the transaction is finalized.

Agency Cross Transaction

Another example where the adviser will benefit from the customer's acceptance of the advice given is called an "agency cross transaction." Here, the most important thing to remember is that the adviser can only be *advising* one side of the transaction. They can be advising you to buy 1,000 shares of ABC, and, as it turns out, they will also act as the broker between you and the seller.

Excuse me? So, should you buy these 1,000 shares because they're a good investment, or because the adviser likes to act as a broker, too, in order to pocket commissions in addition to your advisory fee?

It's a conflict of interest, at least potentially. So, the adviser would need to disclose the potential conflict of interest, get the advisory client's written consent, and at least once per year send a statement itemizing all the "agency cross transactions" effected on behalf of the client. Why? This way clients can ask themselves if the adviser is executing trades on their behalf because it's a good investment strategy for the client, or a nice way for the adviser to pocket commissions on each trade. Full disclosure of all material facts is what all regulators demand and what all investors deserve.

Earning Compensation in Addition to Advisory Fees

As we said, the regulators hate it when advisers engage in "self-dealing." Advisers are either telling clients what to do with their money, or they're trading client accounts on their behalf. Either way, everything they do is for the interest of the client. If they start doing things that enrich the adviser without the client's knowledge, we have a problem. For example, what if your "adviser" was charging you an "advisory fee" when he put you into seven different mutual funds that just happen to pay him high 12b-1 fees? Hmm, maybe the "advice" wasn't as objective as it seemed. The adviser would have to disclose the 12b-1 fee so that you can decide if his advice is actually objective and in your best interest. Advisers might receive compensation from various broker-dealers when executing trades—that needs to be disclosed to clients. Why? It might explain the frequent trading. Hmm, maybe the adviser isn't being as "objective" as he's supposed to be. Compensation received from broker-dealers could come in the form of hard dollars (money) or "soft dollars," including research, software aiding in research, and custodial & clearing services. Advisers may not accept the following forms of soft-dollar compensation: office overhead, salaries, cell phones, computers, vacations, and, in general, anything that clearly benefits the adviser but not the clients.

Recommending Securities the Adviser Also Trades In

Just to make sure advisers aren't trying to pump up the price of the stocks they hold, the regulators require advisers to disclose that they recommend securities to clients that they also trade in themselves. In some ways, this doesn't seem like a scary practice—wouldn't I prefer that my adviser have a stake in the stocks and bonds they put me into? But, when we talk about "conflicts of interest," we're including *potential* conflicts of interest, even *unconscious* conflicts of interest.

Acting Contrary to Recommendations

If an adviser is advising an investor to do things contrary to what the adviser is doing, that should be disclosed. For example, I would like to know that my adviser is selling Google short if he's telling me that I should buy it. Why is he telling me to do something contrary to what he's doing? Maybe it makes sense in some cases.

If I charged clients an hourly rate to draw up an investment strategy, I would make sure the strategy met *their* needs, not mine. I would not likely park all of my money in T-bills, but if this client has an extreme need for liquidity, no ability to withstand a loss or even fluctuation in principal, and wouldn't be able to sleep knowing her account could drop 20% this year, T-bills is what I'm going to recommend. And, I'll tell her that this is contrary to what I would do.

Disclose or Abstain

Usually, disclosing potential conflicts of interest ahead of time and obtaining the client's consent will take care of the problem; however, sometimes the conflict is so great that the adviser must simply abstain. What would be so bad that mere disclosure would not take care of the problem? How about if the portfolio manager manages an account for just the three partners, including himself? In this account there are 1 million shares of XYZ common stock. XYZ common stock has also been placed in many client accounts, based on the portfolio manager's discretion. Well, one morning the portfolio manager reads in the *Wall Street Journal* that XYZ's CEO is about to be indicted for fraud and the company is also going to re-state earnings for the past five years, so he unloads the 1 million shares in the partners' account before selling the shares he's put in client portfolios.

Big mistake. Advisers are fiduciaries, who must put the needs of their clients first. In this case the adviser would have put the needs of the adviser ahead of the client, to the detriment of the client, and no amount of prior disclosure would make it okay. The adviser should have simply abstained from this self-serving activity, or at least made sure nobody found out.

CUSTODY OF CLIENT FUNDS/SECURITIES

The Uniform Securities Act states, "It is unlawful for any investment adviser to take or have custody of any securities or funds of any client if: the Administrator prohibits custody, or if the investment adviser fails to notify the Administrator that he has or may have custody." So, if the Administrator has a rule prohibiting custody, advisers registered in that state had better not take custody of client assets. If there is no rule against custody of client assets, the firm still needs to notify the Administrator, which they would do by updating or indicating this rather important fact on Form ADV.

It always shocks me that someone who is neither a bank nor a custodial broker-dealer would actually try to maintain client assets, keeping track of interest earned, dividends received, purchases and sales of securities, deposits and withdrawals in the account, etc. Most advisers would agree, which is why they use a "qualified custodian" to hold client assets and keep track of them. Banks/savings institutions insured by FDIC, registered broker-dealers, "registered futures commission merchants, and foreign financial institutions" are listed as "qualified custodians" in the NASAA Model Rule on Custody. When an adviser uses a qualified custodian, the custodian sends the quarterly account statements to the client. The adviser sends a billing statement (invoice) to the custodian and a copy to the client as well, representing the amount of the management fee to be deducted and how he arrived at that figure. With this arrangement, the adviser won't have to maintain high net capital requirements or submit an audited balance sheet to the regulators or the clients. They also won't have to pay a CPA to come in unannounced once a year to audit the books and records to see if client assets are, in fact, being properly maintained. To avoid the higher financial requirements, the annual audit, the massive record-keeping requirements, and the frightening responsibility of acting like a bank for thousands of people, most advisers want to "avoid being deemed to have custody" of client assets. The NASAA website has a very helpful Q & A on custody issues from which several potential test questions could be pulled.

First, what does it mean to have "custody" of client funds and securities? Basically, it means that the adviser is holding the funds/securities or has the ability to appropriate them. An exam question might ask what an adviser should do if somebody sends client securities inadvertently to the adviser's office, and the adviser—like most sane people—would like to "avoid being deemed to have custody." The adviser needs to keep records of what happened—the securities that were sent, when they were returned. And, he needs to return them within three business days to the sender. If he does that, he won't be required to meet the financial requirements, or update Form ADV to indicate the firm has custody. Another question might say that the adviser is sent a check from the client payable to a third party—a mutual fund or annuity company, for example. Does the adviser have custody of client assets? Not if he forwards the check to the third party within 24 hours, and not as long as it's really a "third party," not another company related to the adviser's firm.

The typical model is for an adviser to get written discretionary authority from the client to manage/trade the account. The account is held at the custodial broker-dealer, who keeps track of the securities and cash balances that change every single day the market is open, and sends the quarterly account statements showing the positions of securities and cash to the client. The adviser gets written authorization from the client to bill the custodian for the advisory fee. As long as the adviser sends a billing statement (invoice) to the custodian and also the client, and has the client's authorization to do this, everything is fine. The adviser would not have to meet the higher net capital, record keeping, and auditing requirements associated with maintaining custody of client assets.

Some advisers do maintain custody, though, so let's see what they have to do. As we mentioned, before taking custody the adviser first has to check with the state securities Administrator to see if there is a rule prohibiting custody of client funds. If there's no rule against it, the adviser can take custody so long as they notify the Administrator in writing. If the adviser actually does maintain custody, they must:

- Segregate each client's securities and keep good records as to who is who and what is what
- Deposit client funds into a bank account holding only client funds. The accounts must be maintained in the name of the adviser as agent or trustee. Records must be kept for each account showing where it is maintained, all deposits and withdrawals, and the amount of each client's ownership in the account
- Notify each client, in writing, of the place and manner in which the funds and securities will be maintained
- Send statements at least quarterly to each client that are itemized showing all the client's funds and securities and transactions
- Arrange to have an UNANNOUNCED annual inspection by an independent accountant to verify that everything's on the up-and-up. The accountant must then promptly file a report with the Administrator following the examination

ADVERTISEMENTS

Advertisements for Investment Advisers must be fair and accurate. An adviser may not use testimonials from satisfied clients. They can't use testimonials from *dissatisfied* clients, either, though, of course, they wouldn't want to pay somebody big money to go on television and bash the firm. The adviser can list past stock picks provided that they don't imply that future results are somehow guaranteed because of past successes, and if the adviser lists past stock picks, they have to include all recommendations—winners and losers—over the same period. And, the period covered must be at least one year. Some advisers have gotten 10% returns in a month and then bragged about a "120% annualized rate of return" in an advertisement.

Big problem. I saw another adviser put out a list of profitable "stock picks" without mentioning one little caveat—he never actually purchased any of those stocks. They represented a "hypothetical portfolio" only.

In other words, advertising cannot be misleading. If the adviser's stock picks are up 50%, how does that compare to the market in general? If the S&P gained 52% and this guy's stock picks gained 50%, I'd want to know the *whole* story, right? If the recommendations listed pertain only to a select group of clients, that needs to be made clear. It also needs to be clear whether the performance figures are including the management fees (deducted from the returns, right?). If the advertisement claims that a graph, chart, formula or any other device being offered will assist an investor in making his own decisions, the advertisement has to disclose the limitations and the difficulties involved in trying to implement the thing. If the adviser offers "free services with no obligation" those services had better actually be free, with no obligation. In general, advisory advertisements need to go to great lengths to avoid misleading prospects and clients.

NASAA MODEL RULES/STATEMENTS OF POLICY

NASAA's Policy Statement for Broker-Dealers and Agents is fertile ground for test questions. In fact, I would expect 5–10 questions pulled almost verbatim from the following document. I've already pointed out several items from this one; I just didn't want you to feel cheated by not seeing the original document in the original legalese. Luckily, I follow the NASAA statement with an explanation written in a language you are probably more comfortable with.

English.

NASAA's "Dishonest or Unethical Business Practices of Broker-Dealers and Agents"

[Adopted May 23, 1983]

[HIGH STANDARDS AND JUST PRINCIPLES.] Each broker-dealer and agent shall observe high standards of commercial honor and just and equitable principles of trade in the conduct of their business. Acts and practices, including but not limited to the following, are considered contrary to such standards and may constitute grounds for <u>denial, suspension or revocation of registration</u> or such other action authorized by statute.

1. BROKER-DEALERS
a. Engaging in a pattern of unreasonable and unjustifiable delays in the delivery of securities purchased by any of its customers and/or in the payment upon request of free credit balances reflecting completed transactions of any of its customers;

b. Inducing trading in a customer's account which is excessive in size or frequency in view of the financial resources and character of the account;

c. Recommending to a customer the purchase, sale or exchange of any security without reasonable grounds to believe that such transaction or recommendation is suitable for the customer based upon reasonable inquiry concerning the customer's investment objectives, financial situation and needs, and any other relevant information known by the broker-dealer;

d. Executing a transaction on behalf of a customer without authorization to do so;

e. Exercising any discretionary power in effecting a transaction for a customer's account without first obtaining written discretionary authority from the customer, unless the discretionary power relates solely to the time and/or price for the executing of orders;

f. Executing any transaction in a margin account without securing from the customer a properly executed written margin agreement promptly after the initial transaction in the account;

i. Entering into a transaction with or for a customer at a price not reasonably related to the current market price of the security or receiving an unreasonable commission or profit;

j. Failing to furnish to a customer purchasing securities in an offering, no later than the due date of confirmation of the transaction, either a final prospectus or a preliminary prospectus and an additional document, which together include all information set forth in the final prospectus;

k. Charging unreasonable and inequitable fees for services performed, including miscellaneous services such as collection of monies due for principal, dividends or interest, exchange or transfer of securities, appraisals, safekeeping, or custody of securities and other services related to its securities business;

l. Offering to buy from or sell to any person any security at a stated price unless such broker-dealer is prepared to purchase or sell, as the case may be, at such price and under such conditions as are stated at the time of such offer to buy or sell;

m. Representing that a security is being offered to a customer "at the market" or a price relevant to the market price unless such broker-dealer knows or has reasonable grounds to believe that a market for such security exists other than that made, created or controlled by such broker-dealer;

n. Effecting any transaction in, or inducing the purchase or sale of, any security by means of any manipulative, deceptive or fraudulent device, practice, plan, program, design or contrivance, which may include but not be limited to;

(1) Effecting any transaction in a security which involves no change in the beneficial ownership thereof;

(2) Entering an order or orders for the purchase or sale of any security with the knowledge that an order or orders of substantially the same size, at substantially the same time and substantially the same price, for the sale of any such security, has been or will be entered by or for the same or different parties for the purpose of creating a false or misleading appearance of active trading in the security or a false or misleading appearance with respect to the market for the security

(3) Effecting, alone or with one or more other persons, a series of transactions in any security creating actual or apparent active trading in such security or raising or depressing the price of such security, for the purpose of inducing the purchase or sale of such security by others;

o. Guaranteeing a customer against loss in any securities account of such customer carried by the broker-dealer or in any securities transaction effected by the broker-dealer or in any securities transaction effected by the broker-dealer with or for such customer;

p. Publishing or circulating, or causing to be published or circulated, any notice, circular, advertisement, newspaper article, investment service, or communication of any kind which purports to report any transaction as a purchase or sale of any security unless such broker-dealer believes that such transaction was a bona fide purchase or sale or such security; or which purports to quote the bid price or asked price for any security, unless such broker-dealer believes that such quotation represents a bona fide bid for, or offer of, such security;

q. Using any advertising or sales presentation in such a fashion as to be deceptive or misleading; or

r. Failing to disclose that the broker-dealer is controlled by, controlling, affiliated with or under common control with the issuer of any security before entering into any contract with or for a customer for the purchase or sale of such security, the existence of such control to such customer, and if such disclosure is not made in writing, it shall be supplemented by the giving or sending of written disclosure at or before the completion of the transaction;

s. Failing to make a bona fide public offering of all of the securities allotted to a broker-dealer for distribution, whether acquired as an underwriter, a selling group member, or from a member participating in the distribution as an underwriter or selling group member; or

t. Failure or refusal to furnish a customer, upon reasonable request, information to which he is entitled, or to respond to a formal written request or complaint.

2. AGENTS
a. Engaging in the practice of lending or borrowing money or securities from a customer, or acting as a custodian for money, securities or an executed stock power of a customer;

b. Effecting securities transactions not recorded on

the regular books or records of the broker-dealer which the agent represents, unless the transactions are authorized in writing by the broker-dealer prior to execution of the transaction;

c. Establishing or maintaining an account containing fictitious information in order to execute transactions which would otherwise be prohibited;

d. Sharing directly or indirectly in profits or losses in the account of any customer without the written authorization of the customer and the broker-dealer which the agent represents;

e. Dividing or otherwise splitting the agent's commissions, profits or other compensation from the purchase or sale of securities with any person not also registered as an agent for the same broker-dealer, or for a broker-dealer under direct or indirect common control; or

f. Engaging in conduct specified in Subsection 1.b, c, d, e, f, i, j, n, o, p, or q.

[CONDUCT NOT INCLUSIVE.] The conduct set forth above is not inclusive. Engaging in other conduct such as forgery, embezzlement, nondisclosure, incomplete disclosure or misstatement of material facts, or manipulative or deceptive practices shall also be grounds for denial, suspension or revocation of registration.

PLAIN-ENGLISH VERSION

As you noticed, the policy statement starts with the conduct of broker-dealers and then moves on to the agents who represent them. Item A prohibits unreasonable and unjustifiable delays in delivering securities that customers have purchased or paying out a request from the cash balance. Broker-dealers would probably prefer to sit on client cash a while, but if the client has $2,000 of "cash" in her account, the firm has to pay her promptly upon request. Regular way settlement is "T + 3," so once that trade is completed on the third business day, the customer can request a check for that amount. Also, stocks that pay dividends and bonds that pay interest will build up the cash balance in the investor's account. NASAA is just reminding broker-dealers that if their customers want their cash paid out to them, or their stock certificates shipped to them, the firms cannot unreasonably delay these requests.

Item b is the legalistic definition for "churning." Notice how churning involves excessive size as well as frequency of trading. Remember that suitability is the name of the game, and frequent trading is unsuitable for the vast majority of investors working with a registered representative. Of course, frequent trading does seem to help the registered rep's paycheck, and broker-dealers do know who their "big producers" are, but NASAA is reminding broker-dealers not to let registered reps encourage frequent trading or trading huge positions relative to the account balance. Administrators in the real world frequently write orders of revocation that explain how a particular rep was engaging in a "turnover ratio" of, say, 15, or possibly higher. A "turnover rate/ratio of 15" would indicate that if the customer's average account balance is, say, $20,000, the registered rep somehow talked the guy into executing $300,000 worth of trades over the year. Frequent trading might be suitable if the client is a former commodities trader and a multimillionaire who knows what he's doing, but given the character of the account, if the rep is encouraging trading that is too frequent, the Administrator can definitely move to suspend or revoke the license. Often, FINRA would catch it first and then just forward the information on over—either way, regulators hate churning. It's an obvious way in which a registered rep can put the client's entire life savings at extreme risk while the registered rep faces no financial risk himself and, in fact, benefits on every trade whether the client wins or loses.

Item c is a reminder that when the firm recommends the purchase, sale, or exchange of a security, they have to have reasonable grounds to make the recommendation based on an investigation of the client's situation. This brings up many important concepts. First, if the customer calls the firm to place an order, that's an unsolicited transaction in which the broker-dealer has no suitability requirements. But, if the broker-dealer recommends a transaction, they have to know that it's suitable. If the client is unsophisticated, the firm has to know that the client understands the complexities or risks of products such as collateralized mortgage obligations, variable annuities, or viatical settlements. Senior investors generally have a major need of liquidity—if the broker-dealer gets compensated handsomely for selling deferred variable annuities, that doesn't mean they can sell them to a lot of 75-year-old investors unless the firm knows for sure that the investors don't need any of this money during the surrender period, and that they all understand that "subaccounts" are just a fancy term for "stock and bond market," both of which can be a little, well, unpredictable from time to time. FINRA inserts a few phrases into their suitability rule that NASAA leaves out here. FINRA uses the word "non-institutional," so that we understand the firm doesn't have to hand-hold with the big institutional investors. And, they insert the notion that to recommend a security, the firm needs the customer's financial information and profile, but that the firm could recommend a money market mutual fund even without having the client's information. That makes perfect sense, actually. I mean, if a money market mutual fund is too hot for an investor to handle, she isn't an investor. She's a bank customer who took a wrong turn somewhere—somebody please point her back to the large FDIC signs before anyone gets hurt.

Item d reminds the firm not to buy or sell securities for a customer if the customer hasn't authorized the broker-dealer to do so. You might be shocked to see how many firms seem to forget this idea, but if the customer hasn't talked to anyone about buying or selling securities, the customer should *never* end up seeing that purchases or sales have been taking place in the account, right ? If your roommate came home one night and said, "I bought you the nicest pair of shoes for $1,200—here's your credit card," how would you feel? Would you be thankful that someone had the good sense to spend your money on something you didn't even know you needed? Of course not. That's why unauthorized transactions are a very serious violation. Spending clients' money without their knowledge has gotten many broker-dealers in hot water with the regulators, as it should. Broker-dealers make recommendations to clients, and as long as those recommendations are suitable, the broker-dealer isn't responsible for the outcome of the investment. However, if they're placing orders that no one actually ordered, their license could certainly end up being suspended or revoked before or after FINRA disciplines them.

Item e is very closely related. Before a broker-dealer can choose the activity (buy/sell), asset (which stock/bond), or the amount (# of shares/bonds), the customer must grant written discretionary authorization. So, if the firm does not have written discretionary authorization from the customer before making any of those choices, they've made a big mistake. Thus, a Series 63 question might ask what the broker-dealer can do once the client informs the firm that the discretionary authorization form is in the mail. Not much at this point—the broker-dealer needs it signed, in writing, on file, before they choose the asset, the activity, or the amount of shares. The time and price at which an order is executed is not considered such a major aspect, so the firm could take a market order from a customer and then have the "discretion" to enter it later, when they're convinced the customer can get a better price—those are called "market not held" orders, by the way, in case you don't have enough to remember at this point. The firm does not need written discretionary authority to choose time/price for a customer order. So, to make sure we understand this highly testable concept, if the customer says, "Buy 1,000 shares of a software company," the firm would need written discretionary authority to insert the name of a particular company into that order, e.g., Oracle, Microsoft, or IBM. But, if the customer said, "Buy 1,000 shares of MSFT at a good price today," the broker-dealer does not need written discretionary authority to execute that as a "market not held" order that will be executed when they think they can get a better price.

Item f reminds the firm not to let a customer start trading on margin unless the firm gets a signed margin agreement promptly *after* the initial transaction. I would have expected the rule to require the agreement ahead of time, but nobody asked my opinion. And, you can see why the Series 63 has such a nasty reputation—you have to remember that the firm needs discretionary authorization signed before using discretion, but they can execute a margin transaction and *then* get the signed margin agreement. And, trust me, the Series 63 will try to trick you on these points—it could easily ask you which of the following four is a violation and make it look like the firm is screwing up by executing the margin transaction and then promptly getting the signed margin agreement. Most people who kind of half-studied will grab that answer choice as a violation and somehow overlook some obvious example of churning or unauthorized transactions. You really have to know your stuff, and this particular NASAA policy statement will likely generate up to 10 of your Series 63 questions.

Item g speaks to the bookkeeping requirements for broker-dealers holding customer securities, some of which have been pledged as collateral for the loan in a margin account. NASAA is reminding broker-dealers to keep the customers' fully paid securities separate from the firm's securities or securities pledged as collateral. Item h reminds broker-dealers not to pledge customer securities as collateral unless they have written authorization from the customer. In other words, in a margin account, the customer signs a hypothecation agreement, giving the broker-dealer the authority to pledge the securities as collateral. But, if a broker-dealer just started pledging the securities that customers thought were in "safekeeping" as collateral for loans to the firm, we would have a very ugly situation on our hands. It would be like finding out that a neighbor just borrowed $300,000 and put *your* house up as collateral. Even funnier, he can't repay the loan, so the bank is foreclosing on *your* property. To protect customer assets, broker-dealers need to keep their books stringently so that it's crystal clear that these shares belong to the firm's account, and these belong to the customers.

Item i is pretty straightforward. Let's say that a municipal bond issued by a small school district seldom trades. A customer comes in and wants to liquidate 100 of these bonds. There isn't much of a secondary market for these things, but the firm knows that the most recent transactions occurred yesterday at $1,100 per bond. Therefore, they can't give this guy $900 for those same bonds because that price is not reasonably related to the market price. The firm also can't charge commissions that are way out of line with the industry norms.

Item j requires underwriters to deliver a prospectus "no later than the due date for confirmation." Sometimes, rather than a final prospectus, a final statement is sent out that completes any information not already covered in the preliminary prospectus. Either way, NASAA is reminding firms to deliver a prospectus in a new offering. Why wouldn't a firm always want to deliver a prospectus? Because those things lay out a lot of gloom-and-doom scenarios that can easily scare an investor away from the table. One minute the investor is ready to buy an additional offering of Starbucks common stock, the next minute she's reading about the risk of a "global pandemic" or "possible negative health effects associated with the company's products." Oh well. Investors have to be fully informed of all the important risks—otherwise, the broker-dealer would be selling securities fraudulently.

Item k reminds firms not to charge unreasonable or inequitable fees for services performed, including a host of various services that broker-dealers provide. The regulators don't spell out maximum fees, but they expect firms to keep their charges reasonable and fair among their various customers. If not, the Administrator can always schedule a hearing at the firm's earliest convenience.

Point l is talking about a violation called "backing away." If a broker-dealer puts out a firm quote, they had better be prepared to trade at the price they indicate. Point m is admonishing broker-dealers not to mislead customers by saying that a security is being offered "at the market" if there is really no secondary market out there for the security. I have seen several examples of investors getting duped into buying "preferred stock" in some shaky company and then finding out later that the stock isn't listed or traded anywhere. Maybe one of those investors wants to liquidate and get some of her money back—the broker-dealer can't say that they're offering to buy those shares "at the market" unless they know an actual secondary market for the security exists. If they're the only firm willing or crazy enough to buy that preferred stock, they need to be clear about that.

Item n goes into great detail in explaining that market manipulation will get you into all kinds of trouble. We can't just get together with another firm and buy a huge block of thinly traded stock, then start creating the illusion of an active market for a particular stock, so that we can later dump our stock at a much higher price, all based on our deception and manipulation of the market. It makes for some entertaining scenes in "The Sopranos" or *Boiler Room*, but we should probably not model our business conduct on any of the characters represented in either highly entertaining work of fiction.

Item o reminds the firm not to guarantee the customer against a loss. Broker-dealers make suitable recommendations, but they don't protect customers from market losses. If the word "guaranteed" is used, it has to be explained clearly to the investor to avoid misleading him. A US Treasury security is definitely guaranteed as to interest and principal by the US Treasury, but it still has interest rate and market risk. A corporate bond could be "guaranteed" if a third party promised to pay interest and/or principal in the event of a default, but that also needs to be explained clearly to an investor. A broker-dealer could sell someone a "puttable bond" or a bond with a "put option" that gives the investor the right to sell the bond back for a set price in exchange for some kind of premium. In this case, there would be a written agreement, and it would be clear what the customer paid and what the customer gets. But a broker-dealer doesn't tell a customer that if the trade they're recommending goes sour, they'll eat the losses for them. They're not insurance companies accepting premiums in exchange for protection against market loss. And, if they tell an investor her money is "guaranteed" when, in fact, it isn't, that would be a very serious violation.

Item p reminds broker-dealers not to publish that a transaction has occurred unless they actually know it occurred. Otherwise the firm might be engaging in market manipulation, or being used as pawns by those who are.

Item q reminds the firm not to circulate material that is misleading or deceptive. For example, it might be tempting to put out a flyer that shows how much Company XYZ would be worth if over the next 6 months they simply eliminated $5 billion in debt, increased revenues 10,000% and slashed costs 89% without resorting to layoffs or pay cuts. You could even show graphs of this wonderful turnaround effort. Trouble is, it's all based on wild conjecture, is so improbable as to be nearly impossible, and, therefore, should not be circulated at all. It is "nonfactual," misleading and probably deceptive.

Don't do that.

If the broker-dealer is owned by the issuer of the stock that the firm is selling to investors, that important detail should be disclosed, as Point r reminds us. Right? The broker-dealer is recommending that you buy stock, bonds, or commercial paper in the parent company? Doesn't that sort of directly benefit the broker-dealer even beyond the typical commissions earned? Item s reminds underwriters not to get greedy when they realize that the stock they're bringing to the primary market is likely to take off like a rocket ship. Might be tempting to hang onto the stock for their own accounts and cancel all the indications of interest, but that would be "failure to make a bona fide offering" and would get the firm into all kinds of trouble.

Item t is a very clear reminder to give customers the information they are entitled to. Customers are certainly entitled to trade confirmations, account statements, mutual fund prospectuses, etc. They're entitled to a copy of the firm's most recent balance sheet. They are even entitled to independent research on companies generated by other firms. Broker-dealers have to respond to written customer complaints, as well, and they have to keep detailed records on how the complaint was handled.

And then the policy statement addresses agents specifically.

Item a reminds agents not to borrow money from customers unless the customer happens to be a lending institution: bank, savings & loan, thrift, credit union, building & loan, etc. If an agent wants to borrow from a customer who is a human being, the agent needs to check the broker-dealer's policy on this. Maybe it's okay to borrow money from a client if the client is an immediate family member or a business partner. But many agents out there try to borrow money from clients under the table, promising to "pay it right back." Maybe the agent borrows $100,000 from a client and then goes bankrupt, gets fired, or dies…then what is the client supposed to do about the hundred grand he foolishly lent to his former agent?

That's basically the situation the regulators are hoping to avoid.

An agent cannot "act as a custodian for" customer money or securities. Once the client's money goes into the agent's bank or brokerage account, it has no chance of survival. Many investors have been swindled by cutting personal checks to their sales agent or handing him cash. I recall an enforcement action in Arkansas in which an investor gave an agent over $50,000 cash money, and the agent gave the investor a personal check "as a receipt for the cash," instructing the customer not to try and cash the check or anything but to, instead hang onto it as a, you know, receipt for the cash. The most shocking part was that *most* of the investor's money did eventually make it into his brokerage account. Well, all but six grand, but now we're just splitting hairs.

Item b warns against executing transactions not recorded on the books and records of your firm unless you have written authorization from the firm to do so. An official order to deny an agent's license in the State of Washington told a sad story of an agent who got an elderly investor to cut him three personal checks for $50,000, all of which ended up in the agent's brokerage account. So, right there, he has "acted as a custodian for client money" and "commingled client funds with his own," which is, like, really bad. But then when he started executing trades, the Administrator could also add item b to the list of allegations, since those transactions were certainly *not* recorded on the regular books and records of the broker-dealer, who knew nothing about the scheme.

Item c is pretty clear. If there is an offering of stock open only to accredited investors, and your customer isn't close to meeting the net worth and income requirements, would it be okay to indicate a higher net worth and income on the required paperwork in order to allow him to buy the limited offering?

No.

Item d reminds us that, basically, you shouldn't be sharing profits and/or losses with a customer. The only exception is when you're in a joint account with the customer and you've received the customer's authorization as well as your broker-dealer's. If you get any test question on the sharing arrangement, remember that you must share in proportion to your investment in the account. Unless it's an immediate family member and then nobody cares how you share.

Item e makes it clear that you can only split commissions with registered agents at your firm or a firm directly related to your firm, as a subsidiary, for example. So, you can split commissions, as long as the agent is registered and works for your firm directly or indirectly. Many agents' assistants get their licenses in order to take client orders and share commissions with their agents. That's fine. But it wouldn't be fine for an agent to tell 20 of his friends that he'll split commissions with them in exchange for referrals. Refer me a new client with $1 million net worth, and I'll give you 1/3 of the commissions I make for the first year—what do you say?

The regulators say, "Don't do it."

The policy statement then tells the agent not to do the stuff it told broker-dealers not to do, except for the stuff that would only relate to the firm.

And then the policy statement ends with a reminder that these prohibited activities are not inclusive, meaning there's still plenty of other stuff that could get you in hot water with the regulators. They just felt like pointing out *some* of the things not to do in this policy statement.

NASAA MODEL RULE: UNETHICAL BUSINESS PRACTICES OF INVESTMENT ADVISERS, INVESTMENT ADVISER REPRESENTATIVES AND FEDERAL COVERED ADVISERS

[Amended 2005, Adopted in 1997]

[Introduction] A person who is an investment adviser, an investment adviser representative or a federal covered adviser is a fiduciary and has a duty to act primarily for the benefit of its clients. The provisions of this subsection apply to federal covered advisers to the extent that the conduct alleged is fraudulent, deceptive, or as otherwise permitted by the National Securities Markets Improvement Act of 1996 (Pub. L. No. 104-290). While the extent and nature of this duty varies according to the nature of the relationship between an investment adviser or an investment adviser representative and its clients and the circumstances of each case, an investment adviser, an investment adviser representative or a federal covered adviser shall not engage in unethical business practices, including the following:

(a) Recommending to a client to whom investment supervisory, management or consulting services are provided the purchase, sale or exchange of any security without reasonable grounds to believe that the recommendation is suitable for the client on the basis of information furnished by the client after reasonable inquiry concerning the client's investment objectives, financial situation and needs, and any other information known by the investment adviser.

(b) Exercising any discretionary power in placing an order for the purchase or sale of securities for a client without obtaining written discretionary authority from the client within ten (10) business days after the date of the first transaction placed pursuant to oral discretionary authority, unless the discretionary power relates solely to the price at which, or the time when, an order involving a definite amount of a specified security shall be executed, or both.

(c) Inducing trading in a client's account that is excessive in size or frequency in view of the financial resources, investment objectives and character of the account in light of the fact that an investment adviser or an investment adviser representative in such situations can directly benefit from the number of securities transactions effected in a client's account. The rule appropriately forbids an excessive number of transaction orders to be induced by an adviser for a "customer's account."

(d) Placing an order to purchase or sell a security for the account of a client without authority to do so.

(e) Placing an order to purchase or sell a security for the account of a client upon instruction of a third party without first having obtained a written third-party trading authorization from the client.

(f) Borrowing money or securities from a client unless the client is a broker-dealer, an affiliate of the investment adviser, or a financial institution engaged in the business of loaning funds.

(g) Loaning money to a client unless the investment adviser is a financial institution engaged in the business of loaning funds or the client is an affiliate of the investment adviser.

(h) Misrepresenting to any advisory client, or prospective advisory client, the qualifications of the investment adviser or any employee of the investment adviser, or misrepresenting the nature of the advisory services being offered or fees to be charged for such service, or to omit to state a material fact necessary to make the statements made regarding qualifications, services or fees, in light of the circumstances under which they are made, not misleading.

(i) Providing a report or recommendation to any advisory client prepared by someone other than the adviser without disclosing that fact. (This prohibition does not apply to a situation where the adviser uses published research reports or statistical analyses to render advice or where an adviser orders such a report in the normal course of providing service.)

(j) Charging a client an unreasonable advisory fee.

(k) Failing to disclose to clients in writing before any advice is rendered any material conflict of interest relating to the adviser, or any of its employees which could reasonably be expected to impair the rendering of unbiased and objective advice including:

(1.) Compensation arrangements connected with advisory services to clients which are in addition to compen- sation from such clients for such services; and

(2.) Charging a client an advisory fee for rendering advice when a commission for executing securities transactions pursuant to such advice will be received by the adviser or its employees.

(l) Guaranteeing a client that a specific result will be achieved (gain or no loss) with advice which will be rendered.

(m) **[Alternative 1]** Publishing, circulating or distrib- uting any advertisement which does not comply with Rule 206(4)-1 under the Investment Advisers Act of 1940.

(m) **[Alternative 2]** (1.) Except as otherwise provided in subsection (2.), it shall constitute a dishonest or unethical practice within the meaning of [Uniform Act Sec. 102(a)(4)] for any investment adviser or investment adviser representative, directly or indirectly, to use any advertisement that does any one of the following:

(i.) Refers to any testimonial of any kind concerning the investment adviser or investment adviser representative or concerning any advice, analysis, report, or other service rendered by such investment adviser or investment adviser representative.

(ii.) Refers to past specific recommendations of the investment adviser or investment adviser representative that were or would have been profitable to any person; except that an investment adviser or investment adviser representative may furnish or offer to furnish a list of all recommendations made by the investment adviser or investment adviser representative within the immediately preceding period of not less than one year if the advertisement or list also includes both of the following:

(A) The name of each security recommended, the date and nature of each recommendation, the market price at that time, the price at which the recommendation was to be acted upon, and the most recently available market price of each such security.

(B) A legend on the first page in prominent print or type that states that the reader should not assume that recommendations made in the future will be profitable or will equal the performance of the securities in the list.

(iii.) Represents that any graph, chart, formula, or other device being offered can in and of itself be used to determine which securities to buy or sell, or when to buy or sell them; or which represents, directly or indirectly, that any graph, chart, formula, or other device being offered will assist any person in making that person's own decisions as to which securities to buy or sell, or when to buy or sell them, without prominently disclosing in such advertisement the limitations thereof and the difficulties with respect to its use.

(iv.) Represents that any report, analysis, or other service will be furnished for free or without charge, unless such report, analysis, or other service actually is or will be furnished entirely free and without any direct or indirect condition or obligation.

(v.) Represents that the [Administrator] has approved any advertisement.

(vi.) Contains any untrue statement of a material fact, or that is otherwise false or misleading.

(2.) With respect to federal covered advisers, the provisions of this section only apply to the extent permitted by Section 203A of the Investment Advisers Act of 1940.

(3.) For the purposes of this section, the term "advertisement" shall include any notice, circular, letter, or other written communication addressed to more than one person, or any notice or other announcement in any electronic or paper publication, by radio or television, or by any medium, that offers any one of the following:

(i.) Any analysis, report, or publication concerning securities.

(ii.) Any analysis, report, or publication that is to be used in making any determination as to when to buy or sell any security or which security to buy or sell

(iii.) Any graph, chart, formula, or other device to be used in making any determination as to when to buy or sell any security, or which security to buy or sell.

(iv.) Any other investment advisory service with regard to securities.

(n) Disclosing the identity, affairs, or investments of any client unless required by law to do so, or unless consented to by the client.

(o) Taking any action, directly or indirectly, with respect to those securities or funds in which any client has any beneficial interest, where the investment adviser has custody or possession of such securities or funds when the advisor's action is subject to and does not comply with the requirements of Rule 102e(1)-1. and any subsequent amendments.

(p) Entering into, extending or renewing any investment advisory contract, unless such contract is in writing and discloses, in substance, the services to be provided, the term of the contract, the advisory fee, the formula for computing the fee, the amount of prepaid fee to be returned in the event of contract termination or non-performance, whether the contract grants discretionary power to the adviser and that no assignment of such contract shall be made by the investment adviser without the consent of the other party to the contract.

(q) Failing to establish, maintain, and enforce written policies and procedures reasonably designed to prevent the misuse of material nonpublic information contrary to the provisions of Section 204A of the Investment Advisers Act of 1940.

(r) Entering into, extending, or renewing any advisory contract contrary to the provisions of Section 205 of the Investment Advisers Act of 1940. This provision shall apply to all advisers and investment adviser representatives registered or required to be registered under this Act, notwithstanding whether such adviser or representative would be exempt from federal registration pursuant to Section 203(b) of the Investment Advisers Act of 1940.

(s) To indicate, in an advisory contract, any condition, stipulation, or provisions binding any person to waive compliance with any provision of this act or of the Investment Advisers Act of 1940, or any other practice contrary to the provisions of Section 215 of the Investment Advisers Act of 1940.

(t) Engaging in any act, practice, or course of business which is fraudulent, deceptive, or manipulative in contrary to the provisions of Section 206(4) of the Investment Advisers Act of 1940, notwithstanding the fact that such investment adviser or investment adviser representative is not registered or required to be registered under Section 203 of the Investment Advisers Act of 1940.

(u) Engaging in conduct or any act, indirectly or through or by any other person, which would be unlawful for such person to do directly under the provisions of this act or any rule or regulation thereunder

The conduct set forth above is not inclusive. Engaging in other conduct such as non-disclosure, incomplete disclosure, or deceptive practices shall be deemed an unethical business practice. The federal statutory and regulatory provisions referenced herein shall apply to investment advisers, investment adviser representatives and federal covered advisers to the extent permitted by the National Securities Markets Improvement Act of 1996 (Pub. L. No. 104-290).

PLAIN ENGLISH VERSION

The first point this adopted model rule makes is that an investment adviser, investment adviser representative, or federal covered adviser is a fiduciary and has a duty to act primarily for the benefit of its clients. Of course, we've already mentioned that, but notice how NASAA mentions it right off the bat in this model rule. It's that important—hello, somebody. Also, by listing all three terms (investment adviser, investment adviser representative, federal covered adviser), the document reminds us that each term is related yet different. The investment adviser and federal covered adviser are business entities, while the investment adviser representative is the individual who represents one of those business entities. Also, there is a difference between an "investment adviser" and a "federal covered adviser." The difference is simply that the federal covered adviser is registered with the SEC, while the "investment adviser" is subject to the state's registration, books & records, and net capital requirements. Notice how the provisions laid out in this document (written by a group of *state* regulators) "apply to federal covered advisers to the extent that the conduct alleged is fraudulent, deceptive, or as otherwise permitted by [NSMIA]." A federal covered adviser could have a big office in Bakersfield, California, and have 7 bazillion dollars under management. Clearly, they register with the SEC and are federal covered. But, this model rule is also making clear that the big, federal covered advisory firm is still subject to the state's powers to enforce anti-fraud rules. In other words, the federal covered adviser sends Form ADV to the SEC, and tells the SEC to send a copy to the State of California, called a "notice filing." The adviser also provides a U-4 to the state on each investment adviser representative with a place of business in the state or with more than 5 non-institutional clients. As long as they do that, this adviser will not have to hear from the State of California again, unless "the conduct alleged is fraudulent, deceptive, or as otherwise permitted by NSMIA." So, a federal covered adviser registers only with the SEC, but the adviser is still subject to both the SEC's and the state's ability to protect investors from fraudulent, deceptive practices in the securities business. And, really, how could it be any other way? If the SEC is too understaffed to go after a federal covered adviser destroying senior citizens' accounts all across the fine state of California, is the California Securities Administrator just supposed to stand there powerless to do anything about it? Not a chance.

All right. Since we had so much fun dissecting the *introduction* to this NASAA model rule, let's now have some fun looking at the specifics. Item (a) reminds investment advisers not to recommend the purchase or sale of any security unless they have reasonable grounds to believe it's a suitable recommendation. Notice how the item specifically mentions clients "to whom supervisory, management or consulting services are provided." Another type of advisory service is called "impersonal advice," and this advice does not even purport/claim to be specific for the individual client. There is a world of difference between delivering the same advice to a group that is generally interested in, say, value investing, and providing "supervisory, management or consulting services" to a specific client. If I'm supervising your investment activities, actually managing your portfolio, or getting paid a big hourly rate as a consultant, the regulators would be tickled to death if I actually knew something about your situation before I start running my mouth or running the meter.

The second item is a little surprising. Most readers would have figured the adviser needs written discretionary authority from the client *before* using discretionary power, but it turns out the client can give oral authorization to get the discretionary nature of the account going. The adviser then has 10 business days after the first discretionary order is placed to obtain written authorization. If the client fails to return the signed written authorization within 10 business days, the adviser would only be able to recommend transactions to the client or place unsolicited orders, just like an agent/broker-dealer without written discretionary authority.

So, broker-dealers and investment advisers are treated differently for purposes of using discretion. Broker-dealers need written discretionary authority before making any discretionary trades because they get compensated per transaction, and the temptation to just start buying stuff in their clients' accounts would be overwhelming, like asking my two cats to baby-sit your pet hamster for a week without an adequate supply of Friskies on hand. I mean, after a while, what are you gonna do? It's a hamster—we're hungry predators with sharp claws. But an investment adviser really gets compensated by charging a percentage of the assets, so if he makes some dumb purchases he'll not only not gain from it, but also his fee will start going down with the assets. One percent of $100,000 is better than 1% of $80,000, right? Would the Series 63 actually try to trick you on the subtle difference between broker-dealers and investment advisers in terms of using discretion to place client trades?

Maybe. The Series 65 and 66 definitely do that, and they both overlap with the Series 63 enough to bring it up in detail here. Remember, our goal is to *over*-prepare you for the exam. We're just not sure it's actually possible to be over-prepared for the Series 63. Seriously. This test can go into areas no one expected or simply ask about a familiar concept in such a convoluted way that test-takers either panic or truly don't recognize what the heck they're being asked. But, if you know the big concepts, it becomes exceedingly difficult for the test to have its way with you—it will push you around, no matter who you are. But, if you know the concepts inside out, you can push back pretty hard yourself.

Item (c) simply says that advisers should not try to induce their clients to become frantic traders, especially if the adviser is getting compensated for those transactions. Remember that plenty of advisers get legal kickbacks from the broker-dealers used to place all the trades their clients make. Sometimes it's cold, hard cash. Sometimes it comes in the form of "soft dollars." So-called "soft dollar compensation" includes services such as research reports or analytical software that might be given in exchange for placing trades with the broker-dealer. Remember that vacations or travel are not allowable "soft dollar" compensation. The allowable soft dollar compensation benefits clients—the stuff that isn't allowed would only benefit the adviser. Either way, if the adviser gets compensated when their clients trade through a particular broker-dealer, that needs to be disclosed. Also, "wrap fees" could be structured as to give the adviser incentive to trade more frequently, so the adviser needs to remember that he/she/they are a fiduciary to the client, and should not try to milk him for every last possible dollar.

Item (d) reminds IAs and IARs not to purchase or sell securities when they have no authorization from the client to do so. I can't imagine trying to manage a client's portfolio unless I had the discretion to make trades as I saw fit, but that doesn't mean that all investment advisers have been granted that discretion. If the adviser or IAR is unauthorized to execute transactions without talking to the client, doing so would be a violation known, not surprisingly, as an "unauthorized transaction." Spending the client's money without the client's knowledge—kind of tough to square that with meeting one's fiduciary duties, isn't it? An investment adviser is in a position of trust. How quickly would you lose a good friend's trust if she found a charge on her credit card for $800 that you forgot to tell her about from back when you house-sat a few weeks ago? She trusted you enough to watch her house and you end up using her credit card to ring up purchases—even if they are "gifts" purely for her use, you don't spend someone else's money unless she has given you that authority.

Item (e) is saying that if your client's husband calls up and says his wife wants you to sell 1,000 shares of MSFT, you can only do so if the client has given her husband written trading authorization and you have that on file. Otherwise, you have to talk to your customer, the wife. Don't take orders from anybody but your client, unless the third party has been granted written third-party trading authorization.

Borrowing money from clients is a practice that makes regulators very nervous. An investment adviser can only borrow money from a client if the client is a broker-dealer, an affiliate of the adviser, or a financial institution in the business of making loans (Bank, Savings & Loan, Thrift, etc.). So, don't borrow from customers unless the customer is in the business of lending money. And, don't lend money to a customer unless your advisory firm is in the business of making loans, or the customer is an affiliate of your advisory firm. One example of an "affiliate" of an investment adviser would be the investment adviser representatives and their supervisors. Another example would be a business entity affiliated with the adviser. But, in general, how could an investment adviser fulfill their fiduciary obligation to a client when borrowing the client's money? Are they giving the client every last basis point of yield that she's entitled to based on their credit rating? Or, are they tying up money that would be better served in Treasury bonds that never miss an interest payment and have no risk of default? Or, if the adviser is going around borrowing money by selling promissory notes in the firm, he's not really an investment adviser—he's an issuer of securities. How can he advise you to put money into his firm in an objective, unbiased fashion? On the test, watch out for investment advisers "who act as issuers of securities." That's a major red flag to a regulator.

Item (h) really takes the fun out of being an adviser. These heavy-handed regulators insist that I refrain from lying about my qualifications, the qualifications of my employees, or the services we will provide through our contract with the client and the fees we will charge for performing those services.

Item (i) is a little tricky and, therefore, fertile ground for harvesting exam questions. If I provide a report or a recommendation to a client when, in fact, that report or recommendation was actually prepared by someone else, I have to disclose the fact and tell you who provided it. However, if I order prepared reports or use published research/statistical analyses to come up with my recommendations, that's different. No disclosure there. I'm just doing my homework to come up with a better plan for my customer. In fact, on the adviser's disclosure brochure (ADV Part 2) prospects are already informed whether the adviser uses research and analyses prepared by others, along with other information sources such as prospectuses, annual reports, financial periodicals, company press releases, etc. So, if you get a tricky question on this, try to determine if the adviser is trying to pass off somebody else's work as their own, or if they order reports and analyses to help them come up with better recommendations. I mean, I'd kind of like to think my adviser is constantly poring over published reports, just crunching data with his nose to the grindstone and shoulder to the wheel 10–12 hours a day, and I do not really care which websites or newsletters or reports he subscribes to. On the other hand, if he's paying another firm to come up with the recommendations for my portfolio, I want to know that rather than find out my adviser was just trying to make it *look* like he actually knew something about investing himself.

Item (j) also takes all the fun out of the business by prohibiting advisers from gouging their clients. What would make the fee "unreasonable"? The regulators are indicating that you and your firm have two options here: 1) you can charge fees that are reasonable or 2) we can have ourselves a hearing.

The next item, (k), would probably produce a test question. Basically, it's just saying that if the advice being given will also lead to the advisory firm or any of its employees receiving a commission or any other compensation should the client act on the advice, that potential conflict of interest must be disclosed in writing in advance of giving/rendering the advice. In other words, wouldn't you feel better about paying for investment advice knowing that the advice is being given by a totally objective professional, rather than someone who will make a big commission check if you take the advice? If the adviser or adviser rep is giving you advice to do something that will put more money in their pocket, that fact needs to be disclosed. For example, if the IAR or adviser receives 12b-1 fees on the mutual funds recommended or purchased for the client, that fact needs to be disclosed.

Item (l) is the very familiar prohibition against guarantees. Don't guarantee a profit. Don't guarantee against a loss. I have recently seen many instances at the state regulatory websites of representatives who have horribly dropped the ball and then tried to appease the client by cutting a personal check. You know, maybe after you accidentally sell 1,000 of the client's B-shares three years after purchase when you were sure they were A-shares, costing her $3,500 by your little gaffe, you invite her to lunch, slip her a check for $3,500, pick up the tab, and everybody's happy.

Not a good idea. In another instance, a shady operator sold an Illinois resident shares of stock in a company that was not even public yet, telling her that "when" the company did their IPO, she would make "a return at least equal to her original investment" and that by investing in said stock "she would become a millionaire." Of course, the stock never went public, the investor never made a return *on* her original investment, and now can't seem to get a return *of* her original investment.

Item (m) probably threw you for a loop, what with the whole "[Alternative 1], [Alternative 2]" thing. Either way, the item is telling advisers to be careful about the advertisements they put out. NASAA knows that some state regulators would rather not refer to the federal legislation, while some are quite comfortable letting somebody else spell things out. I mean, if those high-energy types in Washington, DC, have already exhausted all kinds of time and effort laying out a set of perfectly good stipulations, why not use them? This way, we don't even have to go to the trouble of copying and pasting them into our own rules. Instead, we can just refer to the rule spelled out in the Investment Advisers Act of 1940 and call it a day.

In any case, whether we just point the adviser to the federal rule or kind of spell the same thing out for him in our own words, as state regulators we want advisers to know that their advertising had better not be misleading in any way. You can't list the excellent performance of stock picks that you didn't actually pick. And when you do actually pick the stocks you claim to have picked, the period covered has to be at least one year, and all types of disclosures have to be provided, too. Also notice that testimonials from clients are not allowed by either the federal or the state regulators. As the Investment Adviser Act of 1940, Rule 206(4)-1 says:

> It shall constitute a fraudulent, deceptive, or manipu-
> lative act, practice, or course of business for any
> investment adviser to publish, circulate, or distribute
> any advertisement…which refers, directly or indi-
> rectly, to any testimonial of any kind concerning the
> investment adviser or concerning any advice, analysis,
> report or other service rendered by such investment
> adviser:

Item (n) is a likely testable point: don't divulge the identity, affairs, or investments of your client to anyone else without the client's written permission or some sort of subpoena order to turn the information over to the Administrator, or to the courts. Might be tempting to show prospects what you've done for, say, Oprah Winfrey's account, but both Ms. Winfrey and the state securities Administrator would have a real problem with that. So, on a test question, don't let the adviser reveal the *identity*—not just the affairs—of the client without the client's written permission or some sort of legal demand for the information.

Item (o) basically boils down to, "Be real careful what you do with client funds/ securities under custody." The Rule 102e(1)-1 referenced in this item is also currently viewable at the NASAA website and could easily help you snag a test question or two. We address custody issues elsewhere in the book, where we explain that most advisers use qualified custodians, who send account statements to clients. The adviser sends a billing invoice to the custodian and an invoice to the client when it comes time to deduct money for the advisory fee. If they follow the safeguards, they are not deemed to have custody. If they inadvertently receive client securities, as long as they return them to the sender in three business days and keep records of the event, they are not considered to have custody of client assets. Same thing for a 3rd-party check—as long as it is forwarded to the unrelated third party within 24 hours, the adviser is not considered to have custody. If they *are* deemed to have custody, the adviser has higher net capital requirements and will have to file audited balance sheets and pay a CPA to do an annual surprise audit of the books and records. In all cases, an adviser with custody must notify the Administrator of that fact, which they would do by updating Form ADV.

Item (p) looks like a test question waiting to be written. It reminds us that all advisory contracts must be in writing and must stipulate: services provided, term of the contract, advisory fees, formula for computing the fees, the amount of prepaid fees that are refundable, whether the adviser has discretion, and that no assignment of contract can occur without client consent. Also note that even if the adviser did not end up assigning a client's contract to another party without consent, the fact that their contract with the client failed to state that provision could lead to problems with the regulators. Advisers file a sample of the client contracts with the Administrator, though not a copy of *each* client contract.

Items (q) has to do with the adviser's Code of Ethics policy, which has to make sure that employees are not violating insider trading rules or trying to take advantage of large customer orders that are about to be placed. Advisers now require their "access persons" to provide account statements and trade confirmations for all of their personal brokerage accounts. Some transactions, IPOs and limited offerings of securities, specifically, require pre-approval and not just reporting. Item (r) is stating the obvious—advisory contracts are part of the books and records of the firm and the prototype is shown to the regulators when the firm registers. So if there is anything in these advisory contracts that violates the provisions of the Investment Advisers Act of 1940, that would be a big problem. Why do state regulators refer to the federal Investment Advisers Act of 1940 so often? Because it is so amazingly thorough in its treatment of *everything* related to the advisory business. The Uniform Securities Act looks like a little pamphlet compared to that bad boy, so when the state regulators need a standard for advertising or advisory contracts, or, basically, the final word on what is and isn't allowed of investment advisers, the federal act is extremely useful.

Item (s) reminds us that no waivers of any provision are allowed. In other words, let's say that you and your advisory clients don't like the fact that they can't compensate you as a share of capital gains, so you get an attorney to draw up a waiver that says it's okay, since both parties agree that it's okay.

No. It's not okay. No waivers of compliance are allowed. Everybody lives by the same rules, even the ones who don't like the rules. Any such "waiver of compliance" would be considered null and void in an Administrative or court proceeding, anyway, which means it would not be worth the paper it's printed on, much less the legal fees spent having the worthless thing drawn up.

Item (t) points out that whether an adviser or IAR is subject to state registration, federal-only, or exempted from registration at the federal level, they can still get busted for fraudulent, deceptive practices by the state Administrator. Of course, we've mentioned that a few times ourselves, so let's keep moving.

Item (u) points out that beyond fraudulent/manipulative practices, an investment adviser or IAR can get in trouble for engaging in any conduct that is a violation of the securities laws of the state and the rules thereunder.

And the final blurb is very typical of these detailed lists. It reminds us that this list is "not inclusive," meaning this is just *some* of the stuff we felt like talking about in THIS particular publication. It does not represent ALL of the stuff that can get you in trouble.

So be on your best behavior.

NASAA STATEMENT OF POLICY: DISHONEST OR UNETHICAL BUSINESS PRACTICES BY BROKER-DEALERS AND AGENTS IN CONNECTION WITH INVESTMENT COMPANY SHARES

NASAA Broker-Dealer Sales Practices Committee

[Adopted 4/27/97]

Any broker dealer or agent who engages in one or more of the following practices shall be deemed to have engaged in "dishonest or unethical practices in the securities business" as used in Section 204 of the Uniform Securities Act and such conduct may constitute grounds for denial, suspension or revocation of registration or such other action authorized by statute.

A. Sales Load Communications:

1. In connection with the solicitation of investment company shares, failing to adequately disclose to a customer all sales charges, including asset based and contingent deferred sales charges, which may be imposed with respect to the purchase, retention or redemption of such shares.

2. In connection with the solicitation of investment company shares, stating or implying to a customer that the shares are sold without a commission, are "no load" or have "no sales charge" if there is associated with the purchase of the shares: (i) a front-end load; (ii) a contingent deferred sales load; (iii) a SEC Rule 12b-1 fee or a service fee if such fees in total exceeds .25% of average net fund assets per year; or (iv) in the case of closed-end investment company shares, underwriting fees, commissions or other offering expenses.

3. In connection with the solicitation of investment company shares, failing to disclose to any customer

any relevant: (i) sales charge discount on the purchase of shares in dollar amounts at or above a breakpoint; or (ii) letter of intent feature, if available, which will reduce the sales charges.

4. In connection with the solicitation of investment company shares, recommending to a customer the purchase of a specific class of investment company shares in connection with a multi-class sales charge or fee arrangement without reasonable grounds to believe that the sales charge or fee arrangement associated with such class of shares is suitable and appropriate based on the customer's investment objectives, financial situation and other securities holdings, and the associated transaction or other fees.

B. Recommendations:

1. In connection with the solicitation of investment company shares, recommending to a customer the purchase of investment company shares which results in the customer simultaneously holding shares in different investment company portfolios having similar investment objectives and policies without reasonable grounds to believe that such recommendation is suitable and appropriate based on the customer's investment objectives, financial situation and other securities holdings, and any associated transaction charges or other fees.

2. In connection with the solicitation of investment company shares, recommending to a customer the liquidation or redemption of investment company shares for the purpose of purchasing shares in a different investment company portfolio having similar investment objectives and policies without reasonable grounds to believe that such recommendation is suitable and appropriate based on the customer's investment objectives, financial situation and other securities holdings and any associated transaction charges or other fees.

C. *Disclosure:*

1. In connection with the solicitation of investment company shares, stating or implying to a customer the fund's current yield or income without disclosing the fund's most recent average annual return, calculated in a manner prescribed in SEC Form N-1A, for one, five and ten year periods and fully explaining the difference between current yield and total return; provided, however, that if the fund's registration statement under the Securities Act of 1933 has been in effect for less than one, five, or ten years, the time during which the registration statement was in effect shall be substituted for the periods otherwise prescribed.

2. In connection with the solicitation of investment company shares, stating or implying to a customer that the investment performance of an investment company portfolio is comparable to that of a savings account, certificate of deposit or other bank deposit account without disclosing to the customer that the shares are not insured or otherwise guaranteed by the FDIC or any other government agency and the relevant differences regarding risk, guarantees, fluctuation of principal and/or return, and any other factors which are necessary to ensure that such comparisons are fair, complete and not misleading.

3. In connection with the solicitation of investment company shares, stating or implying to a customer the existence of insurance, credit quality, guarantees or similar features regarding securities held, or proposed to be held, in the investment company's portfolio without disclosing to the customer other kinds of relevant investment risks, including but not limited to, interest rate, market, political, liquidity, or currency exchange risks, which may adversely affect investment performance and result in

loss and/or fluctuation of principal notwithstanding the creditworthiness of such portfolio securities.

4. In connection with the solicitation of investment company shares, stating or implying to a customer: (i) that the purchase of such shares shortly before an ex-dividend date is advantageous to such customer unless there are specific, clearly described tax or other advantages to the customer; or (ii) that a distribution of long-term capital gains by an investment company is part of the income yield from an investment in such shares.

5. In connection with the solicitation of investment company shares, making: (i) projections of future performance; (ii) statements not warranted under existing circumstances; or (iii) statements based upon non-public information.

D. Prospectus:

In connection with the solicitation of investment company shares, the delivery of a prospectus, in and of itself, shall not be dispositive that the broker dealer or agent provided the customer full and fair disclosure.

PLAIN ENGLISH VERSION

The first item under "Sales Load Communications" makes the very basic point that all sales charges must be disclosed to investors. The "asset-based" charges are commonly called 12b-1 fees, and these need to be disclosed, just as the front-end charge for A-shares and back-end or "contingent deferred sales charge" for B-shares must be made clear. Does this mean the agent simply has to hand the client a prospectus? No, the agent has to do that for sure, but the agent is only doing his job properly if he can explain all the important information to the investor. Many investors would probably prefer to hear something like, "You don't need to read this thing—nobody can understand it anyway," but if an agent did that, he could tell the regulators that he, A, delivers the prospectus to all clients and B, does his best to make sure nobody reads it. So, if the test asks if delivering the prospectus relieves the agent and broker-dealer of their duty to disclose material facts, the answer is, no. A carrier pigeon could deliver a prospectus; we need a human being called an "agent" to explain the important information to investors. So, agents need to know that A-shares often charge front-end loads of over 5% and the sooner the investor sells her B-shares, the higher the back-end or "contingent deferred" sales charge she will leave on the table. The higher the ongoing "asset-based sales charges" or "12b-1 fees," the lower the investor's total return. So, as in any business, trying to hide the charges from the customer is a bad idea. It's just that with mutual funds, variable annuities and other investment company products, the job of explaining the charges is especially challenging.

Since sales charges can scare away investors, many funds are sold as "no load." That is fine, as long as there is no deception. As the second point under "Sales Load Communications" states, telling an investor that she is buying a "no-load fund," when, in fact, she isn't, is a very bad idea. In fact, it's the perfect example of fraud—selling a security by misleading the investor about how much she's being charged. If there is a front-end load (A-shares) or contingent deferred sales charge (B-shares, some C-shares), and the agent pretends the investment product is a "no-load fund," we would soon see this agent up on several regulatory websites. Also, no-load funds can charge 12b-1 fees of up to .25% of net assets. But, if the 12b-1 fee is higher than .25% (1/4 of 1%), then the fund is no longer a "no-load" fund. See, if the 12b-1 fee gets too big, the investor would end up losing a lot more to these ongoing sales charges over time than she would have paid on a front-end load. So, basically, you need to know the definition of a "no-load fund" and understand that presenting a fund as "no-load," when, in fact, it isn't would be a very bad idea. No-load funds have no front- or back-end sales charges to cover marketing/distribution costs. They can cover the costs with an "asset-based" 12b-1 fee, as long as they keep that fee to no more than .25% of average net assets. T. Rowe Price, in the real world, takes it up a notch, offering "100% no-load funds." How can they get by with saying that?

Because it's 100% true. They don't impose sales charges, and they do not charge an ongoing, asset-based 12b-1 fee. They figured out long ago that "100% no load" brings more dollars into the fund, and then the fund can charge a management fee against a much bigger pile of money. Mutual funds are investment products, but there are also businesses behind these products. The goal is to make as much revenue as possible. Clearly, the ideal business model is to impose the highest sales charge, management fee, and asset-based sales charge that you possibly can. American Funds uses this model and as of this writing is the largest mutual fund company in terms of assets under management. On the other hand, convincing people to ignore a front-end sales charge of, say, 3–5.75% is no easy feat, so no-load funds such as Fidelity can waive the front-end sales charge to attract more dollars into the fund. Once those dollars come into the fund, management fees and a nice steady 12b-1 fee will pull in massive amounts of revenue, allowing the fund to cover all the marketing/sales expenses and live off a healthy management fee. Remember, a management fee of just ½ of 1% is still a huge pile of money for a fund with, say, $1 billion of assets. In fact, it would be $5 million a year. And, as we mentioned, T. Rowe Price decided to take the no-load model up one notch and offer "100% no-load funds." As we said, this is not an act of charity; it simply pulls in more dollars against which management fees can be charged.

Don't worry. Mutual fund companies have figured out how to make a profit. There are funds with loads, funds without loads that charge 12b-1 fees, and there are even funds that have neither a load nor a 12b-1 fee. NASAA and your state securities regulators want you to be able to clarify it all for your investors.

The third point is an obvious companion with the second—if the fund has a front-end sales charge, the investor needs to be informed of any methods of reducing that sales charge. Breakpoints offer lower sales charges at various levels, and most funds let investors achieve breakpoints through a letter of intent (LOI) that allows investors to put the money in gradually over a 13-month period. Of course, it would be more fun for the folks getting compensated with the sales charge to sort of ignore the whole breakpoint/LOI angle, but it would also be a guaranteed route to regulatory problems. The exam might call this infraction "breakpoint selling."

The fourth item has given many firms headaches, leading to several multimillion-dollar fines by NASD/FINRA. The item points out that if the fund offers A-, B-, and C-shares, the agent must make sure that the share class being recommended is appropriate. B- and C-shares are not suitable for most investments. The B-shares are only appropriate for small investment amounts, and the C-shares are appropriate only for shorter-term investments. If you download the prospectus for, say, The Income Fund of America®, you will see that as of this writing, American Funds will not even accept an order above $50,000 for B-shares. So, the idea that B-shares are only for investors who can't achieve the breakpoints offered on A-shares is built right into the system. See, investors might think they're saving big money through the B-shares, which charge no front-end load. Unfortunately, as they wait for the back-end load to decline to zero, the higher 12b-1 fees on B-shares might be taking an extra .75% of the account value from the investor year after year. It's like "reverse compounding," in which the investor *loses* more money to the 12b-1fee as the account, presumably, grows. So, if the agent puts an investor with $500,000 to invest into B-shares, we're going to see him up on FINRA's website, followed by any state regulators who care to join the disciplinary party. That $500,000 should have gone into A-shares, because the breakpoint at 500K would knock the front-end sales charge down to a very low amount, and then the investor would save a ton going forward, paying maybe 75 basis points less each year on a substantial sum of money.

Download a prospectus from American Funds at www.americanfunds.com and check out the tables explaining "fees and expenses" of the fund. And, just so we're clear here, American Funds isn't endorsing me, this book, Pass the Test, etc. They just happen to make my job very easy by putting their prospectuses up on their website, color-coding them according to volatility, and offering A-, B-, and C-shares, which are all testable on your exam.

Recommendations are always a big deal, so let's take a look at what NASAA has to say about making recommendations to investors considering the purchase of mutual funds, variable annuities, etc. The first point here is that if the agent is recommending that an investor purchase large cap growth funds in five different mutual fund companies, all of which have similar sales charges and breakpoint/LOI structures, that agent is going to be hard-pressed to explain why this is suitable. Mutual funds with similar objectives are much more similar than most people realize, so there is seldom a reason to hold five "different" large cap growth funds, since the funds would likely not be much "different" at all. Remember that $200,000 going into one mutual fund company's products will knock down the front-end sales charge, while investing $40,000 in five different mutual fund families will cause the investor to pay the highest possible sales charge each time. Which, again, might be rather enriching for the folks selling mutual fund shares, but, once again, the pesky regulators are insisting that we not take advantage of investors like that.

The second point goes along with this, coming from the "sale" side of the equation. It just means that the agent would be in trouble for talking someone into selling her current holdings, just so the agent can earn a commission by putting the proceeds into a different fund. If there is a good reason in terms of suitability, that's different, but with mutual fund families offering something for every investor under the sun, it would be tough to justify that advice. If the investor is doing okay in her current "long-term investment grade bond fund," there would be little reason to talk her into selling that just so the agent can put her into a similar long-term investment-grade bond fund issued by a company that will pay him through the sales charge, 12b-1 fee, or both.

Section C, Disclosure brings up several points that could pop up on the exam. If the agent is quoting the "yield" of a fund, he needs to make sure the customer understands how that differs from "total return." The "yield" for a bond fund, for example, would factor in the dividend payment only. Total return factors in the dividend, the capital gains distribution, and the rise or drop in NAV. So, telling an investor that the yield is 10% would be misleading if the agent didn't also explain that since interest rates went up, the fund is actually down 1% in terms of "total return." Yes, it's nice to get the dividends, which are usually paid monthly by a bond mutual fund. But, the investor needs to also know about total return, since the fund's total return could easily be negative for the year, or much, much lower than the "yield" that an unscrupulous agent could otherwise focus on.

The next point is fairly obvious. An agent can't compare a growth fund's total return of 5% to current CD rates, without pointing out a few important facts. First, stock funds often lose a quarter or half their value in a single year, and many simply fold up completely, unlike a bank CD that is fully insured by the FDIC up to $250,000. And, a 5% total return for the stock market is extremely unimpressive; while CDs simply pay whatever current interest rates happen to be. So, don't make unfair and deceptive comparisons.

Also, remember that *all* securities are subject to anti-fraud rules. Yes, a United States Treasury Bond is guaranteed by the United States Treasury as to interest and principal payments, and, yes, no one has ever been stiffed buying US Treasury Bonds. But, if interest rates rise, market values drop. An investor could purchase a T-bond and then need to sell when rates have risen. She might have to sell $10,000 par value for just $9,000 or less, depending on how high rates have risen. And, investors can just start panicking and suddenly decide that Treasuries aren't safe, or there are simply much better investments out there—rapid selling will depress the price of T-bonds, as it does to any other commodity. Explain all that to an investor before putting her into a US Government Bond fund, and explain that while the underlying bonds are guaranteed by the US Treasury, the mutual fund itself isn't guaranteed.

The fourth point is talking about the NASD/FINRA violation called "selling dividends." It would be easy to sucker investors with this one, because human beings love to get checks. What the investor might not understand about an upcoming dividend is that, by definition, when the fund pays a $1 dividend, the net asset value drops by *exactly* $1 per share. See, the NAV of a fund is simply the value of one slice of the net assets. Cash represents an asset. If the fund reduces that asset by $1 per share, the NAV per share goes down $1 per share. So, what's the hurry? The investor can avoid paying tax on the dividend by waiting and will simply buy the shares for the price, reduced by $1. So, you should definitely sell mutual funds that pay dividends to investors looking for income, but you can't make it appear that the investor needs to hurry up and buy the upcoming dividend.

And, as we discussed, yield and total return are separate things. If the agent tried to boost the yield by including the long-term capital gains distribution, that would be misleading. The fund occasionally gets lucky and sells stocks or bonds for much more than they bought them. But that's not a reliable, yield-producing strategy. Yield comes from dividends paid on stock and interest paid on bonds. It's a fairly steady, reliable income stream, especially compared to attempting to buy low and sell high with any consistency.

Projections of the fund's performance are simply not allowed. You can talk about the past performance, as long as it's clear that this does not imply or guarantee anything in the future. I mean, the Chicago White Sox won the World Series in 2005, so there is obviously no connection between past and future performance. As in the world of sports, last year's hottest mutual fund has no statistical chance of being next year's hottest mutual fund.

Section D makes a point I made earlier, but in legalese. "In connection with the solicitation of investment company shares, the delivery of a prospectus, in and of itself, shall not be dispositive that the broker dealer or agent provided the customer full and fair disclosure." What that means is that your job as a securities salesperson is to explain material facts to investors. Handing someone a prospectus is a requirement, but it does not necessarily relieve you of your responsibility to disclose other material facts to the investor.

Securities

(15 of 60 questions on exam)

The only way that the state *securities* Administrator could have any authority over an investment is if the thing actually met the definition of a "security." The exam will ask several questions designed to determine if you know which investments are securities, which ones need to be registered, which transactions are special, etc. Let's start with the most fundamental question: is the investment a security or not?

NOT SECURITIES

Earlier we pointed out that not every single investment of money is a security. Even though part of my investment strategy could be to put $100,000 into a fixed annuity so that I know I'll have an income stream when I retire backed up by a solid insurance company, I am not investing in a "security" in that case. A "security" is not an insurance product or a commodity futures contract. That means that the following are not securities and are not being regulated by the Uniform Securities Act:

- Fixed annuity
- Whole life, term life, universal life, endowment policy
- Commodity futures contract

That means that you could not possibly commit securities fraud selling those things deceptively. Why not? Because they aren't securities. Similarly, it would be tough to get nailed for clipping in baseball, or icing in basketball. I mean, clipping is definitely a violation, but only if we're inside the world of football. Icing is a violation, assuming we're actually playing hockey. So insurance and commodities investments are in different sports, each with its own set of officials/umpires. We're talking about the sport called "securities," on this exam and in the Uniform *Securities* Act.

So, now we've laid the groundwork for one of the few easy questions on the exam. If the test asks, "Which of the following is not a security," look for one of the bulleted items above. Or, maybe they'll make you stretch a bit further and ask, "Which of the following is least likely an investment adviser?" If so, remember that if the advice is on one of the bulleted items, we're probably not talking about an investment adviser. Why? Investment advisers give advice on *securities*.

THESE ARE SECURITIES

The Uniform Securities Act lists examples of securities:
- Note
- Stock
- Treasury stock
- Bond
- Debenture
- Evidence of indebtedness
- Certificate of interest or participation in any profit-sharing agreement
- Collateral-trust certificate
- Pre-organization certificate or subscription
- Transferable share
- Investment contract
- Voting-trust certificate
- Certificate of deposit for a security
- Stock option or option on a commodity futures contract
- Certificate of interest or participation in an oil, gas, or mining title or lease
- In general, any interest or instrument commonly known as a "security"
- Certificate of interest or participation in or warrant or right to subscribe to or purchase, any of the foregoing

So, of course, the exam may try to mess with you about commodity futures contracts. While the futures contract is not a security, the option to buy or sell that contract *is* a security. Also, watch out for this—a "single stock futures contract" IS a security. Why? Because a single stock futures contract is a security.

When the Administrator issues a notice of hearing to the respondent, they typically write something like, "The stock referenced in paragraph 6 is a 'security' as that term is defined in the Uniform Securities Act under Section..." The regulators are establishing why they have authority over the activity. The respondent's attorneys will likely try to argue that the investment did not meet the definition of a "security," putting it outside the reach of the securities Administrator. Football referees have no authority to call a balk, right? Basketball referees don't get to call a lot of high-sticking violations, right? Unfortunately, most investments of money that are at risk do fit under the definition of a "security," and are, therefore subject to registration and disclosure requirements.

Did you happen to notice the bulleted item "in general, any interest or instrument commonly known as a "security"? That casts a wide net, doesn't it? Basically, it means that if there is some legal or regulatory precedent calling this thing a "security," guess what? It's a security—get it registered and watch what you say and don't say about it to investors in our state. You also noticed "investment contract" above. That was what the "Howey Decision" defined for us. Casting a very broad net, the Howey Decision says that an "investment contract," which is a security, is anything that fits this description:

- an investment of money in a common enterprise where the investor's fortunes are bound together with those of other investors or the promoter
- the investor hopes to profit solely through the efforts of others

The "solely through the efforts of others" above means that this person is providing money, not labor, to the enterprise. If I sell you a 10% ownership interest in my dairy farming operation for $100,000, and you have no pre-existing relationship with me or any work/managerial duties, that ownership interest is an investment contract and, therefore, a security. That means that I'm offering and intend to sell a "security," which means I could end up committing securities fraud, whether I'm in the securities industry or not. If I gave you an offering document representing that I own 300 head of cattle, when it's really only 100 that I keep shuffling around on you, that would be misleading. Same thing if I give you an income statement or balance sheet full of bogus numbers.

And, since this thing fits the definition of a "security," it probably needs to be registered. Remember the very first phrase in the Uniform Securities Act, which explains that the whole thing is designed to prevent fraud and to make securities get registered before they're offered and sold to investors.

REGISTERING SECURITIES

Not all securities have to be registered at the state level, but we haven't gone there yet—don't worry, it's coming. We're still talking about the securities that *do* have to be registered. If the security has to be registered with the state, this is what the state wants from the person filing the registration statement:

- Filing fee (big surprise)
- Total amount of the offering
- Amount of securities offered in <u>their</u> state
- <u>Names</u> of other states where securities will be offered (not the amount offered in *each* state)
- Any adverse order, judgment, or decree entered by a court, the securities agency or Administrator in any state, or the Securities and Exchange Commission in connection with the offering

Also, know that:
- Registrations are effective for one year
- Securities offered by coordination or qualification may require an escrow account whose proceeds are impounded by the Administrator and not released to the issuer/underwriters until they have raised the specified amount
- Securities offered by coordination or qualification may need to be sold through a specified form as stipulated by the Administrator
- The securities registration statement must include a consent to service of process
- Underwriters can file the registration on *behalf of* the issuer

At www.nasaa.org you can take a look at a uniform securities registration form, which will show you pretty much what I just listed above. Also, note that securities registrations are effective for one year going forward from the effective date. See, if an agent gets registered on August 15th, her license is still going to expire on December 31st unless properly renewed. But if a security's registration is declared effective on August 15th, it will be effective for one full year going forward.

Offerings of securities sometimes take awhile to complete. If so, the Administrator can require the issuer to provide progress reports, but not more frequently than quarterly.

You may also need to know that any document filed within the preceding five years can be incorporated into the registration statement by reference. That means that if the issuer has recently filed a financial statement with the Administrator, the registration statement can merely refer to that filing rather than reproduce it.

Once the offering of securities is registered, the issuer and underwriters go into a cooling off period. During the cooling off period, no sales are allowed and no advertising. The cooling off period is a time for risk disclosure and objective facts that investors should consider—not sales hype. To that end, a tombstone advertisement can be placed during the cooling off period, because it is simply an announcement that publishes basic facts about the offer of securities. The name of the issuer and under-writers is given, and a basic description of the securities. For example, maybe we see that the ABC Corporation is offering 6½ % preferred stock, 1,000,000 shares at $100 par value. We would see the name of the lead underwriter and the syndicate members. And, there would be a disclaimer that the tombstone is just an announcement and is not to be "construed as an offer to sell securities or as a solicitation of an offer to buy securities." The *Wall Street Journal* typically has a tombstone advertisement that you can look at—not every day, but they are in there with some regularity.

As the Uniform Securities Act states, "The Administrator may require the filing of any prospectus, pamphlet, circular, form letter, advertisement, or other sales literature or advertising communication addressed or intended for distribution to prospective investors, including clients or prospective clients of an investment adviser unless the security or transaction is exempted by Section 402 or is a federal covered security." In other words, unless there's something special about the security or the way it's being sold, the Administrator can review the prospectus, form letter, pamphlet, advertising copy, etc. before it ever goes out to investors. Why? Well, fraud is like mold; it grows best in a dark place. If the issuer can keep the regulators and investors in the dark about their shaky finances, they can probably extract hard-earned money from people without too much trouble. But, once the state has a chance to review all the literature connected with the offering, the issuer will end up having to disclose risks, which will either scare investors away from the table or maybe delay the offering until the issuer gets their little company on more solid footing. Bring it all into the light, the regulators are saying, and let's all have ourselves a careful look at this whole offering of securities before anybody turns over the first dollar to you.

ADMINISTRATIVE STOP ORDERS

So, as long as you fill out your registration statement and pay your little filing fee, you'll get to issue the securities and raise the money you need to raise, right?

Not right. The Administrator gets *really* nervous when some little company decides it would be fun to raise money by selling securities to people who don't know any better. Many of the enforcement actions at various state regulatory websites involve people selling promissory notes or preferred stock in some company who has no ability to pay interest or dividends and no intention of bothering to register the securities.

Which is pretty rude, since the Uniform Securities Act goes so far out of its way to point out how important it is to register a security in the state before even *offering* to sell it. When you register a security, the state is going to want to see all the sales literature and advertising to be used in connection with the offering. They'll probably want to see a specimen of the security and, of course, all the offering documents. They'll want to know if the security has been registered with the SEC and if any other regulator including the courts might have a problem with it. They'll want to see a copy of the agreement between the issuer and the underwriters and the agreement *among* the underwriters. That point seems to shock many students, but, trust me, the regulators want to know if the underwriters and/or promoters of the whole scheme are planning to get rich while everybody else is left holding some high-risk security not worth the paper it's printed on.

If so, no way.

That's right, just as they can do with the registration/application of an agent, broker-dealer, or investment adviser, the Administrator can prevent a security from getting registered. Why would he do a thing like that?

Because, it's in the public interest and:

- The registration statement contains any statement that is incomplete, misleading, or false
- Any provision of the Uniform Securities Act, or any rule or order by the Administrator, has been willfully violated in connection with the offering
- The security registered or sought to be registered is the subject of an administrative stop order or a court injunction entered under any other federal or state act applicable to the offering
- The issuer's enterprise includes or would include activities which are illegal where performed
- The offering has worked or tended to work a fraud upon purchasers (or would so operate)
- The offering has been or would be made with unreasonable underwriter compensation or excessive promoters' profits, or unreasonable amounts or kinds of options
- A security seeking to be registered by filing is not eligible for such registration
- A security seeking to be registered by coordination has failed to comply with the requirements of that process
- The proper filing fee has not been paid (but only a denial order can be entered and shall be vacated once the fee is paid)

As with registrations of persons, before a denial, suspension, or revocation order is entered, the issuer would get a prior notice of an opportunity for a hearing and all the written findings of fact, conclusions of law. Of course, as before, there are emergency cease & desist orders and there are also "summary suspensions pending final determination of a proceeding," but, what kind of nonsense are they up to that would make the Administrator go and do a thing like that? Remember that if the security's registration is "summarily suspended," the issuer can request a hearing and must get one within 15 days of the request.

Also, did you notice the item concerning illegal operations? That means that if Crystal MethCorp decides to do an IPO, they'll probably run into some snags with the Administrator.

Finally, the Administrator cannot institute a stop order (deny, suspend, revoke) against a registration that is already effective based on facts already disclosed to him unless the proceedings begin within 30 days.

METHODS OF REGISTRATION

There are three different ways to register securities with the state securities Administrator. Let's start with Registration by Coordination.

Coordination

Why would they call this method "registration by coordination"? Because the issuer has to first register the securities with the SEC under the Securities Act of 1933, and then they *coordinate* the process with the states where the securities will be offered for sale. What if the issuer is not going to register with the SEC? Then, they can't use this method. Also, the securities can generally not already be declared effective by the SEC. Actually, the Administrator *could* allow that to happen, but the greater the interval between the SEC effectiveness and filing with the state, the more likely the Administrator will deny the registration.

Typically, the test question would indicate that the company is doing an inter-state IPO. The prefix "inter" means "between" or "among." Since these securities are being sold among many states, this is inter-state commerce, which the federal government typically feels is their business. You have probably noticed that some of the road signs in your state indicate the name of your state, but if you're driving on I-80, I-57, I-10, I-95, etc., the signs are suddenly red, white, and blue. Why? Those are inter-state highways, over which inter-state commerce is conducted, and interstate commerce is the domain of Uncle Sam.

So, the issuer is subject to registration with the SEC under the Securities Act of 1933, and, since the issuer is not big enough to be granted a break at the state level, they also have to register with the states.

That's the deal with registration by coordination.

And, we wish it were that simple. Unfortunately, the folks who write the Series 63 may also expect you to spit back a bunch of bullet points. As the Uniform Securities Act indicates, "A registration statement under this section shall contain the following information and be accompanied by the following documents in addition to the [requirements of all registrations] and a consent to service of process."

And those documents are:

- Three copies of the prospectus and all amendments filed with the SEC under the Securities Act of 1933
- If the Administrator requires it, a copy of the articles of incorporation and by-laws currently in effect, a copy of any agreements with or among underwriters, a copy of any indenture, and a specimen/copy of the security
- If the Administrator requests it, any other information, or copies of any other documents, filed under the Securities Act of 1933
- All future amendments to the federal prospectus

So, as you can see, the issuer and its underwriters are really sweating it out with the SEC and also showing the state regulators what they've shown the federal regulators. The state wants to see what the stock or bond actually looks like, and they'd like to see how much the underwriters are going to make by selling securities in their state. The effective or release date, which is the day that the underwriters can sell to investors, will be declared by the SEC. Just means that as long as you meet the following conditions, your effective/release date at the state level will be whatever day the federal regulators (SEC) declare, assuming:

- No stop order is in effect and no proceeding is pending (deny, suspend, revoke)
- The registration statement has been on file with the Administrator for at least 10 days
- A statement of the maximum and minimum proposed offering prices and the maximum underwriting discounts/commissions has been on file for two full business days

The test could easily throw a question at you concerning the different "cooling off" periods under the federal Securities Act of 1933 and the state requirement under registration by coordination. As of this writing, the federal cooling off period is 20 days, while we see in the preceding bulleted list that the number is 10 days at the state level.

Filing/Notification

As with registration by coordination, issuers using the "registration by filing" method must have a federal registration filed with the SEC. The issuer simply notifies the Administrator that it is meeting the requirements mandated by the state. Note that this method can be referred to as either "registration by filing" or "registration by notification." But, neither one is a "notice filing," which we will look at elsewhere.

Let's use a bulleted list here for the requirements of this method:

- the issuer has registered a class of equity securities under the Securities Exchange Act of 1934 held of record by 500 or more persons
- issuer must have a total net worth of $4,000,000; or a net pretax income of $2,000,000 for at least 2 of the 3 preceding fiscal years
- the issuer has actively engaged in business operations for at least 36 consecutive calendar months preceding registration
- for a period of at least 30 days during the 3 months preceding the offering of the securities registered there have been at least 4 market makers for the class of equity securities registered under the Securities Exchange Act of 1934
- the aggregate commissions or discounts to be received by the underwriters will not exceed 10% of the aggregate offering price
- neither the issuer nor a subsidiary has failed to pay a preferred stock dividend or defaulted on any bond or long-term lease
- in the case of an equity security, the price at which the security will be offered to the public is not less than $5 per share

Mutual funds and unit investment trusts may use registration by filing if:

- A registration statement has been filed under the Securities Act of 1933
- A prior registration in the state was completed within the previous 24 months
- The terms of the prior registration have not materially changed

When applying to register securities by filing, the issuer must file a:

- Statement of eligibility
- Name, address, and form of organization of the issuer
- Statement describing the offering
- Copy of the prospectus filed with the SEC

If all or part of the offering is for the benefit of someone other than the issuer (which we call a "non-issuer distribution"), the statement must also contain the name, address, and amount of securities held by that person, and the reasons for making the offering. In other words, maybe some of the founders are selling their shares (non-issuer) while the issuer is offering shares to investors.

Notice that the Administrator can require more information under registration by coordination than under registration by filing. The Administrator also requires 10 days to review the paperwork under "coordination" but only 5 days under "registration by filing."

Qualification

As the Uniform Securities Act declares, any security may be registered by qualification, but, as we'll see, this is the most arduous, pain-in-the-neck method of registering securities at the state level. In addition to the requirements for securities registration in general, which includes the consent to service of process, a registration statement under qualification must contain the following:

- Basic information on the issuer: name, address, form of organization, etc.
- Information on the issuer's directors, officers, and persons owning 10% + of the issuer's securities
- If anyone is doing a non-issuer distribution connected to this offering, name and address of the person and amount of securities owned
- Capitalization and long-term debt of the issuer
- Kind and amount of securities to be offered, proposed offering price, estimated underwriter compensation and finders fees
- Estimated cash proceeds to be received by the issuer, purposes for which the proceeds will be used
- Copy of any prospectus, pamphlet, circular, form letter, advertisement, or other sales literature to be used
- Specimen/copy of the security being registered, copy of articles of incorporation and by-laws, and copy of the indenture if applicable

The Securities Act of 1933 offers a transactional exemption under Rule 147. The federal government is in charge of inter-state commerce, but since securities sold in a Rule 147 exemption are offered only to residents of the issuer's state, that becomes the state's responsibility. So, registration by qualification is the method used for a Rule 147 offering.

As the Uniform Securities Act then indicates, the securities registered under this method are effective when the Administrator so orders. Therefore, a test question might ask, "Which of the following methods requires a specific response from the

Administrator?" The answer would be "registration by qualification." Recall that for coordination and filing/notification, as long as the state had 10 days to review the paperwork under coordination and 5 days under filing/notification, the effective date was granted by the SEC.

FEDERAL COVERED SECURITIES

Remember that all securities have to be registered at the state level, except for all the securities that don't have to be registered at the state level.

Federal covered securities don't have to be registered with the states. As their name suggests, these securities are *covered* at the *federal* level. The National Securities Markets Improvement Act of 1996 (NSMIA) is what created this special class of security. Basically, it makes no sense to force the following to be registered with both the SEC and the states, so NSMIA says that the following will *only* register with the federal regulators, the SEC:

- Securities listed, or authorized for listing, on the New York Stock Exchange or the American Stock Exchange, or Nasdaq.
- Securities listed, or authorized for listing, on a national securities exchange that has listing standards that the Commission determines are substantially similar to the listing standards applicable to securities described in subparagraph (A); or
- Securities of the same issuer that are equal in seniority or that are a senior security to a security described in subparagraph (A) or (B).
- Securities issued by an investment company that is registered, or that has filed a registration statement, under the Investment Company Act of 1940.
- SALES TO QUALIFIED PURCHASERS.--A security is a covered security with respect to the offer or sale of the security to qualified purchasers, as defined by the Commission by rule. In prescribing such rule, the Commission may define the term 'qualified purchaser' differently with respect to different categories of securities, consistent

with the public interest and the protection of
investors.

Why should these securities automatically be on the federal government's turf?
If the security is trading on a national exchange, first, we're talking about inter-state
commerce, which is the federal government's domain. Just as there are state highways
and also federal interstate highways, some securities are on the state's turf and some
are on the federal government's turf. Second, the issuer of the security has to provide
lots of disclosure and meet all kinds of rigid criteria just to be trading on this national
exchange—notice the phrase, "has listing standards that the Commission determines
are substantially similar to the listing standards applicable to securities described in
subparagraph (A)." The "Commission" (SEC), also reserves the right to determine
that exchanges created in the future have similar criteria. If so, those securities are
federal covered, too. And, if the issuer's common stock is federal covered, so is their
preferred stock and bonds (senior securities). Investment company securities include
open and closed-end funds, UITs, and variable annuities. Those are federal covered.
They might do a notice filing, but that's just a filing of notice with the states. If the
exam asks what the state Administrator may require for an offering of a federal covered
security, the answer would include: copy of documents filed with the SEC, notice
filing fee, consent to service of process. Note that there is a uniform notice filing
for investment company shares at www.nasaa.org. Stocks listed on AMEX, NYSE,
and NASDAQ do not provide notice filings, but investment company shares are still
subject to this requirement, should the exam decide to dig that deep.

So, let's apply the concept. Since securities such as IBM, Microsoft, or variable
annuities are federal covered, the states have no power to enforce anti-fraud regulations on any offer or sale, right?

Right?

How does the fraud definition go again? Does it say that it's unlawful to employ
any device, scheme, or artifice to defraud in connection *with any security that has to be
registered with the state?*

No, remember that it says "any security." IBM doesn't have to register with the
states—so what? If anybody makes a fraudulent offer or sale of IBM, the states can
still enforce anti-fraud regulations on that person. IBM is still a "security." If an agent
is soliciting money from investors, telling them they're purchasing shares of IBM
and sending them fictitious account statements to conceal the fact that all of their
money has really been going into one of his many "special purpose" bank accounts,
the registration of IBM stock is not a relevant point, right? We're not talking about the
primary offering of IBM common stock, which would have been registered exclusively

with the SEC. We're talking about somebody defrauding investors by pretending to purchase securities with their money but actually misappropriating the customer funds and concealing it through mail or wire fraud.

The list of federal covered securities includes securities sold to "qualified purchasers." We mentioned qualified purchasers earlier, when we pointed out that they can pay investment advisers for capital gains/appreciation. They include a corporation with $25 million of assets, a family-owned corporation with $5 million, or a natural person with $5 million to invest.

EXEMPT SECURITIES

The word "exempt" means excused. What do you suppose the word "non-exempt" means? That's right, *not excused.*

So if a security is "exempt" it is excused from the filing requirements we just spent a lot of time discussing. If the security is "non-exempt," it is *not excused* from the filing/registration requirements.

Which securities have to be registered with the Administrator? Not the exempt securities. The only securities that have to be registered are the non-exempt securities. If this seems preposterous, it's only because we're using two words that you're probably not used to seeing in any other context. Their meaning is actually quite simple: securities have to be registered unless they are specifically excused from the registration requirements. Exempt securities are specifically excused, so they don't have to register. Non-exempt securities are not excused from the registration requirements.

That's all we're saying. And, whether a security has to be registered or not is one issue. The way the security is being offered and sold is a whole different concern. Remember that an exempt security is still a security subject to anti-fraud rules. It just doesn't have to go through the process of paying fees and filing mounds of paperwork.

So, the following securities are still securities, but since they are excused from registering with the states, they are "exempt securities." Try to re-create this list on your scratch paper at the exam center before starting your test:

- any security issued or guaranteed by the United States, any state, any political subdivision of a state
- any security issued or guaranteed by Canada, any Canadian province, any political subdivision of any such province, or any other foreign government with which the United States currently maintains diplomatic relations, if the security is recognized as a valid obligation by the issuer or guarantor;

- any security issued by a bank, savings institution, or trust company
- any security issued by a federal savings and loan association, or any building and loan or similar association organized under the laws of any state
- any security issued by an insurance company (except variable contracts!)
- any debt security issued by a federal credit union or any credit union, industrial loan association, or similar association
- any security issued or guaranteed by any railroad, other common carrier, public utility, or holding company that is subject to specified regulations
- any security listed or approved for listing upon notice of issuance on the New York Stock Exchange, the American Stock Exchange, or the Midwest Stock Exchange, any other exchanged approved by the Administrator, and any warrant or right to purchase or subscribe to any of the foregoing
- any security issued by a not-for-profit organization such as religious, educational, benevolent, charitable, fraternal, social, or trade and professional associations
- a promissory note or bankers' acceptance that matures in no more than 9 months, is issued in denominations of at least $50,000, and receives a rating in one of the 3 highest rating categories from a nationally recognized statistical rating organization
- any investment contract issued in connection with an employees' stock purchase, savings, pension, profit-sharing, or similar benefit plan if the Administrator is notified in writing thirty days before the inception of the plan

And, just to keep things nice and simple, two of those securities could actually lose their exemption if they aren't careful. Those would be:

- any security issued by a not-for-profit organization such as religious, educational, benevolent, charitable, fraternal, etc.
- any investment contract issued in connection with an employees' stock purchase, savings, pension, profit-sharing, or similar benefit plan

If you look at the list, you find a lot of government securities. They're either the direct obligation of a federal government, or the securities are regulated by insurance regulators. Or, they're registered exclusively with the SEC. Fine, the state regulators have enough trouble trying to stop all the shady characters trying to sell shares of 17% "guaranteed preferred stock" in Billy Bob's Barbecue Barn. Let the federal regulators deal with federal government securities and securities covered by various federal laws.

We'll deal with the little companies nobody's ever heard of. See, those "federal covered securities" are more easily regulated by the SEC, but the weird little promissory notes that pop up in Pendleton are handled more effectively by the state regulators in Oregon. Those are really the securities that have to be registered with the states—the ones that are *not* trading on a national exchange or issued by a government, a bank, savings & loan, credit union, or insurance company. See, if a company has already met the listing requirements of the NYSE, for example, the states know the company has provided disclosure and has been filing quarterly and annual reports with the SEC under the Securities Exchange Act of 1934. But, some small, local company might have $40 in the bank and bills piling up with American Express. American Express gives small business owners 30 days to pay, so if I owe $150,000 to American Express, maybe I can sell $150,000 of promissory notes to investors who actually think a promise is, like, a promise to get paid or something. See, if the shaky company had to register, it would take more than 30 days to get through the process, and they don't even have enough money to pay the registration fee. That's what state securities regulation is all about—trying to make it tough for shaky companies to trick investors into providing their hard-earned money in exchange for some worthless paper called "preferred stock," a "promissory note," or a "can't-lose investment."

I have purposely delayed commenting on the "promissory note" to see if you're still reading that closely. While you will find an exemption for a "promissory note" on our previous bulleted list, when you look at the requirements, you can see how the company above would *not* be exempt—they can't afford to be rated by S&P or Moody's. And, they would never get a high rating, even if they *could* afford to. On the other hand, if a company's debt has been highly rated by S&P, Moody's, Fitch, etc., that's a world of difference from some company on the verge of collapse using investor funds to keep the big, bad creditors from busting down the door.

EXEMPT TRANSACTIONS

So we've done some hard work, and we can now draw three very clear conclusions:

1. If it is a security, it is subject to anti-fraud regulations
2. If it is a security, it has to be registered
3. Unless it doesn't

Federal covered securities are exempt from state-level registration. Other exempt securities are excused from the requirements to register and file sales literature/advertising with the regulators. So, if it is an exempt security, it is a security that does not have to be registered. If anybody sells it fraudulently at *any* time, that's a whole different issue. It would be securities fraud because the thing in question would be a security, whether it's exempt or not.

But exempt securities do not have to be registered. That's all that the term "exempt security" means. Non-exempt securities, of course, would always have to be registered.

Except when they wouldn't.

As the title to this section already gave away, there are transactions that qualify for exemptions. If you took the Series 6 or 7 already, you saw that there is a very important piece of federal legislation called the Securities Act of 1933, which goes hand-in-hand with the Uniform Securities Act. The Securities Act of 1933 says that all securities have to be registered, except all the securities that don't have to be registered. Many securities are exempt from the Securities Act of 1933's registration requirements, including Treasury securities, municipal securities, bank securities, and highly rated, short-term debt securities, to name a few. The Securities Act of 1933 also has exempt transactions that allow securities to be sold without registration. There is the Reg D exemption under Rule 506—since the security is being sold by the issuer to "accredited investors," the SEC is all laid back about it. The purchasers are, in general, the officers and directors of the company, institutions like mutual and big pension funds, or individuals with high net worth or income. If you follow the stipulations of this exempt transaction, you can avoid the typical registration process for non-exempt securities. There is the "Reg A" exemption for small offerings and other exemptions too numerous and detailed to explore here.

So, just like federal law, the Uniform Securities Act lists securities that are exempt from registration requirements and calls them "exempt securities." Like the federal "Act of '33," the Uniform Securities Act also lists transactions that make the security exempt from registration and calls them "exempt transactions." And, as we've mentioned, both federal and state law make it clear that a security that is exempt from filing requirements does not relieve the *persons* selling that security from anti-fraud rules. So, if fraud takes place in any of the "exempt transactions," then we're still talking about fraud. What we're not talking about is requiring the security to be registered.

Why not? Because it's being sold in an exempt transaction, for example:

- any isolated non-issuer transaction, whether effected through a broker-dealer or not
- any non-issuer transaction by a registered agent of a registered broker-dealer provided the issuer of the security is actually engaged in business and

- a non-issuer transaction in an outstanding security if the issuer of the security:
  - is subject to the registration and reporting requirements of the Securities Exchange Act of 1934
  - is registered under the Investment Company Act of 1940
  - has filed with the Administrator information substantially the same as that required by registered issuers by the Securities Exchange Act of 1934 for a period of at least 180 days prior to the transaction
- any non-issuer transaction effected by or through a registered broker-dealer pursuant to an unsolicited order or offer to buy
  - the Administrator may require that the client acknowledge on a specified form that the order was unsolicited and that the broker-dealer maintain the form for a prescribed amount of time
- any transaction between the issuer and an underwriter, or among underwriters
- any transaction in a bond secured by a real mortgage or deed of trust provided that the entire mortgage or deed of trust, together with all the bonds secured thereby, is offered and sold as a unit
- any transaction by an executor, administrator, sheriff, marshal, receiver, trustee in bankruptcy, guardian, or conservator
- any transaction executed by a bona fide pledge without any purpose of evading this act
- any offer or sale to a bank, savings institution, trust company, insurance company, investment company as defined in the Investment Company Act of 1940, pension or profit-sharing trust, or other financial institution or institutional buyer, or to a broker-dealer, whether the purchaser is acting for itself or in some fiduciary capacity
- private placement: any transaction directed to no more than ten non-institutional investors provided:
  - seller believes all non-institutional buyers are purchasing for investment purposes
  - no commissions paid for soliciting any non-institutional buyer
- any sale of a pre-organization certificate provided:
  - no commission is paid for soliciting any buyer
  - the number of subscribers does not exceed 10
  - no *payment* is made by any subscriber
- any transaction with existing security holders of the issuer, including persons

who at the time of the transaction are holders of convertible securities and warrants, provided no commissions are paid for soliciting buyers, or the issuer files a notice specifying the terms of the offer and the Administrator does not disallow the exemption within five days

- any offer (but not a sale) of a security for which registration statements have been filed under both this act and the Securities Act of 1933 if no stop order or refusal order is in effect

- any non-issuer transaction in the outstanding securities of a foreign issuer provided:
  - the issuer has been filing required reports in Canada or another jurisdiction designated by the Administrator for at least 180 days
  - security is listed on the Toronto Stock Exchange or the TSX Venture Exchange or another exchange that the Administrator designates (or is a senior security of the same issuer)

So there are exempt transactions, but they aren't necessarily easy to claim and pull off. There are also exempt securities, but they represent a fairly select group. Let's say that you own a small candy company that needs to raise $3 million to expand. You do not want to register the securities you'll need to sell, so you call in your attorneys. What do we pay attorneys for? Helping us get out of stuff. You want to get out of the huge hassle of registering securities with the Administrator—can they get you out of it?

They can try. Looking at the list of exempt securities, they don't see anything there for you. Obviously, you're not a government, or a bank, or an insurance company. You're *not* federal covered—you're a small, unknown company, not authorized for listing on the New York Stock Exchange or NASDAQ. So, your stock is not an exempt security; I guess you're stuck registering the stock?

Not so fast. At $500 an hour your attorneys see no reason to rush. They point out that you could offer and sell the securities to a bank, insurance company or other financial institution. Since those guys are big boys and girls, this describes an exempt transaction. Cool—can you get a bank to cut a check for $3 million for "stock" in your small, unknown candy company?

Next idea?

You could do a "private placement." If you could get up to 10 non-institutional investors to invest $300,000 each, you could raise the $3 million. What if the 10 investors only want to put in $50,000 each? Then, you'll need to line up some institutional buyers, which puts you back in the same place, trying to convince a bank or insurance company to invest in your small, shaky candy making company that could be crushed just by a short-term spike in the price of sugar, cocoa, paper, etc.

What if you put out the word that if anyone would like to call up and request the opportunity to make a $300,000 investment, you might then fill their unsolicited order for them?

No—that would be an *issuer* transaction in which the issuer would receive the proceeds. The exempt transaction is an unsolicited "non-issuer" transaction effected by a broker-dealer, meaning "not for the benefit of the issuer," just a transaction between two investors on the secondary market.

So, there are ways around having to register our common stock, but it's not necessarily going to be easy qualifying for an exempt transaction. But, we can easily see why most of these transactions qualify for a more relaxed treatment by the Administrator. For example:

- Any transaction by an executor, administrator, sheriff, marshal, receiver, trustee in bankruptcy, guardian, or conservator

Who is an "executor" usually? The executor of an estate is often just the oldest child, or the one who was always "best with numbers." She often has no clue about securities, so when she goes to liquidate Grandma's estate and some of the securities weren't actually registered, let's get over it. It's not going to happen on a regular basis. When other "fiduciaries" are just liquidating assets and some of those assets turn out to be securities, oh well. It's not like this kind of thing happens every day. A receiver placed in charge of a bankrupt entity to *marshal* it will liquidate those assets, some of which could be unregistered, non-exempt securities. Oh well, it's not like this receiver/trustee in a bankruptcy is a securities dealer trying to skirt the registration requirements.

Recently, I actually heard of an investment advisory firm getting a call from a Texas broker-dealer, who said, "By the way, one of your portfolio managers bought a stock that was never blue skied in Texas." What this rather cryptic statement meant was that a portfolio manager (investment adviser) with discretion over an account bought stock in a really small company for a "microcap" portfolio. But, since nobody called up and solicited the client, it was an "unsolicited, non-issuer transaction effected through a broker-dealer." The word "non-issuer" means it was not part of an IPO or other offering where the issuer is raising money.

So, the broker-dealer had the customer sign the unsolicited order acknowledgment, and they had themselves an exempt transaction. And I had myself a fascinating story that, so far, has been very difficult to work into dinner conversation.

A "non-issuer transaction" is a transaction between two parties in which neither one is the issuer. A trade on the NYSE would be a perfect example of a non-issuer transaction. For example, if you buy 500 shares of Microsoft common stock from another investor, the issuer, Microsoft, is not involved in that "non-issuer" transaction on the secondary market. On the other hand, when a customer redeems her open-end fund (mutual fund) shares, that is definitely a transaction with the issuer of the fund. When someone buys interests in a limited partnership from the distributor, that is definitely a transaction for the benefit of the issuer. When someone purchases Treasuries from a Federal Reserve Bank, that is also a transaction with the issuer and, yes, the exam will expect you to know your stuff to this amazing level of detail. Then again, you can miss 18 of the 60 questions and still pass.

Another item mentioned that an offer for a security that is *in the process of registration* is okay. We're talking about those "indications of interest" you studied for the Series 6 or 7. As long as the issuer has filed the registration statement, they can take the indications of interest, providing investors with a preliminary prospectus. They just can't make a *sale* until the effective date.

If the exam wants to play hardball, it could bring up a subtle difference between the private placement and the offer of pre-organization certificates. In the private placement, investors are definitely paying money for the securities. They also generally need to hold the securities for at least one year before selling them. No commissions can be paid for soliciting the 10 non-institutional buyers, but the money is definitely being paid from the investors to the issuing company. In a *pre-organization* certificate offering the maximum number of buyers (period) is 10 and no commissions may be paid for soliciting *any* buyer. And, no *payment* may be made by any buyer.

Okay, so my advice is to use the scratch paper they give you at the testing center and try to write down the following:

- Exempt securities
- Exempt transactions

But, also remember that those terms *only* mean that the security didn't have to be registered. All *persons* are subject to anti-fraud regulations in connection with *any* offer, sale, or purchase of *any* security. And remember that while only a few specific types of exempt *securities* can have their exemption revoked, the Administrator could take action to revoke/deny any of the exempt *transactions*. An exempt transaction saves time and money for the issuer, but if it isn't carried out in accordance with the state securities laws, the state securities Administrator is going to pull the plug on the whole thing. And, since the issuer might blow the Administrator off, the attorney general could seek a court injunction, which is where the fun really begins.

As the Uniform Securities Act utters in a moment of clarity, "In any proceeding under this act, the burden of proving an exemption or an exception from a definition is upon the person claiming it." That is an extremely likely thing for the exam to ask. It just means that the default setting is: register your securities. If you think your securities don't have to be registered, it's up to you to know for sure and be able to prove you qualify for the exemption. It is *not* up to the Administrator to show you why you had to register.

Also, as the SEC indicates in federal securities law, the fact that a securities offering has been registered or is exempt from registration does not imply that the Administrator has approved the security or passed judgment on the merits of the investment. Any representation that the security has been "deemed a good, safe investment" by the Administrator, for example, would be fraudulent.

OFFERS AND SALES

And now let's enjoy the definition of:

> "Offer" or "offer to sell" includes every attempt or offer to dispose of, or solicitation of an offer to buy, a security or interest in a security for value.

> "Sale" or "sell" includes every contract of sale of, contract to sell, or disposition of, a security or interest in a security for value.

Why are these definitions important?

Because the most important part of the Uniform Securities Act is the very beginning. In the beginning, the Uniform Securities Act created the fraud statute, which states:

> It is unlawful for any person, in connection with the offer, sale, or purchase of any security…to employ any device, scheme, or artifice to defraud, etc.

Obviously, we've already defined "security" and pointed out that whether the security is required to be registered or not has nothing to do with this fraud statute.

If it's a "security," it's covered by the anti-fraud statutes. So, if the guy who is the subject of an Administrative action pays his attorneys to argue that the investment did not fit the definition of a "security," he's hoping the hearing officer agrees. But, since most things do fit the definition of "security," they might, instead, try to argue that the conduct in question does not fit the definition of "offer" or "sale." Also, a security only has to be registered if it is to be offered and sold to investors—so, if the activity doesn't meet those definitions, no registration was required in the first place.

Notice how the definition of *offer* uses the phrase, "or solicitation of an offer to buy." That sounds fancy, but it's actually completely necessary. If the lawyers who wrote the statute weren't so good at anticipating what lawyers for the other side will attempt to argue, they might have forgotten to add that phrase. If they had, the other side's attorneys could try to make the following specious argument: No, my client, in fact, did not try to *sell* a security to anyone. What he did, instead, was to call several investors and tell them that he might, in fact, have some securities that they might want to invest in. He then promptly hung up the phone. It wasn't until several days later that the first investor called back and asked if he could *buy* some securities. So my client, in fact, agreed to let the investor buy some securities; however, he, clearly did not try to *sell* the securities to anyone.

Of course, since the individual "solicited an offer to buy a security," it was the same thing as making an "offer to sell" a security. At the top of a tombstone ad for a new offer of securities, you will see the phrase, "This announcement should under no circumstances be construed as an offer to sell or a solicitation of an offer to buy. Offerings are made by the prospectus."

The tombstone is just an announcement of fact. But, when somebody calls up and requests a prospectus, sending that prospectus represents an "offer to sell" a security. So, there had better not be anything misleading in the prospectus or in the conversation connected to it, right?

So, if the conduct in question fits the definition of an offer and/or a sale of securities, it is subject to the anti-fraud statutes and possibly the registration requirements. Okay, let's start with some things that might not seem like offers but actually are. As the Uniform Securities Act states:

```
Any security given or delivered with, or as a bonus on
account of, any purchase of securities or any other
thing is considered to constitute part of the subject
of the purchase and to have been offered and sold for
value.
```

What that means is that if a corporation is offering bonds and also sweetening the deal with some warrants, both securities are part of the offer and sale. Or, if the purchase of 100 preferred shares entitles the buyer to receive 10 shares of common stock, both securities are considered to have been offered and sold. So, if you get a test question about some company who wants to raise capital without actually registering the stock, remember that they can't get cute and tell investors that a purchase of $10,000 par value of debentures entitles them to receive 10 shares of common stock—that common stock is the subject of the offer of bonds and must be registered.

This is very similar to the third item concerning the sale or offer of a warrant or right.

> Every sale or offer of a warrant or right to purchase
> or subscribe to another security of the same or another
> issuer, as well as every sale or offer of a security
> which gives the holder a present or future right or
> privilege to convert into another security of the same
> or another issuer, is considered to include an offer
> of the other security.

This means that if an issuer offers or sells a warrant that allows the holder to purchase common stock at a set price, the common stock has *also* been offered. Therefore, you can't offer or sell the warrant without also registering the stock that can be purchased with the warrant.

> A purported gift of assessable stock is considered to
> involve an offer and sale.

Shares of stock are typically no longer assessable, but they do exist. Assessable shares can be assessed fees for future improvements/expansion, so the regulators decided that a gift of these shares wasn't really a gift. So, a "purported gift of assessable stock" is considered both an offer and a sale of a security. I wish I could tell you otherwise, but your exam will almost certainly expect you to know that, and might even trick you with a gift of *non*-assessable stock, which would simply be a gift of stock. You know those sadistic fraternity members who like to line up the pledges in the middle of the night and break out the paddles, the spotlights, etc.? Guess what many of them do for a living now? That's right—they write Series 63 questions.

Seriously.

Just remember that a gift of assessable stock is an offer and a sale of a security, while a gift of *non*-assessable shares would be neither an offer nor a sale. It would be a gift of stock.

Be ready for some very tough questions on this exam.

NOT OFFERS

Now we get to look at some examples of things that are *not offers* of securities, which means they would not be subject to registration requirements. As the Uniform Securities Act states, the following are not considered to be *offers* of securities:

- any bona fide pledge or loan of a security
- any stock dividend if nothing of value is given by stockholders for the dividend
- any act incident to a class vote by stockholders… on a merger, consolidation, reclassification of securities, or sale of corporate assets in consideration of he issuance of securities of another corporation
- any act incident to a judicially approved reorganization in which a security is issued in exchange for one or more outstanding securities, claims, or property interests

First, if you're pledging securities as collateral, you are not making an offer to sell securities. So, you can pledge a security as collateral even if the security isn't registered. A stock dividend, as you saw on the Series 6 or 7, is really a non-event. The issuer used to cut the big earnings pie into 10 million slices; now they're going to give everybody more slices by cutting the pie into 15 million smaller slices and having everybody pretend they've gained something. That is not an offer—just a way of pushing down the market price for the stock to entice investors to buy more of it. When a corporation merges with another corporation, the acquiring company is not really offering their securities to the other shareholders—the two companies are simply going to become one. And the last bullet point has to do with a bankruptcy proceeding. The bankruptcy judge will approve the plan to wipe out the current shareholders and give the stiffed bondholders shares in the newly organized entity. So, that's a way of dealing with some mighty ticked-off creditors, not an offer of securities.

D-O-A

So, the next question is, "When has an offer been made in a particular state?"" Luckily the Uniform Securities Act tells us that:

> ...an offer to sell is made in this state when the offer
> originates from this state, or is directed by the
> offeror to this state.

If you get a test question stating that an agent in State A calls an investor in State B trying to interest the investor in some securities, tell the exam that an offer to sell has been made in both states. The Uniform Securities Act also gives the Administrator authority when an offer has been accepted in the state. An offer to sell "is accepted in this state when acceptance is communicated to the offeror in this state and has not previously been communicated to the offeror outside this state." That communication could be by phone, text message, email, fax, etc., by the way.

As usual, this is much simpler than it first appears. If an agent in North Dakota calls a customer vacationing in South Dakota and asks if she'd like to buy a variable annuity, an offer to sell a security has been made in both states. If the buyer isn't sure, maybe she calls back a few days later while visiting her Aunt Lorraine in Lincoln, Nebraska. "Sure," she says, "I'd like to communicate my acceptance of said variable annuity to you, the offeror," now the offer has been accepted in Nebraska. Think "D-O-A" here. Where was the offer directed (D), where did it originate (O), and where was it (A) accepted? The offer was D-directed into South Dakota, O-originated in North Dakota, and A-accepted in Nebraska.

What if the investor cuts a check while kickin' it up in Branson, Missouri? Nobody cares where the check is cut. It's all about where the offeror and offeree were when they were communicating. Also, if the agent had been offering shares of General Electric, headquartered in New York, that would not imply that the New York Administrator is somehow involved. GE almost certainly has nothing to do with this North Dakota agent.

Please remember that in the next chapter we'll be saying that the North Dakota agent can call an existing customer just visiting the state of South Dakota without having to *register* as an agent in South Dakota. Fine. The agent could also get into his pickup truck and drive to the other state without getting a South Dakota driver's license. But, in either case, if the dude starts violating the law, the State of South Dakota can nail him. What if the agent doesn't like that fact?

Tell him to stay the heck out of South Dakota.

MEDIA

Finally, just in case the exam loses its mind the day you take it, memorize the following from the Uniform Securities Act:

> An offer to sell or to buy is not made in this state when the publisher circulates any bona fide newspaper or other publication of general, regular, and paid circulation which is not published in this state, or which IS published in this state but has had more than two-thirds of its circulation outside this state during the past twelve months, or a radio or television program originating outside this state is received in this state.

So, the state where the periodical is published is the state in which the offer to sell or solicitation of an offer to buy takes place...except for that funky thing about the publication being published in, say, Connecticut, but two-thirds of the circulation is outside that state. In that case, the offer to sell is being made in the state(s) where the advertisement is received. This seems a little crazy (like the exam itself), but what it means is that if you publish an advertisement in the New York Times, which has a circulation beyond New York, the offer to sell or solicitation of the offer to buy occurs only in New York. It's a New York newspaper, basically. But a magazine with a national subscription could be "published" almost anywhere and circulated across the country. In this case, if the magazine is produced/published in South Dakota, but more than 2/3's of the circulation is outside of South Dakota, then the offer to sell/solicitation of an offer to buy securities did not occur in South Dakota. It occurred wherever the offer was received. Also, the radio or TV advertisement is considered to take place where the TV or radio program originated. The notes to the Uniform Securities Act indicate that "a radio or television program is considered to originate in the state where the microphone or television camera is located, not at any relay station." Would the Series 63 actually reach this deep into triviality just to steal another point from you?

Sure—that's how it maintains its nasty reputation. It won't reach there very often—just often enough to keep you up at night and keep you studying another hour or two after the point of exhaustion.

Exclusions and Exemptions for Persons

(a continuation of "Registration of Persons")

BROKER-DEALERS

As we've said several times, a "broker-dealer" is defined by the Uniform Securities Act as "any person engaged in the business of effecting transactions in securities for the account of others or for his own account." Even though we see the words "person" and "his," we do not assume that a broker-dealer is an individual. And, we also don't make the wild statement that a broker-dealer can *never* be an individual, either. An exam question could try to get you to make that statement, so if it does, tell the test a broker-dealer could be a "natural person" or "individual." But, think of a broker-dealer as a business entity, sometimes an entity as massive as Morgan Stanley, Merrill Lynch, or Goldman Sachs, to name just three. Or, if you prefer the Hollywood version, think of a "broker-dealer" as the kind of insane place where Charlie Sheen's character works in the movie *Wall Street*.

NOT A BROKER-DEALER

The Uniform Securities Act then states that a "broker-dealer" does not include:
- Agent
- Issuer
- Bank, savings institution, or trust company

That simply means that agents, issuers, banks, savings institutions, and trust companies do not meet the definition of "broker-dealer." They don't have to claim an exemption from registration any more than the high school math teacher had to claim an exemption from the gym glass requirement. When the *administrators* of the school established the gym class requirement, they weren't including teachers, janitors, coaches, bus drivers, guidance counselors, etc. They were including only high school students in the requirement to take gym class. Similarly, when the Administrator requires broker-dealers to register and to refrain from unethical business practices, he simply is not talking to banks, savings institutions, trust companies, or the agents who *represent* broker-dealers. So, if a test question is looking for "broker-dealers," skip over any answer choice that's talking about agents, issuers, banks, savings institutions, or trust companies.

Why?

They're not broker-dealers.

EXEMPTION

Then, there are broker-dealers who don't have to register. If a broker-dealer has *no place of business in the state*, there is a good chance that state won't make them register. But make sure in the exam question that the broker-dealer has *no place of business in the state*. Why? Because if they *do* have a place of business in the state, they'll have to register. For an exemption to registration we're talking only about firms *with no place of business in the state*.

See, if I'm the Colorado securities Administrator, I don't care about the broker-dealers with offices in Nebraska. Not unless they start doing business with Colorado residents, that is. I'm out to protect my residents, so if you want to do business with my residents, you'll have to register. However, the out-of-state broker-dealer may only want to do business with my "big kids," known as "institutional investors." If so, I'm not worried about making the firm register. If they try to take advantage of anyone, I'll come after them, but as long as they mind their p's and q's, I'll let them do business exclusively with the following investors without making them register:

- Issuers of the securities involved in the transactions
- Other broker-dealers
- Banks, savings institutions, trust companies, insurance companies
- Investment companies as defined in the Investment Company Act of 1940
- Pension or profit-sharing trusts
- Other financial institutions or institutional buyers

So, if the broker-dealer has an office in the state, they register in the state. If they want to do business with individuals, they'll also have to register, whether they have an office in the state or not. But, if they *don't have an office in the state,* they will *not* have to register if their only clients are those above.

Unfortunately, that's about as simple as we can make that concept, and you'll notice we left it out when first explaining the registration requirements for broker-dealers.

I don't expect that to sink in immediately, but you will have to know which broker-dealers register and which ones are exempt long before you sit for the Series 63. So, let's apply the concepts a bit before moving on. If a broker-dealer in Minneapolis has a customer who chooses to spend a few weeks in Florida each year, can the broker-dealer call the customer in Florida to sell her some securities or convince her to sell some of her current holdings? Or, would they need to get licensed in Florida first?

This is a broker-dealer who has no place of business in the state of Florida and who is not doing business with any Florida residents. So, as long as the customer is in the state of Florida no more than 30 days, the broker-dealer does not need to register in the state of Florida.

What if the broker-dealer wants to solicit business from people who *are* Florida residents? They need to get registered in Florida.

In Q & A format, you can think through these issues like so:

Question: does the broker-dealer have an office in the state?
Answer: Yes
Therefore: the broker-dealer must register in the state.

Question: does the broker-dealer have an office in the state?
Answer: No

Follow-up Question: does the broker-dealer have any non-institutional investors in the state?
If YES: the broker-dealer must register in the state.
If NO: the broker-dealer is exempt from registration requirements.

AGENTS

As we saw earlier, the Uniform Securities Act defines an "agent" as "any individual other than a broker-dealer who represents a broker-dealer or issuer in effecting or attempting to effect purchases or sales of securities." If the individual represents a broker-dealer in the state, that individual must register as an agent of the broker-dealer. That means he/she must take pre-license exams, fill out and sign the U-4 form filed by the broker-dealer on his/her behalf, and also pay an initial licensing fee plus an annual renewal fee. So, most people would be pretty excited to discover that they don't have to register as an agent.

NOT AGENTS

The Uniform Securities Act points out that if the individual represents the *issuer* of the securities involved in the transaction, he would not be an agent if:

- The security is exempt
- The transaction is exempt

So, if the individual works for www.treasurydirect.gov, she represents the US Government in helping people buy Treasury bills, notes, and bonds. She isn't getting a commission because there are no commissions charged to buy US Treasuries directly from the US Treasury. Therefore, she does not meet the definition of a "securities agent" subject to registration.

The Uniform Securities Act also then points out that an individual can effect transactions with the issuer's employees, partners, or directors *if no commission or other remuneration is paid.* Maybe you work in the human resources department and help employees buy their employer's stock for the 401(k) plan. As long as you don't get a commission for the transactions, you're not an agent. But, clearly, if your company offered you, say, $50 for every sale of stock, you would start pestering and pressuring the employees to buy stock, and that would be a different situation.

Officers and directors of the issuer can offer and sell the issuer's securities in exempt transactions, but if you get a test question about an officer "offering securities to the public," make that guy register as an issuer agent. Why? Well, I am the "officer" of my own little S-Corporation. In fact, to cut down on disagreements, I elected myself to ALL of the offices—president, vice-president, secretary, and (my favorite role) treasurer. Gee, I guess I'm an "officer of the issuer" and can go around "offering shares to the public."

Sure—I could do that as long as A) I got myself registered as an agent or B) was pretty sure the regulators would never find out.

Clerical/ministerial personnel of a broker-dealer are not agents, either. If you get a question about an individual working at a broker-dealer who merely gives out quotes or sales information, that individual is not an agent and is not subject to registration. Read carefully, though. If the question indicates that a sales assistant is authorized to accept purchase and sale *orders* from customers, that "sales assistant" is really an agent who really needs to pass her Series 7 and 63, possibly the 6 and 63.

Finally, the Uniform Securities Act says, "A partner, officer, or director of a broker-dealer or issuer, or a person occupying a similar status or performing similar functions, is an agent *only if he otherwise comes within this definition.*"

Wow, so if he's not an agent, he's not an agent?

That's pretty much what they're saying. If the guy is on the board of directors for a broker-dealer, is he automatically an agent? No. Not unless he wants to start offering/selling securities. If he just wants to sit on the board, he's a board member. If he wants to act like an agent, he's an agent.

MUST REGISTER

Notice how the whole idea of squirming out of the registration requirement as an agent is predicated on the fact that the individual represents the *issuer* of the securities involved in the transaction. What if the individual represents a broker-dealer? Then, he *will* have to register if:

- He has a place of business in the state, OR:
- The investors are individuals (not institutions)

EXEMPTIONS

And that means that if the agent has no office in the state, and the customers are all institutional investors, he does not have to register in that state. Also, the agent can do business with an *existing customer who is not a resident of the state* without having to register. Remember that agents represent broker-dealers, so the idea of the Minnesota resident vacationing in Florida applies both to the broker-dealer and the agent who represents the firm. If her existing client is just visiting Florida, the agent in Minnesota is not required to register in the other state.

Of course, if the agent deceives the client while the client is in the other state, the other state could crack down on her. But that's another issue. Which is why the exam will likely try to trick you into thinking that because the Minnesota-based agent is not required to register in Florida, the Florida securities Administrator has no authority whatsoever over her activities. No—as we saw, any time an offer to sell a security is directed into the state, the state has authority over the offer, should something funky take place. It's just that this out-of-state agent way up in Minnesota does not have to *register* as an agent in Florida.

LIMITED REGISTRATION OF CANADIAN BROKER-DEALERS

NASAA stands for the "North American Securities Administrators Association," which includes the regulators in the Canadian provinces and the state regulators in the US. Some students ask in live classes, "Hey, if it's North America, what about Mexico?" To which I can only offer a heartfelt, "No sé, amigo. Lo siento mucho. Quizás debes escribir a tu senador."

Canadian broker-dealers that have no place of business in a particular state and are properly registered in Canada would not have to register in a state if they wanted to serve a temporary resident of the state who was already a client of theirs in Canada. So, several test questions could be written to mess with you on that point—what if the broker-dealer wants to sign up a new client? Then, they would have to register. What if they have a place of business in the state? Then, they need to register. What if this existing client is in the state permanently, as opposed to staying here to complete a temporary job assignment? Then, the firm would have to register. But, if the individual is an existing client and is staying temporarily in the state, the broker-dealer has no place of business in the state, and the firm is properly registered in Canada, the Canadian broker-dealer is exempt.

Canadian broker-dealers could also claim an exemption if the individual is a temporary resident of the state and is enrolled in a self-directed tax advantaged retirement plan in Canada. It would be impractical to force this Canadian broker-dealer to register for two reasons. One, these plans have to be sited in Canada with a Canadian trustee, and the account cannot be run through the books of a non-Canadian broker. Second, the securities in the account have to be predominantly Canadian, and not many US securities brokers have sufficient trading activity in these stocks to make it practical for a US broker to hold the account.

Also, and as usual, if this Canadian broker-dealer is only effecting transactions with the big institutional investors, no registration in the state is required. In case the test is in an especially foul mood when you sit down to take it, remember that the Canadian broker-dealer would do the following to claim the exemption from registration:

- File a copy of the BD's current application for registration as required by the province in which the BD has its home office
- File proof of membership in a self-regulatory organization or stock exchange in Canada (and maintain such membership)
- File a Consent to Service of Process
- Disclose to clients in the state that the Canadian BD is not subject to the state's full regulatory requirements.
- Make books and records available to the Administrator concerning business conducted in the state
- Inform the Administrator of any criminal or regulatory actions against the firm

The agents representing the Canadian broker-dealer claiming the exemption are also exempt from registration requirements. I would expect your exam to try and trick you into saying that, therefore, they are exempt from anti-fraud statutes.

Remember that there is *no exemption to the anti-fraud statues, ever.*

For a real-world look at the Canadian broker-dealer exemption, visit our extra information at www.passthe63.com/updates.

INVESTMENT ADVISERS

Let's recall the 111-word definition of "investment adviser" in the Uniform Securities Act:

> "Investment adviser" means any person who, for compensation, engages in the business of advising others, either directly or through publications or writings, as to the value of securities or as to the advisability of investing in, purchasing, or selling securities, or who, for compensation and as a part of a regular business, issues or promulgates analyses or reports concerning securities. "Investment adviser" also includes financial planners and other persons who, as an integral component of other financially related services, provide the foregoing investment advisory services to others for compensation and as part of a business or who hold themselves out as providing the foregoing investment advisory services to others for compensation.

Many professionals try to convince the regulators that they don't meet the definition of "investment adviser," so the SEC put out Release IA-1092 back in 1987. This release spells out that if the answer to the following three questions is "yes," then the individual is probably an investment adviser. The three questions or "prongs" are:

- Does the professional provide investment advice on securities through recommendations, research, or opinions?
- Does the professional receive compensation in any form as a result of the activities?
- Does the professional engage in a regular business of providing advice on securities?

What if the professional is advising people on fixed annuities? Chances are, even if receiving compensation, that person does not meet the definition of "investment adviser." Why not? Fixed annuities are not securities. However, things can get tricky here. What if an insurance agent goes around telling people he is a "financial advisor" and underlines people to sell their mutual funds and other securities in order to purchase his equity indexed annuity, which is currently not defined as a "security"? Is he an insurance agent, or is he an investment adviser? The question is important because if the state defines him as an investment adviser and decides he's been acting as such without being registered, things can get ugly. But, how would he fit the definition of "investment adviser" if he's just an "annuity salesman"? The definition of adviser from the Uniform Securities Act and the Investment Advisers Act of 1940 includes the phrase, "or as to the advisability of investing in, purchasing, or selling securities." Then, we apply the "three-pronged approach" put out in Release IA-1092. Does the individual provide investment advice? He's advising on the "advisability of selling securities," right? Does he do this as part of a regular business? Well, if he held five seminars last month explaining why people should abandon their mutual funds and brokerage accounts in favor of his equity indexed annuities, and he's raking in about $35,000 a month in commissions, I'd say it's part of a regular business. Does he receive compensation in any form from the advice? Maybe not directly, but whenever he convinces people to sell their *securities*, he ends up being compensated quite handsomely when they put that money into the equity indexed annuity.

Some state regulators might conclude the individual is just an annuity salesman and leave him alone; however, many states have already cracked down on these individuals for "holding themselves out as an objective adviser" when, in fact, they're not registered as such. Massachusetts has cracked down on several individuals who fit this mold, and I had a recent discussion with a Midwestern state regulator who gave the typical lawyerly answer of, "Well, in some cases, I'd say the individual *is* an adviser, but in other cases, maybe not."

The comments to the Uniform Securities Act address the difficulty of including "financial planner" in the definition of "investment adviser" with the following:

> Financial planners and others who hold themselves out as providing investment advisory services to others for compensation are necessarily in the business of doing so. The provision defining an "investment adviser" to include financial planners and others who hold themselves out as providing investment advisory services to others for compensation should not be construed to

mean that all financial planners fall within the definition by virtue of their designation as "financial
planners." Financial planners rendering advice exclusively in such non-securities areas as insurance and
budget management, for example, would not be covered
by the definition. However, persons offering "total
financial planning" would be holding themselves out
as providing investment advisory services.

So, things are taken on a case-by-case basis, and we can see from the commentary above how easy it would be for a state securities Administrator to fit someone within the definition of "investment adviser" or convince a court to do so. Your best bet is to get yourself registered, or make sure nobody finds out.

NOT INVESTMENT ADVISERS

The Uniform Securities Act then states that the following folks do *not* meet the definition of investment adviser:

- An investment adviser representative
- Bank, savings institution, trust company
- Lawyer, accountant, teacher, or engineer whose performance of these services is solely incidental to the practice of his profession
- Broker-dealer whose performance of these services is solely incidental to the conduct of his business as a broker-dealer and who receives no special compensation for them
- A publisher of any bona fide newspaper, news column, newsletter, news magazine, or business or financial publication or service, whether communicated in hard copy form, or by electronic means, or otherwise, that does not consist of the rendering of advice on the basis of the specific investment situation of each client
- A federal covered adviser

Just as the Uniform Securities Act states that a broker-dealer is by definition not an agent, an investment adviser is not an investment adviser representative. In both cases, the first party is a business entity—the agents and adviser representatives are individuals who *represent* the business entity. The separation between bank, broker-dealer, and investment adviser especially comes into play when we're talking about large financial institutions such as Wells Fargo. I actually have a completed Form ADV

Part 2 right here on my computer, sent to me for free by "Wells Capital Management, Incorporated." That is the name of the investment adviser that was managing some 185 *billion* dollars at the time the disclosure brochure was put together. Page 6 of the adviser's Form ADV Part 2 states, "Wells Capital Management Incorporated (WellsCap) is a registered investment adviser and a wholly owned subsidiary of Wells Fargo Bank, N.A. ("Wells Fargo"), which is wholly owned by Wells Fargo & Company, a diversified financial services company." So, there is this massive financial services company named "Wells Fargo & Company," under which we find a bank called, not surprisingly, "Wells Fargo Bank," and there is also an investment adviser subsidiary called "Wells Capital Management" that manages some $185 billion of assets for institutional clients. The bank and the investment adviser are related, sure, because they have the same parent called "Wells Fargo & Company." But, they're also separate entities. So a bank, savings institution, or trust company might be *related* to an investment adviser, but that doesn't make them an investment adviser.

Why would the LATE (lawyer, accountant, teacher, engineer) item be included? Well, sometimes a lawyer will have to talk about securities in order to perform his job. If your grandmother dies after naming you the executor of her estate, you will come into an attorney's office and deal with a bunch of paperwork. The attorney will ask you about the estate assets, which include Grandma's checking and savings accounts, CDs, house, personal items, etc. The estate assets might include securities, too, so if the attorney asks, "What is the approximate *value of the securities* held by the estate?" does that make him an investment adviser? No, that question is "solely incidental to his profession" of acting as the estate attorney. As long as he doesn't get compensated to tell you whether you should sell the holdings, diversify, etc., he is acting as an attorney and not an investment adviser. Similarly, your accountant may suggest that you make your maximum 401(k) or IRA contribution, but she's just trying to help you with your taxes. Maybe a last-minute IRA contribution could get you a refund from Uncle Sam—that's the kind of service that accountants provide. She's not an investment adviser unless she starts—get this—advising you on your investments. If she says that for $299 the firm can help you allocate your IRA assets, now she has crossed the line and must register. Many states don't make CPAs take the Series 65 or 63 exams, but they would still want this particular accountant to register as an investment adviser. If she's being compensated for advising others on securities investments, she's an investment adviser. If she's helping people get tax refunds, she's just an accountant. Surely a finance professor can explain the benefits of investing in stock through her lectures to students without having to first register with a Form ADV. Of course, if she has a financial planning business on the side, that's different.

Financial planners are the textbook definition of "investment adviser." What is their compensation based on? Advising others on investing in securities. This would be fertile ground for a Series 63 question, too. The folks who write the test know that you know about the little "LATE" thing. That means that many test takers will see "teacher" and automatically assume she's not an investment adviser. But, the tricky question could have something like this inserted: a finance professor who regularly meets with students to discuss the benefits of investing in securities and provides asset allocation formulas for the students' investment accounts in exchange for a small fee.

That would be different, right? So, as always, read carefully when you take the Series 63.

Finally here, an engineer or geologist might be hired to determine if a company should drill for oil or natural gas on a particular field. The existence of oil or natural gas will be sort of important to the survival of this business, but that doesn't make the engineer or geologist an "investment adviser."

Individuals who pass their Series 6 and 63 and get licensed as agents of particular broker-dealers spend much of their time "advising" or "recommending" that investors purchase various mutual funds and variable annuities. If the agent lays out seven prospectuses and "advises" the investor to put 33% in the large cap growth fund, 33% in the long-term bond fund, and 33% in the small cap international discoveries fund, does that make her an "investment adviser"? How much does she charge to *tell* the investor what to do?

Nothing?

Then she's acting as an agent and an agent has to make recommendations just to do her job. She isn't being compensated for the advice—she'll make a commission if the investor purchases the mutual fund products. If she charged $1,000 just to deliver a report on which mutual funds the investor should choose, that would be different and would require her to register as an investment adviser.

Forbes and *BusinessWeek* talk about securities all the time, but they're just magazines, not investment advisers. *Forbes* has some great columnists who are registered investment advisers (John Rogers, Lisa Hess, David Dremann, etc.), but the magazine itself is not acting as an investment adviser when those columnists write about three stocks they really like right now. And the writers are not looking at my financial situation and telling *me* what to do. They're just writing a column. They need to be registered to run their advisory firms, and therein lies their "street credibility," which explains why they write columns in *Forbes*, but somebody writing a column about investing is just exercising his or her First Amendment right to express opinions through the "press." Not sure we needed to go quite this deep, but you may be amazed at how deep some of the Series 63 questions actually go. I prefer to err on the side of caution. Plus, I find this stuff fascinating—I know. No, I already have a good therapist in mind, thanks.

Unfortunately, the Series 63 could get very mean on this topic of writing about investing—are you a publisher, or are you an adviser who needs to register? The "publisher's exclusion" from the definition of "investment adviser" is available when the publication is "of a general and impersonal nature, in that the advice provided is not adapted to any specific portfolio or any client's particular needs," and when the publication is "of general and regular circulation, in that it is not timed to specific market activity or to events affecting, or having the ability to affect, the securities industry." Okay, so if you write an internet newsletter called "Investing in Technology Stocks," and that newsletter is delivered regularly, you can actually charge a subscription without being forced to register as an investment adviser. But, if your little "newsletter" is blasted out to readers/investors based on "market activity," you aren't writing a newsletter so much as telling people to "buy now" or "sell now" in exchange for compensation. You would be required to register as an investment adviser if the "newsletter" came out based on market developments. Again, though, if the newsletter comes out regularly and clearly isn't telling individuals what to do with their individual portfolios, then you are outside the definition of "investment adviser." You're basically exercising your First Amendment right to express your opinion through "the press."

In the real world and in exam questions, it can be very tricky to know exactly who has to register and who doesn't. What if an insurance agent decides that he doesn't want to sell stocks to people and doesn't want to manage their money or tell them what to do, but he is interested in investments and in making some extra money? He cajoles his 14-year-old daughter into designing a website that allows visitors to sign up for a free service in which they enter their financial data and investment goals into a database, which returns a suggested portfolio allocation and detailed strategy for reducing debt, refinancing mortgages, choosing mutual funds, etc. Is he providing advice on investing in securities? Yes. Is it tailor-made to an individual based on the individual's situation? Yes. Is he an investment adviser? So far, I don't see any compensation, and if he isn't being compensated in any way, he isn't an investment adviser. See, this enterprising insurance agent was smart enough to provide the interactive service for free. He only charges the advertisers on his site, who pay a few hundred dollars a month to display banner and text ads on the home page.

Oops.

Now he *is* receiving compensation indirectly for providing investment advice. He is providing individualized recommendations based on specific client information, and if this is part of a regular business, he's an investment adviser. If he has more than 5 clients in any state, he's going to have to register as an investment adviser in those states. Either that, or claim federal covered status, which is also a possibility. This type of predicament is presented on many Series 63, 65, and 66 questions. Unfortunately, the answers are not always clear, but if you know your stuff, you can still get these questions right.

EXEMPTIONS

So those folks are not investment advisers. They are excluded from that definition. The following folks might be investment advisers, but they don't have to register in the state because they have *no place of business in the state* and:

- their only clients in this state are investment companies as defined in the Investment Company Act of 1940, other investment advisers, federal covered advisers, broker-dealers, banks, trust companies, savings and loan associations, insurance companies, employee benefit plans with assets of not less than one million dollars ($1,000,000), and governmental agencies or instrumentalities, whether acting for themselves or as trustees with investment control, or other institutional investors as are designated by rule or order of the (Administrator),
- or, during the preceding twelve-month period the adviser has had no more than five clients, other than those specified above

The exam might refer to having no more than 5 clients as the "de minimus exemption." Why did the regulators choose the number 5? As it turns out, four was too small of a number and six was a little too high. The number 5 only has to do with *non*-institutional clients—remember that an out-of-state adviser can have as many institutional clients as they want, but they can only have 5 non-institutional or "Regular Joe and JoAnn" clients before they have to register.

Again, notice how I put the phrase *no place of business in this state* in italics. If the firm has a place of business in the state, the firm will always have to register in the state.

Unless it doesn't have to register in the state.

FEDERAL COVERED ADVISERS

Remember our old buddy NSMIA? Sure you do, NSMIA stands for the National Securities Markets Improvement Act of 1996, through which the powers-that-be decided that certain advisers should be "federal covered." That means that these folks register with the SEC. So, even if you had an office in Schenectady you would not register with the State of New York if you were a *federal covered* adviser. You would, instead, register with the SEC. Either way, you'd fill out Form ADV, but you would indicate on it that you were registering with the SEC, who would provide a notice filing to the State of New York. But a notice filing is simply a filing of notice, not a registration with the state, not a submission to their books and records or net capital requirements. The following are federal covered advisers:

- Adviser with > $30 million of assets under management (advisers with $25 million + *may* register with the SEC)
- Adviser doing business in 30+ states
- Adviser to a registered investment company
- NRSROs (Nationally Recognized Statistical Rating Organizations, e.g., Moody's and S&P)
- Pension consultants providing advice to employee benefit plans with assets of at least $50 million
- Affiliates of federally registered IAs if the principal office and place of business of the affiliate is the same as that of the SEC-registered adviser
- Newly formed advisers that reasonably believe that they will become eligible for federal registration within 120 days

Federal covered advisers are still subject to the state's power to enforce anti-fraud regulations. But, as long as they don't plan on defrauding investors, they can have an office in the state without registering with the state. They would register with the SEC and have the SEC send the state Administrator a copy of Form ADV. The firm would pay a notice filing fee and a renewal each year and provide U-4s for each representative with an office in the state or with more than 5 clients in the state. Which probably looks an awful lot like "registering with the state," but it isn't. It's a notice filing. The federal covered firm is registered with the SEC, subject to their inspection authority, licensing fees, books & records requirements, net capital requirements, etc.

What about the investment adviser *representatives* working for a federal covered adviser? Those individuals still register with the states. The firm registers with the

SEC, but the individuals register with the states where they have a place of business or where they have more than 5 non-institutional investors.

Just to keep everything nice and simple.

INVESTMENT ADVISER REPRESENTATIVES OF FEDERAL COVERED ADVISERS

Even though the adviser is a federal covered adviser, the representatives of the firm are still subject to registration with the state Administrator. As with agents of broker-dealers, Form U-4 must be completed by the firm and the individual, and it must pass the smell test. Also, the Uniform Securities Act uses the same language, more or less, to point out that it is unlawful for an investment adviser to employ an investment adviser representative unless the IAR is registered. If the IAR has a place of business in the state, he must register there. Or, even if he does not have a place of business in the state, if he has more than 5 non-institutional (Regular Joe) clients in that state, he must register there.

The exam might expect you to know that an adviser representative would "have a place of business" in, say, Rhode Island even if he only meets with clients there once a month. In fact, even if he simply lets it be generally known that he could meet with clients at an office in Rhode Island, he could be considered to have a place of business in Rhode Island and forced to pay a registration fee. Which, if you think about it, isn't the end of the world. If you're already registered in Connecticut, all you would do is submit some paperwork and a check to the Administrator for the State of Rhode Island. If they charge $200 or $300 to register and renew each year, weigh that against the income you make by doing business in Rhode Island or with Rhode Islanders. Maybe it's worth it, maybe it isn't. If it isn't worth it, though, don't try to operate in Rhode Island under the table. A fully compliant securities professional knows that it's better to bite the bullet than take any chances. What is a few hundred bucks a year in registration fees versus the possibility of having your license suspended or revoked?

Federal Acts

A basic understanding of federal securities acts is important when studying for the Series 63 exam. For example, you might get a question on your exam that asks something like, "Under which federal securities act is registration by coordination made possible?" The answer would be: the Securities Act of 1933, and, yes, many questions on the test are exactly that simple. People tend to remember only the most horrible and difficult exam questions, but, trust me, the majority of questions on the Series 63 exam are softballs, provided that you've really studied and really understand the big concepts.

We have already mentioned several of the following federal securities acts, but let's now explore them in more detail.

SECURITIES ACT OF 1933

When we looked at registration methods for securities, we mentioned that the requirement for using registration by coordination and registration by filing/notification is that the issuer also registers with the SEC under the Securities Act of 1933. The Securities Act of 1933 requires issuers who have not been excused from registration requirements to register their securities with the SEC, who would like to see all the information the company plans to disclose to investors. If the disclosure is incomplete or too hard to read, the SEC will make the issuer re-write it. Of course, the SEC neither approves nor disapproves the securities and makes no judgment as to the accuracy of the information or the quality of the investment. Like a state securities Administrator, they're just out to make sure investors receive enough material information to make an informed decision about purchasing a stock, bond, mutual fund, etc. If the issuer inserts bogus numbers into the prospectus, that's fraudulent, so it's their responsibility to make sure that what they're representing is the truth, the whole truth, and nothing but the truth. The SEC can't verify the information even if they wanted to. Please pick up any mutual fund prospectus and read the disclaimer on the front cover that says something like, "These securities have neither been approved nor disapproved by the Securities Exchange Commission or any other regulator."

Once the issuer registers securities with the SEC, they go into a cooling off period of at least 20 days. During this period, no sales or advertising is allowed. Indications of interest can be solicited, which means broker-dealers can talk to people to see if they might be interested in purchasing the securities once they become effective. But, no money changes hands, and no sales literature may be sent at this point, which includes reports by research analysts. And, those who indicate their interest must receive a preliminary prospectus (red herring) which discloses all material information except for two things: final offering price, effective/release date. So, when you get the prospectus, you can see the company's financial statements and read about its competitors, its history, and the risks of the investment. You can see what the company will do with your money should you decide to invest. You just don't know the exact offering price yet or the day the transaction can take place.

If the registered rep were to highlight key sections of the prospectus or provide his own little written summary, that would be a major violation of the act. Or, if he said that the securities had been "approved by the SEC" or other regulator, that would be considered a criminal violation (fraud).

Remember that all securities have to be registered under the Securities Act of 1933, except for all the securities that don't have to be. If they are exempt securities, they are excused from the registration hassle. Or, if they are sold through an exempt transaction, they likewise get a hall pass. But, whether a security has to be registered or not, the people connected to offering or selling it are still subject to anti-fraud regulations. That means that if you sell a Treasury note through deception, you're in just as much trouble as if you sold a non-exempt security through deception.

SECURITIES EXCHANGE ACT OF 1934

The Securities Act of 1933 is often nicknamed the "paper act," while the Securities Exchange Act of 1934 is nicknamed the "people act." Those are fairly helpful nicknames, as they remind you that the first act is about registering paper (securities), while the second act is about registering and regulating people. Remember that many securities are excused from having to register under the Securities Act of 1933, but they are still *securities*. Similar to what the Uniform Securities Act has to say about untrue statements of material fact or employing any "device, scheme or artifice to defraud," the Securities Exchange Act of 1934 says that it is unlawful to deceive anyone "in connection with the purchase or sale of *any* security." So, if you tell me that I can't possibly lose money on a Treasury bond, you're in big trouble. Yes, the Treasury bond is an exempt security, but that means a Treasury bond is still a *security*, so your misleading statement that leaves out interest rate and inflation risk is fraudulent.

Just this morning my SEC e-newsletter has a story about a genius trader who sold a large position of stock short, then circulated rumors that helped knock the stock price down from about $77 to $63 per share. I mean, it was a profitable trade in which he made about $25,000. Unfortunately, his career in financial services is over. You simply cannot use deception and manipulation when offering, selling, or trading securities. Well you can do it, but if you get caught, game over.

The "Act of '34" defines securities the same way we defined them earlier, since federal and state laws are usually very similar. It includes the phrase "investment contract," so the Howey Decision guides us as we try to figure out if the investment of money equals a "security" subject to registration requirements and anti-fraud statutes. And, the mind-numbing list of securities is also provided here so that we soon see that almost everything is a security except the following: fixed annuity, whole, term, or universal life insurance contract, commodities futures.

Exchanges and national securities associations such as the NASD, NYSE, FINRA, and MSRB are all subject to registration and regulation by the SEC. When those SROs change their rules, the rules have to also be approved by the SEC. Broker-dealers register with the SEC by registering with their SRO—NASD, NYSE, FINRA. All these acronyms can seem a bit confusing, but whether they show up on the test or not, you'll need to know them for your career. You can't build anyone's confidence if you don't know what SIPC, FINRA, CBOE, etc., are all about. That would be like somebody claiming to be a baseball expert, but when you ask him how many RBIs a certain player has this season, he has to ask you to remind him what an RBI is.

Ouch.

INVESTMENT ADVISERS ACT OF 1940

As we saw in the NASAA model rule called "Unethical Business Practices for Investment Advisers, etc.," the state regulators tell advisers not to put out advertising that does not comply with rules promulgated under the Investment Advisers Act of 1940, a federal act of Congress. The state regulators also tell advisers with custody to conform to other SEC rules promulgated under the Investment Advisers Act of 1940. One of the many benefits of this profession is that I get to use words like "promulgated" without being pummeled and, admit it, you didn't even flinch at the word "promulgated" a few lines back, which shows how far you've been sucked into this world of pain. In any case, the Investment Advisers Act of 1940 defines an investment adviser as:

> any person who, for compensation, engages in the
> business of advising others, either directly or through
> publications or writings, as to the value of securities
> or as to the advisability of investing in, purchasing,
> or selling securities, or who, for compensation and
> as part of a regular business, issues or promulgates
> analyses or reports concerning securities

Again, notice the word "compensation" rather than "money." Any economic benefit could be construed as "compensation" if it's given in exchange for somebody's advice on securities. What if the advice is on fixed annuities? Those are not securities, just like icing is not a violation of baseball rules. But, if the thing is a security, and you receive compensation for advising others on that security, you fit the definition of "investment adviser." And, you'll have to register as an investment adviser, unless you don't have to register as an investment adviser. The Investment Advisers Act of 1940 says:

> it shall be unlawful for any investment adviser, unless
> registered under this section, to make use of the
> mails or any means or instrumentality of interstate
> commerce in connection with his or its business as an
> investment adviser

Then, after stating that investment advisers have to register, it follows up with a list of:

> Investment advisers who need not be registered:

The SEC grants exemptions to advisers, which means these folks don't have to register with the federal regulators. These lucky advisers include:

> • any investment adviser all of whose clients are
> residents of the State within which such investment
> adviser maintains his or its principal office
> and place of business, and who does not furnish
> advice or issue analyses or reports with respect to

```
    securities listed or admitted to unlisted trading
    privileges on any national securities exchange
 ·  any investment adviser whose only clients are
    insurance companies
 ·  any investment adviser who during the course of
    the preceding twelve months has had fewer than
    fifteen clients and who neither holds himself out
    generally to the public as an investment adviser
    nor acts as an investment adviser to any investment
    company registered under title I of this Act
```

It's possible that a state(s) will make the firm register, but the SEC is giving those folks a hall pass.

We talked about "federal covered advisers" in an earlier chapter. Remember that these firms are covered by the federal regulators—that means they register exclusively with the SEC, or they are excluded from the definition of "investment adviser." We pointed out that if your assets under continuous, supervisory management are at least $25 million or you advise registered investment companies, you send your Form ADV to the SEC. We gave other examples of federal covered advisers so let's skip the tedious bullet points here.

Above, we see a list of investment advisers who don't have to register because they are exempt. The Investment Advisers Act of 1940 also excludes several entities from the definition of "investment adviser," and the list is exactly as we gave it earlier. So, if you are excluded from the definition of "investment adviser" under the Investment Advisers Act of 1940, or you are told to register with the SEC under this Act of Congress, you are a federal covered adviser. You provide notice to the states where you are subject to "notice filings," but you are either registered with the SEC or not required to be registered with anybody.

Just to keep things nice and simple.

Also, remember that an investment advisory firm can be federal covered, but the representatives of the firm are still subject to state registration. So, the firm files Form ADV with the SEC. They also provide U-4s to the states where the IARs are working. And, the individual investment adviser representatives apply for their state license and pay their little application and renewal fees whether they want to or not.

INVESTMENT COMPANY ACT OF 1940

The Investment Company Act of 1940 defines an investment company as a company whose primary activity is investing. Seriously. If the company's primary activity is investing, if they issue face-amount certificates, or if more than 40% of their total assets are invested in securities, they are probably an investment company. As you saw for the Series 6 and 7, there are three types of investment companies:

- Face-amount certificate companies
- Unit Investment Trusts (UITs)
- Management Companies

And, in case we aren't clear how a "management company" differs from a face-amount certificate company or a unit investment trust, the Investment Company Act of 1940 is kind enough to clear it all up for us:

> "Management company" means any investment company other than a face-amount certificate company or a unit investment trust.

Gee, thanks. Anyway, a face-amount certificate is a debt security where the investor either pays a lump sum or a series of installments. In exchange for these payments, he receives a stated amount on a date at least 24 months in the future. A unit investment trust is a trust that holds investments and sells units to investors, thus the clever name "unit investment trust." A UIT also "has no board of directors," in case the exam brings that up, and its shares are "redeemable." A management company is either a closed-end fund or an open-end fund. Open-end fund shares are redeemable with the issuer, while the close-end fund shares have to be traded on the secondary market among investors.

Investment companies have to register with the SEC because of this Act. As we said, investment company securities are "federal covered."

In general, investment companies are prohibited from:

- Purchasing securities on margin
- Engaging in short sales
- Participating in joint accounts
- Owning more than 10% of another company

Of course, as usual, there is more to it than those generalizations, but you have certainly suffered enough at this point.

INSIDER TRADING AND SECURITIES FRAUD ENFORCEMENT ACT OF 1988

The Securities Exchange Act of 1934 already prohibited insider trading, but in 1988 Congress decided it had to do more to prevent manipulation of the markets. Under the Insider Trading and Securities Fraud Enforcement Act of 1988, which amends the Act of 1934, the SEC can sue violators for "treble damages," which means three times the amount of the profit or the loss avoided by using inside information. People who pass around the information can get busted, not just those who trade on the information. For the people who are in a position to control those who violate insider trading rules, the maximum civil penalties are three times the amount or $1 million, whichever appears to make the person cry harder.

The US Attorney's office can also make a criminal case against insider traders. Inside information is just material information about a security that the public doesn't know yet. Maybe you work for a full-service financial firm. Up on the 7th floor are the investment bankers, who are always cooking up mergers and acquisitions. Maybe they let it slip that GE is about to announce plans to purchase XYZ. Well, gee, maybe you and all your clients should buy puts on GE and calls on XYZ ahead of the big announcement. And, maybe you'll all end up wishing you hadn't, especially if you get caught.

SECURITIES INVESTOR PROTECTION ACT OF 1970

A quick visit to www.sipc.org will reveal the mission of the Securities Investor Protection Corporation, which is:

> SIPC is an important part of the overall system of investor protection in the United States. While a number of federal, self-regulatory and state securities agencies deal with cases of investment fraud, SIPC's focus is both different and narrow: Restoring funds to investors with assets in the hands of bankrupt and otherwise financially troubled brokerage firms. The Securities Investor Protection Corporation was not chartered by Congress to combat fraud.

A Series 63 question might test your knowledge of the difference between SIPC's mission and that of the FDIC. SIPC's website has a section called "Why We Are Not the FDIC," which says:

> "Insurance" for investment fraud does not exist in the U.S. The Federal Trade Commission, Federal Bureau of Investigation, state securities regulators and other experts have estimated that investment fraud in the U.S. ranges from $10-$40 billion a year.
>
> With a reserve of slightly more than $1 billion, SIPC could not keep its doors open for long if its purpose was to compensate all victims in the event of loss due to investment fraud.
>
> **It is important to understand that SIPC is not the securities world equivalent of FDIC—the Federal Deposit Insurance Corporation.** Congress specifically considered creating a Federal Broker-Dealer Insurance Corporation, but lawmakers wisely concluded that such a designation would be both misleading and out of step in the risk-based investment marketplace that is so different from the world of banking.

So, if the person in the test question is telling somebody that the SIPC protection is "just like FDIC insurance," that is completely misleading. SIPC protects customer assets held by a financially troubled broker-dealer. If creditors try to seize assets of the deadbeat firm, your securities are protected by SIPC. However, if you buy a stock for $104 a share and that stock goes to zero, SIPC would like you to know that you probably shouldn't have done that.

As their website says, even though "SIPC was created by an Act of Congress," it is not a government agency or regulatory authority. It is a nonprofit, membership corporation, funded by its member securities broker-dealers. That means that broker-dealers pay into SIPC and proudly display the logo on business cards, along with their NASD/NYSE membership.

SIPC covers stocks and bonds held by a broker-dealer. It does not cover commodities futures or currency, fixed annuities, or limited partnerships. Most mutual funds would be held by the transfer agent, but if the broker-dealer holds them, they would be covered by SIPC, in case you don't have enough to keep straight at this point.

ERISA

The Employee Retirement Security Act of 1974 was designed to clean up abuses by pension funds. Of course, it doesn't cover government plans because the government generally opts not to follow any rules they impose on others. If you work for a company with a qualified plan, they have to cover you as soon as you meet eligibility requirements under ERISA. Generally, this means that as soon as you work 1,000 hours in one year, they have to include you. As long as you're at least 21 years old, that is. Your 401(k) plan works this way, as would a defined benefit pension plan. ERISA has vesting requirements. That means that within a maximum number of years the company's contributions fully belong to the worker. Of course, over the first few years, the worker will probably be only partly vested. If the employee is "50% vested," that means that she owns ½ of the contributions her employer has made. When she's 100% vested, she gets to keep all of her employer's contributions, whether she stays at the company or not. There are funding requirements that tell the company how much money needs to be put into the plan. Participants get to choose a beneficiary who would receive the money if the participant dies. And, there are reporting requirements that require the company to send account statements to the employees on a regular basis.

Each pension plan has at least one fiduciary. The fiduciaries of a plan usually include:

- Trustee
- Investment advisers
- All individuals exercising discretion
- All members of the plan's administrative committee
- Those who select committee officials

The key to determining whether someone is a fiduciary is whether they are exercising discretion or control over the plan. Attorneys, accountants, and actuaries are generally not fiduciaries when acting in their professional roles. The investment manager (adviser) of a pension fund is using discretion/control to invest the plan assets; therefore, the investment manager is a "fiduciary" with huge obligations to the participants and beneficiaries of the plan. As ERISA makes clear:

- a fiduciary shall discharge his duties with respect to a plan solely in the interest of the participants and beneficiaries
- and for the exclusive purpose of: (i) providing benefits to participants and their beneficiaries;

- and (ii) defraying reasonable expenses of administering the plan
- with the care, skill, prudence, and diligence under the circumstances then prevailing that a prudent man acting in a like capacity and familiar with such matters would use in the conduct of an enterprise of a like character and with like aims
- by diversifying the investments of the plan so as to minimize the risk of large losses, unless under the circumstances it is clearly prudent not to do so; and
- in accordance with the documents and instruments governing the plan insofar as such documents and instruments are consistent with the provisions of this subchapter and subchapter III of this chapter.

The "documents and instruments governing the plan" might be referred to on the exam as an "investment policy statement." If the policy statement says that no more than 40% of the plan assets are to be invested in equities, guess what? Don't put more than 40% into equities. Even if you ended up having a good year because of your renegade stock picks, you'd still be in trouble. The only time to override the policy statement is if it clearly violates ERISA. Also notice how diversification is presumed to be part of a prudent investment policy, "unless under the circumstances it is clearly prudent not to do so." This is a direct link to the Uniform Prudent Investor Act, which mentions ERISA many times throughout the text. In fact, all of those bullet points overlap with the Uniform Prudent Investor Act. It's just that the UPIA is talking more to the administrators of private trusts while ERISA is concerned with the fiduciaries running pension trusts. Either way, if you're an investment adviser managing assets on behalf of perpetual graduate students or company retirees, you need to use skill, prudence, and absolute honesty-above-reproach. You need to keep the costs of administering the plan reasonable. Why? As the Department of Labor explains on a very helpful website, "Fiduciaries who do not follow the basic standards of conduct may be personally liable to restore any losses to the plan, or to restore any profits made through improper use of the plan's assets. However, fiduciaries can limit their liability in certain situations. One way fiduciaries can demonstrate that they have carried out their responsibilities properly is by documenting the processes used to carry out their responsibilities." In other words, every time you make a decision, keep good notes and make a backup. This stock was purchased for this reason, these bonds were sold for that reason, we used this broker-dealer to execute the sale for these three reasons, etc.

ANTI-MONEY LAUNDERING REGULATIONS

The Bank Secrecy Act (BSA) authorizes the US Treasury Department to require financial institutions such as banks and broker-dealers to maintain records of personal financial transactions that "have a high degree of usefulness in criminal, tax and regulatory investigations and proceedings." It also authorizes the Treasury Department to require any financial institution to report any "suspicious transaction relevant to a possible violation of law or regulation." These reports, called "Suspicious Activity Reports," are filed with the Treasury Department's Financial Crimes Enforcement Network ("FinCEN").

This is done secretly (thus the law's middle name), without the consent or knowledge of bank customers, any time a financial institution determines that a transaction is suspicious. The reports are made available electronically to every US Attorney's Office and to 59 law enforcement agencies, including the FBI, Secret Service, and Customs Service.

Recently, the US Treasury Department used the Bank Secrecy Act (BSA) to require that for transmittals of funds of $3,000 or more, broker-dealers are required to obtain and keep certain specified information concerning the parties sending and receiving those funds. In addition, broker-dealers must include this information on the actual transmittal order. Also, any cash transactions over $10,000 require the same type of uptight record keeping. For these, broker-dealers must file a Currency Transaction Report with The Treasury Department's FinCEN. If a customer makes two cash transactions that total over $10,000 in the same day, that's exactly the kind of thing the broker-dealer needs to report.

Why? Because terrorist organizations fund their operations through money laundering. Since broker-dealers are financial institutions, they're lumped in with banks and required to do all kinds of record-keeping to help the government prevent these operations.

With the passage of the "USA Patriot Act," broker-dealers and other financial institutions have to help the government monitor suspicious activity that could be tied to money laundering. Broker-dealers now have to report any transaction that involves at least $5,000 if the broker-dealer knows, suspects, or has reason to suspect that it doesn't pass the smell test. The NASD/FINRA spells out four specific characteristics that would make a broker-dealer file a "suspicious activity report" (SAR). A SAR would be filed if the transaction falls within one of four classes:

- the transaction involves funds derived from illegal activity or is intended or conducted to hide or disguise funds or assets derived from illegal activity;
- the transaction is designed to evade the requirements of the Bank Secrecy Act
- the transaction appears to serve no business or apparent lawful purpose or is not the sort of transaction in which the particular customer would be expected to engage and for which the broker/dealer knows of no reasonable explanation after examining the available facts; or
- the transaction involves the use of the broker/dealer to facilitate criminal activity.

Broker-dealers now have to have a "customer identification program" whereby they require more information to open an account. They now have to get the customer's date of birth. If the customer is not a US citizen, the firm will need:

- taxpayer ID number
- passport number and country of issuance
- alien ID card
- other government-issued photo ID card

Even the US citizen may need to show a photo ID, just as you do when you go take your Series 63 exam.

Finally, the federal government now maintains an Office of Foreign Asset Control (OFAC) designed to protect against the threat of terrorism. This office maintains a list of individuals and organizations viewed as a threat to the US. Broker-dealers and other financial institutions now need to make sure they aren't setting up accounts for these folks, or—if they are—they need to block/freeze the assets.

REGULATION S-P

Sharing customer information with law enforcement officials is one thing. Providing it to telemarketers is quite another. To fight identity theft and to protect consumers from having too much of their information shared with people they've never met, the SEC enacted Regulation S-P to put into place a requirement from the Gramm-Leach-Bliley Act. Basically, "a financial institution must provide its customers with a notice of its privacy policies and practices, and must not disclose nonpublic personal information about a consumer to nonaffiliated third parties unless the institution provides certain information to the consumer and the consumer has not elected to opt out of the disclosure." Notice how that phrase separated the "customer" from the "consumer." A consumer is a prospect that the firm is checking out before doing any business with him; a customer is someone with whom the firm has started an account or a financial relationship. So, when the firm is checking out a consumer's sensitive information—e.g., their credit report—they need to be very careful to safeguard that information. Broker-dealers now have to deliver initial and annual notices to customers about their privacy policies and practices, and about the opportunity and methods to opt out of their institution's sharing of their nonpublic personal information with nonaffiliated third parties. The initial notice must be provided no later than when the firm establishes a customer relationship with the individual.

Broker-dealers and financial advisers also need to have written supervisory procedures dealing with the disposal of consumer credit report information. Since firms typically look at a consumer's credit history when opening accounts—especially margin accounts—selling annuities, or providing financial planning services, the firms need to safely dispose of the information rather than just setting it all in a big box out back. Or, maybe some sloppy firm tosses out 25 old hard drives that contain all that sensitive information—they could easily lose their license over that.

As you may have noticed, there a lot of ways to lose your license. And knowing those ways is really the whole point of making you suffer through some ordeal called the Series 63.

Background

Most people taking the Series 63 exam have recently taken the Series 7 or Series 6 and, therefore, have some background knowledge of common stock, preferred stock, corporate bonds, etc. Then again, a certain percentage of candidates are taking the Series 63 all by itself. If you belong to the second group, this part of the book is written especially for you. If you belong to the first group, you still might want to read this section as a review of what you learned while studying for your Series 6 or Series 7 exam.

INVESTMENT SECURITIES

Investments come in three main categories: equity, fixed income, and money market. Your portfolio is probably allocated so that a certain percentage is devoted to equity investments, a percentage to fixed-income investments, and a percentage to money market or "cash" investments. The money you invest in equity securities is generally the money you don't need to touch for a while, the money that is supposed to grow into a pile large enough to achieve some long-term goal such as retirement, education, or, perhaps, world travel. Fixed-income securities are generally less volatile and provide a more dependable stream of income than equity. The money market component of your portfolio is for the money you might need to spend at a moment's notice. Liquidity and safety of principal are the main advantages of money market securities. That means that your account tends to be worth at least what you invested, and you can make a withdrawal without taking a hit if you need to.

CASH EQUIVALENTS (MONEY MARKET)

Money market securities are simply debt securities maturing in one year or less. Safe, liquid investments. Money market securities are called "cash equivalents" because, basically, they are just as good as cash. Better, actually, because unlike cash sitting in a drawer somewhere, money market instruments are earning interest. It's not necessarily a high *rate* of interest, but at least you're putting your cash to work and you're not risking it in the stock market where anything can happen, or the bond market, where interest rates could rise and knock down the value of your holdings. From a money market mutual fund account, investors can actually write checks—that's how stable the value of the investment is. On the other hand, a retiree making withdrawals from an account holding stocks, bonds, and most types of mutual funds can end up selling her holdings at a loss. So, if the investor will need to make frequent withdrawals from the account, that account needs to hold a money market mutual fund or money market securities. The problem with investing too much of your money into cash equivalents is that you will miss out on the big growth opportunities that arise when the stock or bond markets decide to go off on a tear, which is known as "opportunity cost." Also, short-term debt securities do not keep pace with inflation very well, leaving the investor with purchasing power or inflation risk.

T-bills

Buying T-bills is about as safe as it gets. Remember that the "T" is for "Treasury," and T-bills are guaranteed by the United States Treasury. That's right, the interest and principal are guaranteed, and the US Treasury has never stiffed anyone. So, if you don't need to withdraw a certain amount of money for several months or longer, you can buy the 3-month or 6-month T-bill and usually earn higher yields than you'd earn in a savings account. T-bills don't pay regular interest checks. Instead, investors buy them at a discount from their face value. In a high interest rate environment, a 6-month $100,000 T-bill might sell for just $97,000, allowing the investor to keep the $3,000 difference at maturity. When interest rates are low, the 6-month T-bill might sell for only a slight discount below the face amount. Suddenly, we're all paying $99,000 for a $100,000 T-bill, making just $1,000 over that 6-month period. In either case, though, we are buying high credit quality securities that leave us with virtually no default risk.

Bank CDs usually yield about the same as T-bills, but the bank's FDIC insurance usually stops at $250,000 per account. T-bills, on the other hand, are simply guaranteed no matter how large the denomination. Any given Monday T-bills are available by auction from as small as $100 par value and as large as $5 million. No matter how big your bill, it's insured/guaranteed by the US Treasury.

Negotiable/Jumbo CDs

Some people like to step outside the realm of FDIC insurance and purchase "jumbo" or "negotiable" CDs. The denominations here are at least $250,000 and often several millions of dollars. Therefore, jumbo CDs are often not fully insured by the FDIC but are, rather, backed by the issuer. That makes their yields higher. Also, if you've ever pulled out of a bank CD early, you know how painful that can be. With a jumbo CD you have a negotiable/marketable security that you can sell to someone else. That's what the word "negotiable" means. CDs do make interest payments, unlike T-bills, which are purchased at a discount from their face value.

Banker's Acceptance

When an American company imports, say, computer parts from Japan, they typically "pay" for the shipment by presenting a letter of credit from a bank. If the shipment is worth $10 million, maybe it would be better to get most of that cash right now. So, a "banker's acceptance" is created whereby a pension or mutual fund buys the $10 million banker's acceptance for, say, $9.9 million. In other words, they'll make the $100,000 difference in a few weeks or months. Not a ton of money to make, but there's also not much risk. As with a T-bill, banker's acceptances are so short-term that it would make no sense to send interest checks to the buyer. Instead, these short-term debt securities are purchased at a discount from their face value. The difference between what you pay and what you receive *is* your interest income.

Commercial Paper

Commercial paper is a major component of money market mutual funds. In order to build an $800 million factory, it probably makes more sense to issue bonds and pay the lenders back slowly, as you are currently paying off the mortgage on your house. But if GE needs a mere $50 million to tide them over for a few months, they would probably prefer to borrow it short-term at the lowest possible interest rate. If so, they issue a piece of commercial paper with a $50 million face amount, selling it to a pension or mutual fund for, say, $49.8 million. Again, the difference between the discounted price and the face amount *is* the interest earned by the investor.

Repurchase Agreements

Large financial institutions borrow money at low interest rates over the short term by taking your money and paying whatever a savings account or CD currently offers. They then lend your money out to someone else long-term at a higher interest rate. As long as they're able to borrow at a lower rate than they lend, they're fine. But, the business model also puts them at risk in terms of fluctuating interest rates. In order to shield themselves from interest-rate risk over the next 30, 60, or 90 days, large financial institutions engage in repurchase and reverse repurchase agreements. Basically, one party sells the other party something today with the agreement to repurchase it at a set price in the near future. The difference between what you pay today and receive in the near future would be your fixed rate of return over that time frame. So, if one bank calls another one to propose the arrangement, that's a repurchase agreement. If they call the other bank and ask to do it the other way around, that's a reverse repurchase agreement. Although definitely part of the money market, they're more of a private arrangement than a piece of paper that gets bought and sold.

Tax-Exempt Municipal Notes

We'll look at municipal securities in a moment, but for now just know that cities, counties, school districts, etc., can borrow money long-term by issuing bonds, and they can borrow short-term by issuing notes. Anticipation notes are very common, and their name tells you exactly what's going on—there is money coming into the city's coffers in the near future, but there are some bills due *right now*. For example, property taxes are collected twice a year. If the city wants some of that money now, they can issue a tax anticipation note or TAN. If it's backed up by revenues, from sewer and water services for example, it's a revenue anticipation note or RAN. If the note is backed up by both taxes and revenues, they call it a "tax *and* revenue anticipation note" or TRAN. But, my personal favorite of these short-term municipal notes has to be the "bond anticipation note" or BAN. In this case, the issuer borrows money from somebody now and backs it up with part of the money they're going to borrow in the near future when they issue more bonds.

Seriously.

The interest paid on these municipal notes is lower than the nominal rates paid on a corporation's commercial paper, but that's okay—the interest paid is also tax-exempt at the federal level. So, if an investor or an institution is looking for safety, liquidity, and dependable, tax-exempt interest over the short-term, they purchase these anticipation notes directly or through a tax-exempt money market mutual fund.

Last Word

While the textbook definition of a money market security is a debt security maturing in one year or less, the usual maturity is a maximum of 270 days. There is an exemption to registration under the Securities Act of 1933 and the Uniform Securities Act for short-term debt securities based on that 270 days, and no one wants to register a short-term debt security, since by the time they got it through registration interest rates would have changed. Also, if the test writers want to make you sweat, they might ask if a T-bond could be a money market security. At first glance you think, no, a T-bond matures in 10 to 30 years, so there's no way it could be in a money market portfolio. Well, when it's issued the thing might have a 10-year maturity. The next year it would be nine years from maturity. Eventually, it would be one year or less from maturity, so, yes, *any* debt security one year or less from maturity is a money market instrument, regardless of the original maturity.

DEBT SECURITIES (FIXED INCOME)

Even though money market securities are also fixed-income securities, the phrase "fixed-income" generally refers to longer-term debt securities. These longer-term debt securities go by many names, but whether we're calling them bonds, debentures, notes, or certificates, we're just talking about debt securities. Stock holders are part owners of the corporation. Bond holders are not owners of the corporation—they are lenders *to* the corporation. Debt securities (bonds) are loans that investors make to the corporation. The corporation, in other words, goes into debt when they issue debt securities (bonds) to investors. The debt securities pay regular interest to investors and return the principal of the loan at the end of the term. These loans that investors make have a liquid secondary market, so investors can sell their bonds and get some or all of their money back whenever the markets are open. Bond market prices do fluctuate, but, generally bond prices are not as volatile as stock prices. So, a bond mutual fund is more volatile than a money market mutual fund, but still not in the same category of risk with equity (stock) mutual funds. If your daughter were already 15 years old and headed to college, you'd probably be a lot more comfortable putting your money into investment-grade bonds than in the stock market. Over a 3–5-year period, it's a pretty sure bet that stock prices will fluctuate much more than bond prices. Also, bonds pay a stated rate of interest; with stocks, we assume the dividends will continue and we hope that the market price will go up in our favor. But assumptions and hope are not much good at paying tuition bills, so if the investor has a shorter time horizon or a major need to protect her invested principal, bonds (fixed income) would be much more suitable than stocks or stock mutual funds.

Bonds have a par value of $1,000. This is the amount an investor will receive with the very last interest payment from the issuer. Up to that point, the investor has only been receiving interest payments against the money he loaned to the corporation by purchasing their bond certificates. So the bond certificate has "$1,000" printed on the face, along with the interest rate the issuer will pay the investor every year. This interest rate could be referred to as the coupon rate or "nominal yield." We have to pick a number for an example, so let's use 8%:

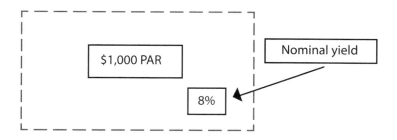

This bond would pay 8% of $1,000 in income to the investor every year, and then return the $1,000 with the final payment—end of story. This one pays $80 a year. A 5% bond would pay $50 a year. An 18% bond would pay $180 a year, and I sure hope somebody checked the credit rating on that one.

How often does this nominal yield change?

It doesn't. This nominal yield is what is paid to the investor every year. It represents a fixed payment, similar to a fixed-rate mortgage. Since the investor's income is fixed, they got all creative and decided to call bonds "fixed-income securities." The exam might also point out that borrowing money from investors or other lenders is called using "leverage," so a company that has issued a lot of debt securities and/or done a lot of long-term borrowing from banks is a "highly leveraged" company.

US Government Debt

As we mentioned briefly in the money market section, some of the safest debt on earth is US Government debt, also called "Treasury" securities. This stuff is produced by the United States Treasury, the same folks who issue the ten-dollar bills in your wallet. Therefore, if you've never doubted the ability of the US Treasury to back up a ten-dollar bill, you have no reason to doubt their ability to back up the T-bills, T-notes, and T-bonds we're about to look at in some detail.

So, the US Treasury borrows money and also happens to have the ability to print more money to pay back the lenders. This "national debt" you've no doubt heard of from the chattering media is the amount of debt that has been issued by the US Treasury and still needs to be paid off. So, whenever the federal government wants to spend billions of dollars they don't actually have, they simply issue more of these debt securities and leave it to future administrations and taxpayers to either pay it off or pass it on to future generations.

Amazingly, the US Treasury has *always* managed to pay investors back plus interest, end of story. So, if you buy a bill, note, bond, or STRIP from the United States Treasury, you do not have to worry about default risk. You're going to get your interest checks on time, and you're going to get your money back. You just aren't going to get rich in the process. In fact, you usually need to be rich already to get excited about US

Government debt, but that's another matter. For the test, just remember that US Government/Treasury debt is safe and liquid. If you can't stand the "risk" presented by owning Treasuries, you must drive to work in an armored vehicle and chew your food 29 times before swallowing.

Not that there's anything wrong with that.

T-bills

As we saw, T-bills are short-term debt securities issued by the US Treasury. T-bills pay the face amount at maturity, and investors try to buy them for the steepest discount possible. If the T-bill pays out $1,000, you'd rather get it for $950 than $965, right? In the first case you make $50 interest; in the second case you make only $35. It's tough to get excited about making $35 or $50 in interest, but if you add some zeros to your investment, things get a bit more interesting.

These bills mature in one year or less—4 weeks, 13 weeks, 26 weeks, 52 weeks—so there are no coupon payments. As we just saw, you buy the T-bill at a discount and receive the full face amount when it matures—the difference is your interest income. T-bills are the shortest maturity of the Treasuries, and they are offered in minimum denominations of $100. Every Monday excluding federal holidays, T-bills are offered at auction, allowing regular folks to buy a T-bill as small as $100 or as big as $5 million by putting in a "non-competitive tender." For further information on T-bills and auctions, please visit www.treasurydirect.gov. You might be shocked at how simply the federal government explains these things on their helpful website.

T-notes, T-bonds

So, T-bills do not pay interest per se—rather, they pay back more than they took from you a few weeks or months ago. If you want regular interest checks, you buy a T-note or T-bond. T-notes are offered with 2–10-year maturities. T-bonds go from 10 to 30 years.

T-notes and bonds both make semi-annual interest payments, and are both quoted in 32nds. A quote of 98.16 means $980 plus 16/32nds or ½. So a T-bond priced at 98.16 costs $985. It's not worth delving into—trust me.

T-notes and T-bonds would generally offer higher yields than T-bills, with the bonds offering slightly higher yields than the notes. Of course, that's when we have a normal yield curve. With any luck, the Series 63 will not sweat you on yield curves, which usually comes up on the Series 65 or Series 7 exam, if at all.

STRIPS

Anyway, the Treasury Department can also take T-notes and T-bonds and "strip" them into their various interest and principal components. Once they "strip" the securities into components, they can sell interest-only or principal-only zero coupon bonds to investors. We call these STRIPS, which stands for the "separate trading of registered interest and principal of securities." For the test, if an investor needs to send kids to college and needs to have an exact amount of money available on a future date, put him into STRIPS, especially if the question says he wants to avoid reinvestment risk. This way, he'll pay a known amount and receive a known amount on a future date, without having to reinvest coupon payments every six months at varying interest rates. He won't get rich, necessarily, but he won't lose the kid's college fund in the stock market, either.

Treasury Receipts

Broker-dealers sell the same basic product, only they call them Treasury Receipts. Even though they have the word "Treasury" in their name, Treasury Receipts are not direct obligations of the US Government. Rather, they are backed up by the Treasury securities the broker-dealer holds in escrow. Close, but yet so far from being a *direct* obligation of the US Treasury. So, STRIPS are direct obligations; receipts are not. For both receipts and STRIPS, remember that they are purchased at a discount and mature at the face value. The interest earned by investors on T-bills, T-notes, T-bonds, STRIPS, and even Treasury Receipts is all taxable only at the federal level.

TIPS

As if Treasury securities weren't already safe enough, the government created TIPS, which stands for "Treasury Inflation Protected Securities." When inflation rises, the payout increases, and when inflation drops, the payout goes down. As usual, we use the CPI to measure the rate of inflation.

Mortgage-backed Securities

The US Government also has agencies that issue debt securities. The Farm Credit System and Federal Land Bank help farmers finance equipment and land purchases. Like a bank, they also issue debt securities in order to borrow money from one party and lend it to somebody else at a higher interest rate. These debt securities are not a direct obligation of the US Treasury, so they're not as safe as the T-bills, T-notes, T-bonds, and STRIPS we just looked at. Then again, if these things scare some investors, I'm not sure how they manage to get out of bed in the morning. But, a testable point could be that agencies are not direct obligations of the US Treasury.

I would expect the exam to focus more on the mortgage-backed securities guaranteed by Ginnie Mae, or issued by Fannie Mae and Freddie Mac. Those are the nicknames for the Government National Mortgage Association (GNMA), the Federal National Mortgage Association (FNMA), and the Federal Home Loan Mortgage Corporation (FHLMC).

To create a mortgage-backed security, some really smart people take a pool of mortgages and then create debt securities out of the money paid into this pool so that the investors who buy the funky things will receive most of the interest and principal that is being paid by the homeowners in the pool. When will all of this principal be paid off? Ask yourself that question—when will you have all of your principal paid off? As soon as you pay it off or refinance your mortgage. When will you refinance? Whenever rates drop again. Since we can't predict when homeowners will pay off their mortgages, mortgage-backed securities carry "prepayment risk." When rates drop, the homeowners refinance, and all of the principal is returned to the investors at once. The investors go to reinvest the proceeds, but rates are now lower upon reinvestment.

GNMA or "Ginnie Mae" is special. Although we said that agency securities are not a direct obligation of the US Treasury, Ginnie Mae actually is because she guarantees all the mortgages in the pool with Uncle Sam's full faith and credit. Most of the mortgages guaranteed by Ginnie Mae are FHA loans, and some are VA (Veterans Administration) and RHA (Rural Housing Authority) loans. But, Ginnie is the only one backed by the full faith and credit of the US Government. Fannie and Freddie are public companies now, sometimes called "quasi-agencies" or "government-sponsored enterprises (GSEs). They have a line of credit with the US Treasury allowing them to borrow money at lower rates than their competitors, but the US Treasury would not have to bail out Fannie or Freddie if they got themselves into trouble. Would they let them fail? Probably not. Could they let them fail? Absolutely. Since Fannie and Freddie are public companies or "quasi-agencies" you can buy stock in them. There is no stock in Ginnie Mae because it's not a company—it's purely a government agency. Fannie and Freddie promote home ownership by providing a liquid secondary market allowing lenders to sell their mortgages and, therefore, make more mortgages at perhaps lower rates. They guarantee the mortgages, but, again, Fannie and Freddie securities are not a *direct* obligation of the US Government.

Agency securities are taxable at the federal, state, and local levels.

CMOs

CMOs are sold by companies who buy up mortgage-backed securities and create a fancy product called a collateralized mortgage obligation, or CMO. This is how a very simple CMO would function: the investors in the CMO are divided up into three classes or "tranches." They are called class A, B or C. Each class differs in the order they receive principal payments, but receives interest payments as long as the principal is not completely paid off. Class A investors are paid principal first with prepayments and repayments until they are fully re-paid. Then class B investors are paid off, followed by class C investors. In a situation like this, class A investors bear most of the prepayment risk, while class C investors bear the least. Prepayment risk is the risk that mortgages will be repaid more quickly than expected when rates drop. It seems unlikely, but the exam could bring up some of the following bullet points. It seems a waste of time to delve into this topic, but it also seems foolish to ignore it, since the Series 63 has a habit of bringing up some very surprising topics from time to time:

- Backed by agency pass-through securities
- CMOs usually offer low returns because they are very low risk and are sometimes backed by government securities.
- Most rated AAA
- They do not have a liquid secondary market, due to their complexities
- Brokers must use extra care to determine suitability due to the complex nature of the product
- CMOs are derivatives (as are options)
- PAC stands for "planned amortization class"
- PACs are protected from prepayment risk and extension risk
- TAC stands for "targeted amortization class"
- TACs present more extension risk, the risk that principal will be paid back too slowly
- TACs generally yield more than PACs

Municipal Bonds

When the US Government wants to borrow money, they issue Treasury Securities and pay folks back out of taxes. When states, counties, cities, school districts, etc., borrow money, they issue municipal bonds and pay investors back either out of taxes or out of the revenues generated by the project being financed with the bonds. If the municipal bonds are paid off through sales, income, or property taxes, we call these general obligation bonds, backed by the "full faith and credit" of the issuer. Maybe you've voted on the issuance of school bonds used to improve your local schools. Those are general obligation bonds. They had to ask your permission to hike your property taxes in order to pay back the buyers of the bonds used to improve the schools. Your community might also want to build fun stuff like a water park, museum, or convention center. Those projects generate revenue in the form of parking fees, entrance fees, and concession sales, so the issuer can borrow the money through a "revenue bond." Remember that the revenue generated (they hope) by the facility represents all that the issuer has to pay the bond interest and retire the principal to the bondholders. So, which bond typically yields more, revenue or "G.O."? In other words, which one carries more risk to the bond holder, the one backed by the full faith and credit/taxing power of the issuer, or the one that is only as solid as the revenues we *hope* are generated?

The revenue bond is riskier, so it yields more.

Municipal bonds generally pay tax-exempt interest at the federal level. See, the federal government wants states/counties/cities to have good schools, roads, sewers, etc. If they don't tax the interest the issuer pays on the bonds, the issuer can pay lower nominal yields to investors, meaning the issuer can borrow money on the cheap. Why would investors take lower coupon payments? Because the coupon payments aren't taxed by the federal government. Therefore, if you're in the 30% tax bracket, a municipal bond could pay you 5%, and you'd still come out better than if you'd bought a corporate bond paying 7%. Just take the .05 the municipal bond pays and divide by the "other side" of your tax bracket (.70) to get the municipal bond's tax-equivalent yield of 7.14%. The corporate bond would have to yield 7.14% to be equivalent to the municipal bond paying just 5%.

So, a municipal bond investment is tax-exempt, right?

Careful now. Depends on what your meaning of the word *is* is.

First, the only thing that could be tax-free is the interest payment; capital gains are fully taxable, so if you buy a municipal bond at $908 and sell it at $950, you pay a capital gain on the $42 difference. Second, if the municipal bond pays tax-free interest, that's at the federal level. Your state and local government could tax the interest if you buy the bond from an issuer outside the state or locality. If you live in Mississippi and buy a bond issued by Birmingham, Alabama, the state of Mississippi can tax the interest, as can your local government.

So, if you buy a municipal bond that qualifies for tax-exempt interest at the federal level, you'll only get a break at the state level if the bond is issued inside your home state, and your local government can tax the interest in any case, unless they happen to be the issuer of the bond. So a New York City resident who buys a general obligation bond issued by New York City gets a break from the federal government, the state of New York, and the government of NYC.

Third, not *all* municipal bonds are tax-exempt or "tax qualified." The ones that provide an essential service (schools, for example) tend to get the break. But Industrial Development Revenue (IDR) bonds are often fully taxed. And any municipal bond that provides what the IRS considers an inessential service (private purpose) is subject to AMT taxes. Milwaukee's third convention center or first domed sports stadium might not seem as essential to the IRS as it does to the mayor and the city council. In that dispute, guess who generally wins the argument?

The IRS, who, as always, is here to help.

Therefore, all municipal bonds pay tax-free interest at the federal level, except all the municipal bonds that don't. Bonds issued to fund schools and necessary infrastructure get the break; those that build parking garages and convention centers often don't. And, that's not even taking the state/local tax into consideration. The official statement for a municipal bond offering would specify whether the bonds will subject investors to AMT, provide tax-exempt interest, or—sometimes—fully taxable interest.

Who buys municipal bonds? Investors looking for income, safety, and tax advantages. You need those objectives plus their state of residence before making recommendations, and—most of all—you need their tax bracket. Low-bracket investors do not buy municipal bonds.

Corporate Bonds

When the US Treasury or a local government borrows money, they have the ability to pay back the lenders with taxes. When a corporation borrows money, they have to pay back the lenders either with profits, or by borrowing more money from other lenders. To protect the folks buying corporate bonds, Congress passed the Trust Indenture Act of 1939. If a corporation wants to sell $5,000,000 or more worth of bonds with a maturity of more than one year, they have to do it under a contract or "indenture" with a trustee, who will enforce the terms of the indenture to the benefit of the bondholders. In other words, if the issuer stiffs the bondholders, the trustee can get a bankruptcy court to forcibly sell off the assets of the company so that bondholders can recover some of their hard-earned money.

Secured Bonds

Sometimes corporations secure the bonds with specific assets like airplanes, government securities, or real estate. If so, they pledge title of the assets to the trustee, who just might end up selling them off if the issuer gets behind on its interest payments. Investors who buy bonds attached to specific collateral are secured creditors, the most likely investors to get paid should the company go belly up. If the collateral used is real estate, we call it a mortgage bond. If the collateral is securities, we call it a collateral trust certificate. And if the collateral is equipment, such as airplanes or railroad cars, we call it an equipment trust certificate. Since these bonds are probably more secure than other bonds issued by the same company, they offer the lowest coupon payment, too. Remember, if you take a small risk, you usually only get a small reward.

Unsecured Bonds

Most corporate bonds are backed only by a promise known as the "full faith and credit" of the issuing corporation. That's why we might want to see what S&P and Moody's have to say about a particular issuer's full faith and credit. Regardless of the rating, if we buy a bond backed simply by the full faith and credit of an issuer, we are buying a debenture. Debenture holders are general creditors and have a claim that is junior to secured bondholders. Therefore, debentures pay a higher coupon than secured bonds, since they carry more risk of getting stiffed. Corporations typically establish a "sinking fund" to make sure they'll be able to repay the principal on the bonds. A sinking fund is an escrow account invested in safe, liquid securities, just like the escrow account homeowners use to pay taxes and insurance. The existence of a sinking fund is a positive sign to an investor.

"Sub" means "below," as in "submarine" for "below the water," or "subterranean" for "below the ground." Subordinated debentures are below debentures when it comes to liquidating a company and paying out money to the bondholders. Since these bonds are riskier, they pay a higher coupon than debentures.

If all the bondholders have been paid with the proceeds of the liquidation sale and there's still money left over, then we start talking about paying out some money to stockholders. Preferred stock gets preference, so we pay them first, and common stock is always last in line.

So, if a company goes belly up, interested parties make their claims on the company's assets in the following order of priority:

1. Employees/wages
2. IRS/taxes
3. Secured creditors
4. Debentures/general creditors
5. Subordinated debentures

6. Preferred stock
7. Common stock

Notice how the IRS makes sure that employees get paid first. That way they can tax the wages as they come for all the taxes the corporation has failed to pay.

Warms your heart, doesn't it?

Convertible Bonds

Even though bonds are safer than common stock, they also aren't going to double or triple in value over the years the way that stocks often do. That's why some really smart people developed convertible bonds. Now, your bond goes up if the company's <u>stock</u> price rises, giving you some growth potential. So, your bond is now less sensitive to interest rates, and because you get some growth potential on the stock, the interest payment is lower. That's the deal—the issuer wants to borrow your money a little cheaper, and you will let them in exchange for the chance that their stock price will rise and take the price of your bond along for the ride.

When a convertible bond is issued, it is given a conversion price. If the conversion price is $40, that means that the bond is convertible into the issuer's common stock at $40. In other words, the investor can use the par value of her bond towards the purchase of the company's common stock at a set price of $40. Bonds have a par value of $1,000, so if she applies that $1,000 toward the purchase of stock at $40 per share, how many shares would she be able to buy? 25 shares, right? $1,000 of par value divided by $40 per share of stock tells us that each bond can be converted into 25 shares of common stock. So, the two securities should trade at a 25:1 relationship, since the big one (bond) can be turned into 25 of the little ones (stock). The company sets the conversion price; they have no control over where their common stock trades on the open market, right? If the price of the common stock goes up, the value of the convertible bonds goes up. If the company's common stock rises to $50, the bond should be trading for 25 times $50, since it is worth 25 shares of common stock.

$$25 \times \$50 = \$1,250$$

And, if the common stock went up to $60 a share, the bond would be worth 25 times that number, right?

$$25 \times \$60 = \$1,500$$

There is no need to convert the bond, either—its market price is being pushed up by the stock, so you could just sell the bond if you wanted to take a capital gain on the investment. When would somebody convert the bonds to the underlying stock? Only if there were an "arbitrage opportunity," which means that the bonds are cheaper than what the underlying shares are worth. In our example above, when the stock rises to $60, the bond should trade for at least $1,500. That means if it's trading for less than $1,500, investors could buy $1,500 worth of stock for less than $1,500 by purchasing the bonds and converting to the stock.

Credit Ratings

When shopping for a mortgage, what determines your interest rate?
- Current interest rate environment
- Length of time (term) on the loan
- Your credit score

As we have seen, interest rates continuously fluctuate, so timing is everything when taking out a mortgage. Also, if you're taking 30 years to pay back the lender, you will have to pay a higher rate than if you're taking just 15 years. Based on these variables, two people could be in exactly the same situation: Joann wants to take out a 30-year mortgage today, and so does her sorority sister, Sheila. So, they both pay the same rate of interest, right?

Not necessarily. The lender uses the credit scores on both borrowers issued by Experian, TransUnion, and Equifax. The higher the credit score, the lower the interest rate the borrower must pay. Joann has a credit score of 750. Sheila has a credit score of 585. In other words, it stinks to be Sheila. Sure hope she enjoyed all those seven-hundred-dollar purses back before they cut up her credit cards.

Consumers pay rates of interest based on the big three credit rating companies. Corporations and municipalities pay rates of interest based on their credit scores from the big three of S&P, Moody's, and Fitch. Let's use a table and understand that as the credit rating drops, so does the *market price* of the bond. As bond ratings and prices drop, their yields increase. So, a "high-yield bond" is simply a bond that has to offer a huge yield to entice anyone to touch it. In other words, a bond rated AA does not have to offer a high yield, just as Joann does not have to pay a high interest rate to get a mortgage. But, a bond rated BB is backed by a shaky issuer, so, like Sheila, the issuer has to offer a high interest rate to entice anyone to lend them money.

S&P	MOODY'S	FITCH	NOTES
AAA	Aaa	Same as S&P	HIGHEST RATING

S&P	MOODY'S	FITCH	NOTES
AA	Aa	"	VERY SOLID
A	A	"	STILL SOLID
BBB	Baa	"	STILL INVESTMENT GRADE
BB	Ba	"	JUNK, BE CAREFUL
B	B	"	JUNKIER
CCC	Caa	"	Watch out!
CC	Ca		
C	C		
D			D = "in default"

As you might imagine, when a bond becomes a "junk" or "high-yield bond," many mutual funds and pension funds have to follow their policy statement and *immediately* sell the junk/high-yield bonds that do not belong in their portfolios. Guess what happens to bond prices when all these huge institutions go to sell at the same time? Right, they drop even further, pushing the yield up even more. So, as the prospectus for the bond fund sitting on my desk explains, there is a risk both of an actual default and of perceived credit risk—if the market suddenly perceives your bond as shaky, you're going down, baby. By which I mean the *price* is going down. By definition, the yield is going *up*.

Callable Bonds

Treasury bonds can be repurchased by the US Treasury during the last five years of maturity, so the 30-year T-bonds issued in 1984 are callable in 2009. Municipal bonds are usually callable, which allows states, cities, and school districts to refinance their debt at a lower rate, just like homeowners. Corporate bonds are often callable, too, which just means that after a certain period of time, the issuer can repurchase the bonds at a certain price already agreed upon. A bond might be callable starting in the year 2015 at 104, meaning that in the year 2015 the issuer can retire the debt by giving each bondholder a check for $1,040 plus any accrued interest.

When might they want to call a bond? Probably when interest rates have fallen, right? Isn't that when homeowners refinance their loans? Works the same way for bond issuers. When rates go down, they start to think maybe the outstanding debt could be replaced with brand-new, much cheaper debt. If interest rates fall to 6%, they reason, let's issue new debt at 6% and use the proceeds to retire the outstanding debt we're currently paying 8% on.

Pretty simple.

Replacing one bond issue with another is called "refunding." It tends to happen when interest rates fall. It allows the issuer to issue less-expensive debt used to retire more-expensive debt. It's not such a great deal for the bondholders, though. What can they do with the proceeds of the call? Reinvest. At what rate? A lower rate. And, what happens to bond prices as rates decline?

They go up. Only they stop going up when the bonds are called, meaning the bondholder doesn't get the full appreciation in price he would have otherwise gotten. Therefore, the bond indenture would tell investors the first legal call date, and the period from now until then is called "call protection" for obvious reasons. You can certainly buy non-callable bonds, but you'll be offered a lower interest rate, since you aren't giving the borrower an opportunity to refinance in that case. The exam might bring up terms such as "advance refunding," "pre-refunding," and "escrowed to maturity." In this case the issuing municipality issues new bonds at attractive interest rates, then parks the proceeds into an escrow account, where it waits until the first legal call date. If they deposit enough money, invested in Treasury and agency securities, to cover the principal and interest, the original bond issue is considered to be "advance refunded" or "escrowed to maturity." Since there are sufficient funds to cover all the debt service, the bonds would pretty well have to be rated AAA at this point and would have "improved liquidity," should the exam care to mention that fact.

Guaranteed Bonds

The word "guaranteed" is always a red flag when used in connection with an investment. What does the seller mean when he says your bond is "guaranteed"? When the US Treasury says their T-bills, T-notes, and T-bonds are guaranteed, they mean that they will do whatever is humanly possible to pay the interest on time and will return the principal. Since their track record is stellar, you have to assume that the only way to lose money on a Treasury security is to sell it before maturity and after interest rates have risen. If you can hold on until maturity, you will get the principal back on a Treasury security and the US Treasury will not miss an interest payment ever.

So, how can a *corporate* bond be "guaranteed"? What the word means in this context is that a third party, such as the parent company, has promised to pay if the issuer of the bond cannot. In other words, it's a co-signer on the loan. ABC Enterprises issues the bond, which is, fortunately, guaranteed by somebody we've actually heard of called General Electric, the parent company. Is it a "guarantee" that the investor can't lose money?

No. But, just like a banker who has the parent's signature on the loan to Junior, bondholders usually feel better knowing there is a second and usually stronger source of payment should things get funky. The exam may want you to say that a security can be guaranteed as to interest, principal, or dividends. Just remember that the "guarantee" is simply a promise from a party other than the issuer.

Quotes

Bonds are quoted either in terms of their price, or their yield. Since the coupon rate or nominal yield doesn't change, if you give me the price, I can figure the yield. And, if you give me the yield, I can figure the price. If we're talking about a bond's price, we're talking about bond points. A bond point is worth $10, so if a bond is selling at "98," that means it's selling for 98 bond points. With each point worth $10, a bond selling for 98 bond points is trading for $980. A bond trading at 102 would be selling for $1,020. Although fractions have been eliminated from stock and options pricing, they are still very much alive in the world of bond pricing. If a bond point is worth $10, how much is ½ a bond point worth? Five dollars, right? A quarter-point would be worth $2.50, right? An eighth is $1.25, and so on. Therefore, if you see a bond priced at 102 3/8, how much does the bond cost in dollars and cents? Well, "102" puts the price at $1,020, and 3/8 of $10 is $3.75. So, a bond trading at 102 3/8 costs $1,023.75.

$$102 \ [\$1,020] + 3/8 \ [\$3.75] = \$1,023.75$$

If we're talking about basis points, we're talking about a bond's yield. Yield to maturity, to be exact. If I say that a bond with an 8% coupon just traded on a 7.92 basis, I'm telling you that the price went up above par, pushing the yield to maturity down to 7.92%. "Trading at a basis of…" just means that the price pushed the yield to maturity to a particular percentage, or number of "basis points." A basis point is the smallest increment of change in a bond's yield. When the media talks about the Fed easing interest rates by fifty basis points, they're talking about ½ of 1 percent. We would write 1% as .01, right? Well, basis points use a 4-digit display system, so .01 is written as:

.0 1 0 0.

Then, we read that figure as "100 basis points." Two percent would be 200 basis points. One-half of one percent would be written as .0050 or "50 basis points." So, a bond trading at a 7.92 basis means that the yield to maturity is 7.92% or 792 basis points.

Bearer, Fully Registered, Book Entry

In the olden days, some bonds were issued as "bearer bonds," which meant that whoever "bore" or had possession of the bonds was presumed to be the owner. No owner name at all on the certificate; it just said "pay to the bearer," and then the principal amount. So, whoever presented the bond at maturity received the principal. Basically, bearer bonds are like the tens and twenties in your wallet. To whom do those bills belong—you?

Prove it.

Luckily, you don't have to prove it. You are "bearing" those unnamed tens and twenties in your wallet, so they are yours. Period. Just like the bearer bonds in your hands—the fact that you're holding them means that you own them.

In order to receive the interest, investors holding bearer bonds used to present coupons attached to the bond certificate every six months for payment. There was no name on the interest coupon, either, so the IRS had no way of tracking the principal or the interest income. And you know how much that irritates the IRS. So, bonds haven't been issued in bearer form since the early '80's—that doesn't mean they don't exist. A few are still floating out there on the market, so you may have to know about them for the test. Just remember: no name on certificate, no name on payment coupons.

Bonds also used to be registered as to principal only. That meant that we had a name on the bond certificate—the person who would receive the <u>principal</u> amount at maturity. But, again, with the silly little unnamed interest coupons. Therefore, only the principal was registered, thus the name "registered as to principal only."

Anyway, the bond market got smart in the early 1980s and started registering both pieces of the debt service. Now, the issuer has the name of the owner [principal] and automatically cuts a check every six months for the interest. Therefore, the IRS—who is here to help—can also help themselves to a bit of the interest income. We call these bonds fully registered, because both pieces of the debt service (interest, principal) are <u>registered</u>.

Book entry/journal entry bonds are still fully registered. It's just that it's done on computer, rather than on paper. The investor keeps the trade confirmation as proof of ownership, but we still have an owner name on computer, and we automatically cut interest checks to the registered owner.

Trade Confirmations

Broker-dealers send trade confirmations to customers. A confirmation for a bond purchase or sale would typically include the following information:

- Name, address, telephone # of the broker-dealer
- Name of the customer
- Purchase or Sale
- Capacity in which the firm acted: principal, agent
- Trade date and time of execution
- Par value of the bonds ($1,000, $5,000, etc.)
- Settlement date
- Yield and dollar price
- Final monies (total dollar amount of transaction, accrued interest, extended principal, any other fees)
- Name of issuer
- CUSIP number
- Maturity date
- Interest rate
- Features: callable, puttable, escrowed to maturity, in default, etc.

EQUITY SECURITIES

The money that investors put into equity securities should be the money they won't need to spend any time soon. In fact, it should be the money they can afford to lose. As many have discovered, sometimes when you try to put your money to work for you, it ends up getting fired. Why put any of your money at risk? Because history has shown that stocks provide some very nice returns over the long haul. The ride is often a wild one, but over time common stock in solid companies can provide some impressive long-term returns through dividends and capital appreciation. Unlike a bond that is eventually worth just the par value, no one can tell you what the value of a particular common stock will be someday. Long-term returns of 1,000 percent are rare, but they do happen; 100% losses are also not uncommon. Therefore, since anything can happen over a three- or five-year period, the time horizon for equity securities investments should generally be longer than a few years. Stock investments are for the long haul.

Common Stock

Remember that holders of common stock are part-owners of a public corporation. They didn't lend money to the corporation; they bought a piece of the profits.

Common stock holders enjoy several important rights the exam might bring up. The first right is the right of common stockholders to vote for any major issue that could affect their status as a proportional owner of the corporation. Things like stock splits, mergers, acquisitions, board elections, and changes of business objectives all require shareholder approval.

Shareholders vote their shares. If you own 100 shares of common stock, you have 100 votes to cast. So, whenever you get fired up about a big issue at the company, here's you with your 100 votes and here's some pension fund with 800 million votes. This explains why a few large shareholders tend to control things at a public corporation. Beyond voting, common stockholders also have the right to inspect the list of shareholders and copies of the minutes from shareholder meetings. Shareholders have the right to receive stock certificates to show proof of ownership. A stock certificate would state the name of the issuing corporation, the owner's name, and the number of shares the stockholder owns. A shareholder can transfer his shares freely, by selling them, giving them away, donating them to charities, or leaving them to his heirs through a will or trust. The issuing company pays a bank or other firm to keep track of all these transfers of ownership, and guess what we call them?

The *transfer agent*. The transfer agent is a record keeper who has a list of all the shareholders. The transfer agent cancels old shares and issues new ones when they're lost, stolen, or destroyed.

The *registrar* is another outside firm that audits the transfer agent and makes sure the company doesn't accidentally issue more shares than their corporate charter authorizes.

Should a corporation go belly-up and have to be liquidated, common stockholders get in line for their piece of the proceeds. Unfortunately, they are last in line. They are behind all the creditors, including bondholders, and also behind preferred stock holders. But, at least they are in line, and if there are any *residuals* left, they get to make their claim on those assets. That's known as a "residual claim on assets," for obvious reasons.

Buying common stock is really all about owning a piece of the corporation's earnings or "net income." As the earnings increase, usually, so does the price of the common stock. The other way to get a return from your common stock is to receive a piece of those earnings or profits *now*, in the form of a dividend. Which would you vote for as a shareholder—dividends now, or have the company reinvest the profits back into the business?

Trick question—shareholders don't get to vote on dividends. That's right, if a corporation's board of directors doesn't declare a dividend, the dividend doesn't get paid. End of story. But, if the board *does* declare a dividend, here's how it works. The day that the Board declares the dividend is known as the declaration date. The board wonders who should receive this dividend—how about investors who actually own the stock as of a certain date? We call that the record date because an investor has to be the owner "of record" on or before that date if she wants to receive the dividend. The board decides when they'll pay the dividend, too, and we call that the payable date.

Now, since an investor has to be the owner of record on or before the Record Date to receive the dividend, there will come a day when it's too late for investors to buy the stock and also get the dividend.

Why?

Because stock transactions don't settle until the third business day following the trade date. To "settle" means that the buyer has become the new official owner of the stock. If a stock is sold on a Tuesday, the trade doesn't actually settle (ownership doesn't officially change) until Friday, the third business day after the trade. This is known as regular way settlement, T + 3.

So, if an investor has to be the owner of record on the record date, and it takes three business days for the buyer to become the new owner, wouldn't she have to buy the stock at least <u>three</u> business days prior to the record date?

So, if she buys it just <u>two</u> business days before the record date, her trade won't settle in time. We call that day the ex-date or "ex-dividend" date, because starting on that day investors who buy the stock will <u>not</u> receive the dividend. On the ex-date, it's too late. Why? Because the trades won't settle in time, and the purchasers won't be the owners of record (with the transfer agent) on or before the record date.

The regulators (FINRA) set the ex-date, as a function of "regular way" or "T + 3" settlement. The ex-date is two business days before the record date.

So, remember DERP. <u>D</u>eclaration, <u>E</u>x-Date, <u>R</u>ecord Date, <u>P</u>ayable Date. The board sets all of them except the Ex-Date, which is set by the regulators. Also remember that cash dividends are taxable for the year received—yes, the tax rate has become quite enjoyable, but cash dividends are still taxable. That's why it's a violation if a registered representative deceives a client by telling her to hurry up and purchase a stock or mutual fund simply because it is about to distribute a dividend. First, the value of the stock or mutual fund will drop by the amount of the dividend—so what's the hurry? And, second, the dividend is taxable, so what was the point in hurrying? The point in hurrying would be that the registered representative wanted to make a commission at the expense of the investor, hoping nobody notices. This violation is called "selling dividends," and it could easily show up in a test question.

Another way an investor could receive a "dividend" is by receiving more shares from the issuer. This is called a "stock dividend," and it's easy to get excited about getting new shares of stock, until you realize that all the shareholders are getting more shares. No value was created. Basically, the company decided to give everybody more slices of the earnings pie by cutting the slices much smaller and giving everybody more of them. So, if an investor had 100 shares of XYZ that she bought @50, what would happen if the company paid a 10% stock dividend? She would have 110 shares worth $45.45 each. The same $5,000 investment divided among more shares, in other words. Perhaps you recall that a stock dividend does not meet the definition of an offer or sale of securities. Perhaps it's easier to see why that's the case now. Or not. Either way, let's keep moving.

The exam might bring up the difference between authorized, issued, treasury, and outstanding shares. The corporation is "authorized" to issue a certain number of shares in their corporate charter. The amount they have issued at this point is called, not surprisingly, the "issued" shares. Companies often buy back shares and put them in "treasury," so to figure out how many shares are left "outstanding," just take the number of shares issued minus the number repurchased and placed in the treasury. For example, if the company has issued 1,000,000 shares and has 400,000 in treasury, there are 600,000 shares outstanding. Many companies like using cash to buy back shares, as it generally boosts the earnings per share and does not get taxed as a dividend to shareholders. Assuming the net income was exactly the same year-over-year, reducing the number of outstanding shares would, by definition, increase the earnings per share. It also shows the markets that this company truly believes its stock is worth more than people realize.

Rights and Warrants

Another feature common stockholders enjoy is the right to maintain their proportionate ownership in the corporation. The corporation can sell more shares to the public, but they have to give the existing shareholders the right to buy their proportion of the new shares before the public gets to buy theirs. For every share owned, an investor receives what's known as a right. It's an equity security with a very short life span. It works like a coupon, allowing the current shareholders to purchase the stock below the market price over the course of a few weeks. If a stock is trading at $20, maybe the existing shareholders can take one subscription right plus $18 to buy a new share. Those rights act as coupons that give the current shareholders two dollars off the market price. So, the investors can use the rights themselves or sell them on the secondary market.

Another type of special security is called a warrant. It has nothing to do with shareholder rights; it's just easier to learn about warrants and rights together. A warrant is a long-term equity security. There are no dividends attached to a warrant. If you own a warrant, all you own is the opportunity to purchase a company's stock at a pre-determined price. If you have a warrant that lets you buy XYZ for $30 per share, then you can buy a certain number of shares at that price whenever you feel it makes sense to do so, like when XYZ is trading for a lot more than $30 per share. When issued, the price stated on the warrant is above the current market price of the stock. It usually takes a long time for a stock's price to go above the price stated on the warrant. But, they're good for a long time, typically somewhere between two and ten years.

Warrants are often attached to a bond offering. Corporations pay interest to borrow money through bonds. If they attach warrants, they can "sweeten" the deal a little and maybe offer investors a lower interest payment.

Preferred Stock

Another equity security that could show up on the exam is called preferred stock. This stock gets <u>prefer</u>ential treatment over common stock if the company has to be liquidated in bankruptcy, and receives dividends whether common stock receives a payment or not. The preferred dividend is printed right on the stock certificate. The par value for a preferred stock is often $100. The stated dividend is a percentage of that par value. Six-percent preferred stock would pay 6% of $100 per share, or $6 per share per year, then.

We hope.

See, dividends still have to be declared by the Board of Directors. Preferred stockholders aren't creditors. They're just owners who like to receive dividends. If the board doesn't declare a dividend, do you know how much an owner of a 6% preferred stock would receive?

Nothing.

However, if the investor owned cumulative preferred stock, that might be different. She wouldn't necessarily get the dividend now, but the company would have to make up the missed dividend in future years before it could pay dividends to any other preferred or common stockholders. If the company missed the six dollars this year and wanted to pay the full six dollars next year, cumulative preferred stockholders would have to get their $12 before anybody else got paid.

This 6% works more like a maximum than a minimum. If an investor wants the chance to earn <u>more</u> than the stated 6%, he'd have to buy participating preferred stock, which would allow him to share in dividends <u>above</u> that rate. Dividends paid on common stock are frequently increased over time, and participating preferred stock holders will also enjoy that increase.

Callable preferred stock may be repurchased by the issuer as of a certain date for a certain price. The "call" generally happens only if interest rates drop. When interest rates go down, the issuer might get tired of paying generous 6% dividends every year. If so, they can buy the preferred stock back and retire the shares. Or replace them with new preferred stock paying lower dividends that reflect the new lower interest rate environment. So, if the exam asks when preferred stock or bonds get called, tell it that it happens when rates are falling…the same time that homeowners refinance. Also, if you give the issuer this type of flexibility, they'll usually pay you a higher rate of return. So, callable preferred stock tends to pay the nicest rate of return. Most types of preferred stock have no maturity date and are, therefore, "perpetual." That's why callable preferred stock is unique. Since this type of preferred stock is callable, it can be repurchased and retired by the issuer instead of paying out preferred dividends indefinitely.

A truly wild type of preferred stock is called convertible preferred stock. As with convertible bonds, convertible preferred stock lets an investor exchange one share of preferred stock for a certain number of common shares whenever the investor wants to make the switch. Let's say the convertible preferred stock is convertible into 10 shares of common stock. Therefore, the convertible preferred stock is usually worth whatever 10 shares of common stock are worth. When the 10 shares are worth exactly the market price of the convertible preferred stock, the two securities trade at "parity," which means "equal." Just multiply the price of the common stock by the number of shares the investor could convert the preferred into. That gives you the preferred stock's parity price. In our example, if the common stock rises to $13, the parity price of the convertible preferred stock is 10 times $13 or $130.

If a security has a fixed payment, the market compares that fixed payment to current interest rates. Current interest rates represent what investors could receive if they bought newly issued fixed income securities. If fixed income securities are paying 4%, and your preferred stock pays you a fixed 6%, how do you feel about your preferred security? Pretty good, since it's paying a higher rate than current interest rates. If somebody wanted to buy it, they'd have to pay a higher price. But, if interest rates shoot up to 10%, suddenly your 6% preferred doesn't look so good, right? In that case the market price would go down. Not the par value—par value is etched in stone. It's the market price that fluctuates. Who cares about the market price? Well, if you have to sell when the market price is down, you take a loss, right? Many homeowners have recently felt the painful truth of this concept. When you plan to hold the stock, bond, or townhouse for a long while, its market value doesn't seem so important, but when you go to liquidate it (turn it into cash), suddenly the market price is supremely important.

American Depository Receipts (ADRs)/American Depository Shares (ADS)

If you wanted to buy shares in Toyota, you would probably prefer to buy them in American dollars and be able to trade them while the American exchanges are open. To accommodate folks like you, ADRs have been created. ADRs make it easier for Americans to buy shares of foreign stocks. You no longer have to deal with a stock priced at, say, 1,167.59 yen, since the Toyota ADR is priced in American dollars and trades alongside any other stock on the NYSE. An ADR might pay a dividend, but the dividend has to be converted from the foreign currency into US currency, which is partly why ADR owners are subject to currency risk. If the US dollar is strong, the dividend won't be worth as much to an American. If the US dollar is weak, then the dividend will convert to *more* dollars. So, tell the exam that a weak dollar is actually beneficial to an American holding an ADR, while a strong dollar is not. Sounds almost backwards, right? And that's what makes it such a natural Series 63 question.

The exam might also mention that ADR holders have the right to exchange their receipts for the actual underlying foreign shares. And that they allow US investors to give their portfolios international exposure without having to utilize foreign markets. Finally, a sponsored ADR would typically give voting rights to the owner, while an unsponsored ADR would not.

REITs and Real Estate Limited Partnerships

Investing in real estate has many advantages and disadvantages. The advantages are that property values usually go up and that real estate provides diversification to a portfolio. A disadvantage is that real estate ties up a lot of capital. And, it isn't liquid. It often takes months to get a house sold, or sold for a decent price, so the lack of liquidity keeps many investors from buying real estate, especially commercial real estate (shopping malls, skyscrapers, factories, etc.).

This is where REITs come in. A Real Estate Investment Trust (REIT) is a company that owns a portfolio of properties and sells shares in the operation to investors. You could buy into REITs that own apartment buildings, office buildings, shopping centers, hotels, convention centers, self-storage units, you name it. Now, if there were no REITs, it's safe to say that I would probably never be investing in shopping centers or office buildings. But through REITs, I can participate in big, commercial (or residential) real estate without having to be rich or putting up with the traditional liquidity problems. I can liquidate my REITs as fast as I can sell most any other stock.

Real Estate <u>Limited Partnerships</u> are different. First, they are extremely *illiquid*. Meaning, if you think you're going to want to sell, don't buy in. If you buy in as a limited partner (LP), you have limited liability. But, you don't get to sell your limited partnership interest. You're in for the long haul. Often, the folks who buy limited partnership interests are looking for tax write-offs. Since the partners take a share of the income and expenses, often a new partnership will generate losses for the first several years that can be used to offset passive income for the partners. But, these partnership losses can *only* be used to offset passive income—not earned income or portfolio income. Passive income is received from partnerships and any rental units an investor might own.

Not all partnerships are about showing a loss. Some provide new construction. Put up a new townhouse development, sell them all real quick, and walk away with a nice profit. That doesn't sound too bad. Some real estate partnerships are more into owning real estate and making money by renting it out. More income oriented, then, as opposed to new construction, which is more about capital gains. The partners may be able to shelter some income during the early years of operations, but eventually the partnership will likely hit the "crossover point," which is where income begins to exceed deductions.

A fairly likely point on an exam would be that real estate partnerships do pass through losses to the partners, while REITs do NOT pass through losses to the shareholders. REITs pass through income, but not losses. If the company had a loss, that would just push the stock price of the REIT down, like any other company. Also, there are no net worth requirements for REITs, which explains why a schmuck like me has owned them for so long. Finally, note that I've been explaining the REITs that own property and lease it out. There are also "mortgage REITs" that focus more on financing real estate projects, in case you don't already have enough to remember at this point.

INVESTMENT COMPANIES

Any one security in a portfolio is always subject to the risk that its price will plummet. That's why most investors spread this "non-systematic risk" among several stocks or bonds, often from several different industries. That way, if one security loses value, maybe another one will increase in value and offset the loss. While it makes good sense to use this practice of diversification, it also takes a lot of time and money to buy stocks and bonds from many different companies in many different industries, doing all your own research and sweating all the details yourself. So, instead of trying to assemble a large, diversified portfolio on your own, you can buy shares of a large, diversified portfolio managed by a professional. That's what a mutual fund is. It's a big diversified portfolio of many securities managed by a professional and packaged as a complete set to the investor. Think of a mutual fund as a big portfolio pie that can serve up as many slices as investors care to buy.

Investors send in money to buy slices of the big pie; the fund uses the money to buy ingredients, like IBM, MSFT, and GM. When an investor sends in money, the pie gets bigger, but it also gets cut up into more slices—however many she is buying. That way each slice stays the same size. The only way for the slices to get bigger is for the pie to get sweeter, which happens when securities in the fund go up in value, or when those securities kick in dividend or interest payments to the fund. Please understand that mutual funds do not rise in value because people are buying them. In fact, that's backwards.

See, the mutual fund adds up the value of the portfolio at the end of the trading day, which is simply the market price of all the stocks and bonds plus any cash those securities throw off in the form of dividends and interest payments. They divide that total value of cash and market value by the number of existing shares and call that the "net asset value" or "NAV" of the shares. *Now* they put new money in on behalf of the buyers at that NAV. Similarly, the NAV does not drop because there are sellers redeeming their shares to the fund. If we have more sellers than buyers, the pie gets smaller, but it also gets cut up into fewer slices. So, net assets of the fund go up and down due to customer purchases and sales, but the number of shares changes right along with the in-flow and out-flow of cash, leaving everything proportional.

NAV goes up and down each trading day the same way as my little SIMPLE IRA. When the stocks in my online account go up in value, I see a little plus sign and some positive numbers in beautiful, glowing green. When the stocks go down in value, I see a minus sign and some negative numbers in dark, depressing red. Whenever dividends are paid into my portfolio, that raises the value of the account. I mean, what else would it do? Abbott Labs cuts a check to my account for $750. If that doesn't raise the value of my account, what does? Only when Abbott Labs rises in market value. What else would do it?

Nothing. That's the whole story of investing. There is growth, there is income, and sometimes there is both growth *and* income. If you were looking for excitement, please tell me you didn't buy a mutual fund. Mutual funds are about as boring as it gets, and we intend to prove it. Just keep reading; you'll see.

Like any portfolio, when the stocks or bonds inside the mutual fund portfolio appreciate, so do the shares of the mutual fund owned by investors. I mean, if I decided to cut my little SIMPLE IRA into slices, the value of those slices would go up just as I explained above with the little green (positive) and red (negative) numbers. Mutual funds are gigantic portfolios cut up into bazillions of shares. Each share is worth the net asset value or NAV per share. If the fund has $10 million in assets and $500,000 in liabilities, that leaves net assets of $9.5 million. If the pie is worth $9.5 million on net, and there are 1 million slices (shares) of the pie, each slice is worth exactly $9.50. So the NAV of this fund would be $9.50. The net asset value fluctuates with market fluctuations and is re-figured every trading day. Mutual funds will repurchase or redeem their shares whenever an investor decides to sell them. The fund pays investors the NAV per share, which is computed the next time the fund computes it. This is known as forward pricing. If an investor has 1,000 shares to redeem, and the NAV is $9.50 when the fund next computes it, how much do you suppose the investor receives for redeeming her shares?

$9,500. If the fund has no front-end load, the buyers would also pay the NAV. If these are front-end-loaded or "A-shares," we simply add a sales charge on top of the NAV. So, if the NAV is $9.50 but we pay a POP (public offering price) of $10, that extra 50 cents is the sales charge that covers the costs of marketing and selling the fund and leaves a handsome profit for those who market and sell the fund to investors. And those people would be the NASD/FINRA member firms who distribute the shares and make money through sales charges and 12b-1 fees, which will be discussed later.

Investment companies are defined and regulated under the Investment Company Act of 1940. That act of Congress classifies investment companies into three types: face amount certificate companies, unit investment trusts, and management companies. We're mostly concerned with the management companies, which are either open-end funds or closed-end funds. Open-end funds issue new shares whenever investors feel like buying them. They will also buy back/redeem shares whenever investors feel like selling them.

Open- vs. Closed-End Funds

On the other hand, we have closed-end funds, which do a fixed offering of shares, and that's it. A fixed number of shares are sold, unlike an open-end fund that issues an unknown number on a continuous basis. Another major difference is that closed-end funds can use more leverage than their open-end counterparts, which is the phrase used for "borrowed money." Unlike open-end funds, closed-end funds also don't redeem their own shares. Investors buy and sell them, just like individual stocks. Therefore, unlike an open-end fund, whose shares are always worth the NAV per share, closed-end funds are worth whatever the market says they're worth. So, for the test, if you see that a fund has a net asset value of $9 per share and is currently trading for only $7.50, you know it's a closed-end fund. Doesn't mean that closed-end funds always trade below the NAV. It means that open-end funds do *not* do that, because open-end funds do not trade among investors—they are redeemed/sold back to the issuer. Closed-end funds trade on the secondary market among investors, so they can end up trading at their NAV, at a discount to the NAV, or at a *premium* to the NAV.

Why?

Supply and demand. If buyers really want the shares of your closed-end fund, they may pay you more than you ever thought possible. Or less. That's the deal with the closed-end fund; you have to trade it just like any other share of stock. By the way, Nuveen here in Chicago is a leader in closed-end funds—check out their website and you'll quickly see the real-world view of clo sed-end and open-end funds (www.nuveen.com).

OPEN-END	CLOSED-END
Continuous offering	Fixed initial offering only
Investors redeem shares to fund	Investors sell shares OTC/exchange
Investors may pay sales charge	Investors pay commissions
Priced by formula	Priced by supply/demand

Sales Charge, Open-End Funds

An open-end fund will redeem/buy back its shares at the NAV. If you want to buy shares in the fund, you often have to pay a little more than that. The "extra" that investors pay to buy the shares is called a sales charge or sales load. It covers the costs of printing up sales literature, running advertisements in magazines, newspapers, TV and radio, mailing out the prospectus, and paying sales people. It also leaves a profit for the distributors and the broker-dealers who market and sell the shares to investors.

If a fund has a net asset value per share of $9.50 and costs $10.00, how much is the sales charge?

Fifty cents.

What is the sales charge as a percentage? Ask yourself how much of ten dollars is the sales charge? Fifty cents. Fifty cents divided by ten dollars equals 5%. The sales charge is 5% of the public offering price. That's how sales charges are expressed, as a percentage of the public offering price, or the "gross amount invested."

Now, if you get an exam question that gives you the NAV and the sales charge percentage, asking you to calculate the POP, remember that the sales charge is a percentage of the POP. If the test doesn't tell you the POP, how can you figure it? Just take the NAV—which the test has to give you—and divide it by the "complement of the sales charge." The "complement of the sales charge" just means to take 100% minus the sales charge and divide the NAV by that. For example, if the NAV is $9.60 and the sales charge is 4%, the POP would simply be $9.60 divided by .96 = $10.00

$$9.60 \text{ divided by } .96 = \$10.00$$

$$\text{NAV divided by } (100\% - \text{sales charge}) = \text{POP}$$

We said that the fund figures the net asset value at the end of each trading day and *then* new money goes into the fund. So, if the fund has a front-end sales charge, different people will pay different charges depending on the amounts they invest into the fund. Therefore, the fund uses the formula above to figure out how much an investor paying the 3% sales charge pays per share and how much another investor paying the 5.5% sales charge pays per share. If an investor is at the 3% breakpoint level, the fund would take the NAV divided by .97. For the investor at the 5.5% level, the fund would take the NAV divided by .945. This type of calculation seems much more likely to show up on the Series 7 or 6 than the 63, but that is just a guess.

Reducing the Sales Charge

Ever noticed that the more you want to buy of something, the better the deal? Doesn't a small bottle of laundry detergent at the convenience store cost a lot more per ounce than a massive, industrial-sized container at Sam's Club®?

Breakpoints

Same with mutual funds. If you want to invest $1,000, you're going to pay a higher sales charge than if you want to invest $100,000. For mutual funds, investors are rewarded with breakpoints. Let's say that Cromwell Funds has the following sales charge schedule:

INVEST	SALES CHARGE
< $50,000	5%
$50,000 – $149,999	4%
$150,000 – $249,999	3%
$250,000 – $399,999	2%

That means that an investor who buys $200,000 worth of the fund will pay a much lower sales charge than an investor who invests $10,000. In other words, less of her money (as a %) will be deducted from her check when she invests $200,000 as opposed to, say, $10,000. A breakpoint means that at this *point* the fund will give you this *break*. A lower sales charge means that an investor's money ends up buying more shares. For mutual funds, we don't pick the number of shares we want; we send in a certain amount of money and see how many shares our money buys us. With a lower sales charge, our money will buy us more shares. Keep in mind that fractional shares are common. For example, $1,000 would buy 12.5 shares if the POP were $80.

Husband and wife get to combine their investments for the purpose of achieving reduced sales charges. A parent and minor child in a custodial arrangement also get to combine their purchases. So, if the mom puts in $25,000 and also puts in $25,000 for her minor child's UGMA account, that's a $50,000 investment in terms of achieving a breakpoint. The child cannot be an adult; he/she must be a minor. Corporations and other businesses qualify for breakpoints. About the only folks who *don't* qualify for breakpoints are investment clubs.

Another important consideration for breakpoints is that a sales rep can never encourage an investor to invest a lower amount of money in order to keep him from obtaining a lower sales charge offered at the next breakpoint. That's called breakpoint selling and is a major violation. Likewise, if a rep fails to point out to an investor that a few more dollars invested would qualify for a breakpoint, that's just as bad as actively encouraging him to stay below the next breakpoint. Remember, sales reps (broker-dealers) get part of the sales charge. It would definitely be to their advantage to get the higher sales charge. Unfortunately, they have to keep their clients' interests in mind, too. Yes, they take all the fun out of this business.

Letter or Statement of Intent

So, what if we didn't have the $250,000 needed to qualify for the lowest sales charge offered by Cromwell Funds? We could write a letter explaining our intent to invest $250,000 in the fund over the next 13 months. Now, as we send in our money, say, $25,000 at a time, the fund applies the lower 2% sales charge, as if we'd already invested the full amount. The lower sales charge means we end up buying more shares, right? So, the fund holds those extra shares in a safe place (escrow), just in case we fail to invest that $250,000 we intended to. If we don't live up to our letter of intent, no big deal. We just don't get those extra shares. In other words, the higher sales charge applies to the money actually invested.

Also, that letter of intent (LOI) could be backdated up to 90 calendar days in order to cover a previous purchase. If an investor bought $10,000 of the fund on

March 10, he might decide in early June that he should write a letter of intent to invest $250,000 over 13 months. He could backdate the letter to March 10 to cover the previous investment and would then have 13 months from that date to invest the remaining $240,000.

Remember that this LOI covers new money only. Reinvested dividends/capital gains do not count toward this total, and neither does account value. Account value comes into play only if we're talking about the next item, rights of accumulation.

Rights of Accumulation

If an investor's fund shares appreciate up to a breakpoint, the investor will receive a lower sales charge on additional purchases. In other words, when an investor is trying to reach a breakpoint, new money and account accumulation are counted the same way. So, if an investor's shares have appreciated to, say $42,000 and the investor wanted to invest another $9,000, the entire purchase would qualify for the breakpoint that starts at $50,000. $42,000 of value plus an additional $9,000 would take the investor past the $50,000 needed to receive the breakpoint. This is known as rights of accumulation. Don't confuse rights of accumulation with a Letter of Intent, because they have nothing to do with each other. If you sign an LOI for $250,000, the fact that your account value later rises $50,000 has nothing to do with the $250,000 you intend to invest.

Concurrent Purchases

Most "funds" are part of a "family" of funds. Many of these fund families will let you combine your purchase in their Income Fund with, say, their Index or Growth Fund in order to figure a breakpoint. They call this, very cleverly, a combination privilege. So, if the individual invests $20,000 in the Income Fund and $30,000 in the Growth Fund, that's considered a $50,000 investment in the family of funds, and that's the number they'd use to figure the breakpoint.

Just trying to keep everybody in our happy family.

Conversion/Exchange Privileges

The fund might also offer a conversion/exchange privilege. This privilege allows investors to sell shares of, say, the Cromwell Growth Fund, in order to buy shares of the Cromwell Income Fund at the NAV, rather than the higher POP. If we didn't do that, the investor might get mad enough to leave our happy family, since there would be no immediate benefit to his staying with us. I mean, if he's going to be charged the POP, why not look for a new family with a growth fund that might actually, you know, *grow?* But remember that buying the new shares at the NAV is nice for the investor, but the IRS still considers the sale a taxable event. So if you get a test question on the tax treatment, tell the exam that all gains or losses are recognized on the date of the sale.

Distribution Expenses

What is this sales charge/sales load for, anyway?

Let's say that you and your friends want to start a mutual fund. How would you get the shares sold to investors? First, you'd have to pay someone to print the prospectus and a whole bunch of sales literature. Then, you'd have to line up some broker-dealers interested in selling the fund, and—guess what—broker-dealers expect to be paid for their trouble. You'll need to buy some advertising in magazines, newspapers, radio, and TV. And, when somebody sees the advertisement and calls the 800-number, you'll have to mail out the prospectus, which is another cost on top of the cost of printing the prospectus and running the advertisement.

Guess you and your friends won't be starting that fund, after all, huh?

But, wait, there is an NASD/FINRA member firm with a big, fat checkbook interested in sponsoring/underwriting/distributing/wholesaling your fund for you. They're so nice, they're willing to bear all those costs we just mentioned, known as "distribution expenses." Why are they being so nice? Because they're going to charge customers a sales load to not just cover those expenses but also make a profit.

So, how much of an operating expense is the sales load?

Trick question—it isn't an operating expense. It's just an extra fee that the distributor takes from the customer's check. The underwriter/sponsor/distributor bears the distribution costs up front, then covers them (plus a profit) by tacking on a sales charge to the customer. The fund invests the customer's money at the NAV; the distributors take the amount above that (the load) and share it with the broker-dealers who sold the shares. Some distributors even cut out the middlemen and sell to the investors directly. And—as we'll see later—some funds cut out everybody and act as their own distributor. If they do that, they don't charge a "load" per se. They usually charge a 12b-1 fee, instead, which is the same thing only different and which will be explained later.

For now, just remember that a sales charge covers distribution expenses and is not an operating expense to the fund. It's a charge taken out of the investor's check. And it cannot cover management fees, which are operating expenses deducted from the fund's assets on an ongoing basis.

The ABCs

These sales loads/charges can be charged when a customer buys the shares or when the customer sells the shares. Again, the sales charge is taken out of the customer's check. A-shares charge a front-end load when the investor acquires them. A = "acquire." When the investor cuts a check for, say, $10,000, maybe 5% or $500 is taken right off the top to cover the distribution expenses plus a nice profit for the distributors and broker-dealers. B-shares don't charge a front-end load. Instead, B-shares charge a back-end load when the investor sells them. B = "back end." For a "B" share, the investor buys in at the NAV, but she will leave a percentage behind when she sells. For a test question on the proceeds of a B-share redemption, just take the NAV and deduct the appropriate percentage from the investor's proceeds. If the NAV is $10, the investor receives the $10, minus the percentage the fund keeps on the back end. So, if she sells 100 shares and there is a 2% back-end load, she gets $1,000 minus $20. The percentage usually starts to decline in the second year, and after several years (6 to 8), the back-end load goes away completely—effectively, the B-shares are converted to A-shares. That's why they associate B-shares with the phrase "contingent deferred sales charges." Break down those words. The sales charge is deferred until the investor sells, and the amount of the load is contingent upon when the investor sells. Often, the back-end load starts at 5% and gradually drops to 1% and then zero as the shares convert to A-shares, just to keep everything nice and simple. B-shares almost always have higher operating expenses than A-shares, so at some point, the load you avoid on the front end—and the back end after 6 to 8 years—could be outweighed by the higher expenses. In fact, unless you have a small amount of money to invest, an amount that would not help you achieve a breakpoint on the A-shares, it is seldom suitable to purchase B-shares. Most funds will not take an order for B-shares above $50,000. That's because that amount would be better invested in the A-shares, where we can knock down the sales charge and go forward with much lower operating expenses.

Just to make the decision harder, there are also C-shares, which are sometimes called "level load" because of a high and level 12b-1 fee. C-shares might charge a contingent deferred sales charge if the investor sells in less than 1 year or 1½ years, just to keep things nice and simple. But, really, if you can stay in the fund long enough for the back-end charge to go away, you will pay the high 12b-1 fee (usually 1%), but no front-end or back-end sales charges. That's why C-shares are suitable for a shorter-term investment. You wouldn't want to keep getting dinged on a 1% 12b-1 fee that never goes away for very long, but it's okay if you're in the fund for just a few years.

So, which share class should an investor buy? Usually, if the investor has at least $50,000 and a long time horizon, the A-shares will work out best. She'll knock down the front-end sales charge with a breakpoint and then go forward with lower operating expenses. The B-shares are for people who don't plan to invest enough to achieve the $50,000 breakpoint offered on A-shares. C-shares are for the shorter-term investor. Putting a long-term investor with lots of money to invest into C-shares would probably be a violation of suitability requirements. If an equal amount of money would have knocked down the sales charges on the A-shares, chances are the A-shares are what the investor should have been buying. And, putting someone with $100,000 into A-shares when she's going to sell in 2 years or sooner would also probably be a bad idea, since the C-shares would have probably worked out better. Salespersons have suitability requirements and helping investors choose the right share class is part of that responsibility. FINRA has fined many member firms huge amounts of money for improper sales of A-, B-, and C-shares.

SHARE CLASS	SALES CHARGE	OPERATING EXPENSES	SUITABILITY
A	Front-End, can be reduced	Lowest	Long-term investor with 50K +
B	Back-End, declining contingent deferred sales charges	High via 12b-1 fee	Investor with < 50K to invest, mid- or long-term holding period
C	Minimal if any	High via 12b-1 fee	Shorter-term investor with under ~ $500,000

Whether you buy A-, B-, or C-sha res, there are different methods of making your purchases. Most funds have a minimum investment that might be different for a retirement plan as compared to a taxable account. Maybe it's $1,000 for an IRA and $3,000 for a taxable account.

Investors can choose to reinvest dividend and capital gains distributions (explained next), and if they do, they reinvest at the NAV, avoiding the sales charge. They get the effect of "compounding" that way, which is why most folks do this. They can certainly take the distributions in cash if they want, as we'll explain in a second. Some investors set up "voluntary accumulation plans," which means they let the fund automatically deduct a set amount of money each month from their bank account or paycheck. If they're putting in a set dollar amount each month, they are "dollar cost averaging."

Types of Funds

We talked about diversification at the beginning of this discussion. Mutual funds can be as diversified as they want to, but if the fund wants to advertise itself as being diversified, it has to follow the 75-5-10 rule under the Investment Company Act of 1940. That means that at least 75% of the fund's assets have to be diversified so that no more than 5% of the fund's assets are invested in any one stock. The 10 means that the fund cannot own more than 10% of a company's outstanding shares.

Mutual funds have to clearly state their investment objectives. Sales representatives like you have to match your investor's objectives with those of a particular fund.

Equity Funds

Growth Funds

If your investor's objective is capital appreciation, you need to find a mutual fund that invests for capital appreciation, which is also called *growth* or "growth of capital." The stocks in this fund might pay dividends, but that's not the objective. This fund wants to buy stocks and hold them until they appreciate significantly in value. The prospectus I'm looking at says "dividend income, if any, is incidental to the objective of capital appreciation." The trouble with growth funds is that when stock prices are on the decline, there is nothing to smooth out the ride. By definition, you won't be receiving much income from this fund, so when the stocks in the portfolio drop, say, 20%, that's pretty much the end of the story. Therefore, investing for growth involves more volatility than investing for income. It also involves more patience, since there is, again, very little income being paid out to the investors.

Growth and Income Funds

As the name implies, these funds invest in stocks for both their growth potential and their propensity to pay nice dividends. Now, if the market price of the stocks drops, say, 2%, but you receive a 3% dividend yield, you don't feel so bad about things. Therefore, growth and income funds are less volatile than pure growth funds. To achieve the income component, most growth and income funds also invest in debt securities.

Equity Income Funds

Not surprisingly, equity income funds focus on equity securities that pay regular or increasing income. Now, if the focus has been placed purely on the dividend/income potential of particular stocks, chances are, the portfolio manager will end up owning some pretty stable, tried-and-true companies that consistently lead their industry, increase their sales, and pay either a consistent or ever-increasing dividend. For example, I read the other day about an insurance company that has paid a dividend every quarter for the past 136 years. That stock belongs in an equity income fund. Since consistent dividends are paid by established, stable companies, it's a pretty safe assumption that equity income funds will be less volatile than either growth-and-income or pure growth funds.

Notice that even though growth, growth-and-income, and equity income funds are all stock funds, they typically are less volatile as the focus shifts more toward the income component of investing. See, some people are so obsessed with buying stocks and hoping they "go up" that they forget how useful dividend income can be. It can be reinvested into more shares to achieve compounding. Or, it can be used to buy other mutual funds, stocks, bonds, etc. It also tends to reduce the volatility of an investment.

Specialized, or Sector Funds

A fund that concentrates its investments in a particular sector of the market is called a sector or specialized fund. The name of the fund usually implies that it's a sector fund. An "aggressive growth" fund just refers to a style of investing—it doesn't say which industry the companies are in. But, a "science and technology" fund or a "precious metals" fund implies that the fund is concentrating in a particular sector, right? The exam may want you to know that sector funds involve high risk-reward ratios. If you invested in any "Internet funds" back in the late '90s, or any "financial sector" funds recently, that concept should be pretty easy to remember. Also, if it happens to be the hot sector of the moment, I would expect management fees and sales charges to be on the high side.

International, Global Funds

International funds come in a few flavors. They might concentrate in a single country, or a particular region (Latin America, Pacific Rim, etc.). Usually the fund concentrates in companies outside the US. A global fund would invest all over the globe, including the US. International and global funds investing requires a higher risk tolerance than purely domestic funds, but it also offers potential returns an American investor would otherwise miss out on while allowing the investor to diversify away from the US economy.

Emerging Market Funds

A particularly volatile type of international fund would be an emerging market fund. As the name implies, these markets are emerging, just getting started. Lots of wild ups and downs in an immature economy. And if the insurgents take over…well, you get the idea. Basically, the economies are transforming from agricultural-based to industrial (Brazil, for example) or from socialist systems to free market systems (Russia, Eastern Europe, China). If there are lots of labor strikes, banking disasters, material shortages, etc., it's going to make stock prices mighty volatile. But, there are also huge potential growth opportunities, so if the investor is aggressive and seeks capital appreciation, put a percentage of his money into emerging market funds and hope for the best.

Growth, Value, Blend

A growth investor is willing to pay high P/E, price-to-book, and other valuation multiples, while a value investor tries to buy stocks on the cheap. Well, some portfolio managers are absolute mavericks who refuse to be tied down to a label such as "growth" or "value." That means they end up investing in both growth and value stocks. Well, the mutual fund industry insists on labels, so they just labeled these portfolios "blend funds" and kept moving.

Balanced Funds

Balanced funds provide us the perfect bridge from the scary stock market to the boring bond market. A balanced fund always maintains a percentage of assets in bonds and a percentage in stocks. It's not a rigid percentage and the prospectus usually only gives us a vague idea of the split between stocks and bonds. Basically, if it looks like a good year for bonds, the investment adviser switches the concentration to bonds, and vice versa when it looks like a bull market for stocks. Since the fund stays in the bond market, the volatility of the fund is generally much lower than a growth fund or any fund that is primarily invested in stock.

A subtle difference arises when the exam talks about asset allocation funds. These funds, as their name implies, allocate the assets according to the perfect mix of stocks, bonds, and "cash," or "money market securities." So the only real difference I see between "balanced" and "asset allocation" funds is that balanced funds have stocks and bonds, while asset allocation funds go one better by throwing in the "cash" or "money market" component. Also, the percentage mixture is probably more rigid in asset allocation funds. But, many companies would consider their balanced fund to also be an asset allocation fund, so one would hope the exam would focus on better topics.

Bond Funds

Remember that mutual funds are just massive investment pies that serve up slices to investors, so anything that was true of corporate bonds individually is true of a mutual fund that invests in corporate bonds. Like, for example, corporate bonds are nowhere near as safe as municipal bonds, and neither one is as safe as bonds issued by the United States Treasury. Corporate bonds are only as solid as the company who issued them. Investment-grade corporate bonds are obviously more solid than high-yield corporate bonds, but don't kid yourself into thinking that Moody's, S&P, or Fitch can always predict which bonds will end up in default.

Anyway, if the investor's objective is high current income, her risk tolerance will tell us whether to use investment-grade bond funds or high-yield bond funds. For maximum income, we'll recommend high-yield bond funds, as long as her risk tolerance is commensurate with the fact that some of these bonds could implode without warning. Of course, these bonds are commonly referred to as "junk bonds," but the mutual fund industry is too smart to roll out the new "Junk Fund of America." Call that thing the "High-Income Trust Series B," though, and now you'll get yourself some customers.

Income investors looking for tax advantages should buy municipal bond funds. Municipal bond funds receive income from interest payments on municipal bonds, which are generally exempt from *federal* taxation. So, if an investor wants some tax-free dividends, he will get that from a municipal bond fund. Remember that municipal bond funds might pay tax-free dividends, but capital gains are still taxable, just as they are on municipal bonds purchased a la carte. And your state could even tax the dividends you receive, depending on who issued the bonds inside the mutual fund portfolio. Because of this ugliness, fund families have rolled out tax-exempt bond funds specifically for residents of high-tax states including California, Virginia, and Maryland. Investors who live in those states can then purchase mutual funds that pay dividend income exempt from both federal and state taxes. But—as always—capital gains are another story.

And then there are US Treasury funds for people who want to preserve their capital and earn a rather low rate of interest in exchange for that safety. The only way to lose money on Treasuries is to have interest rates go up and you decide to sell anyway. But, the interest payments will always be there on time and you will receive the principal when the thing matures. So, the NAV of the US Treasury fund definitely drops when interest rates rise, but if you have no need to sell, you'll come out okay.

Money Market

Not surprisingly, money market mutual funds invest in money market instruments. They are no-load and maintain a stable value of $1 per share. Actually they "strive to maintain the share price at $1," but that is not guaranteed—it is possible to lose money by investing in a money market mutual fund. Highly unlikely, but possible. Money market mutual funds are good for people who need monthly income or have a near-term goal such as purchasing a house. You don't know how long it will take to find the right house, let alone when the deal will close, so a money market mutual fund is even better than a T-bill. A T-bill matures on a particular day, and God help you if you want to sell it early. For a money market mutual fund, you can simply write a check for $250 or more without paying any fees. Money market mutual funds are good for short-term liquidity and reducing the volatility of your portfolio, but they don't provide much growth of capital, if any.

Also remember that there are tax-exempt money market funds. These funds buy short-term municipal obligations (BAN, TAN, RAN, TRAN), or municipal bonds that are set to mature in a year or less.

Index Funds

The ugly truth is that not many active portfolio managers can consistently beat a comparable index. If you can't beat the S&P 500 index, why not join it? An actively managed stock fund is going to deduct sales charges that can easily be 5% or more for small investments, plus there are annual operating expenses that usually exceed 1%. If you don't like paying sales charges and operating expenses in order to lose to an unmanaged index, why not just buy an unmanaged index fund? Typically, there is no sales charge, and the annual expenses are often about 1/10th of what you'd pay for actively managed stock funds. The exam may point out that if somebody abhors expenses and has no faith in active portfolio management, the index fund is probably appropriate. There are also ETFs, which are index funds that are organized as UITs (unit investment trusts) and traded just like shares of GE or MSFT among investors. Again, we have low operating expenses, but the ETF allows the investor to bet against the market by selling short, purchasing on margin, and taking advantage of the intra-day movements of the index.

Wrap-up

Keep in mind that mutual funds are just packages made up of many individual securities. So, if there is preferred stock, you know there are preferred stock funds. They would be primarily for income investors. If there are GNMAs, then there are, of course, GNMA funds for income investors looking for higher income than that offered by Treasuries. Could there be a convertible bond fund?

Absolutely. Whatever an investor could buy a la carte, she could buy as a complete dinner package through a mutual fund. She pays for the expenses of the fund plus sales charges in many cases, but she gets immediate diversification and professional management in return.

So, if you review the different styles of investing, and throw in the market caps, you see why we could really come up with a variety of fund types. For example:

Equity
Growth Funds
- Aggressive Growth
- Conservative Growth
- Small Cap Growth
- Mid Cap Growth
- Large Cap Growth
- International Growth
- New Economy Growth
- EuroPacific Growth

Value Funds
- Small Cap Value
- Mid Cap Value
- Large Cap Value

Other Equity Funds
- Growth & Income Funds
- Equity Income Funds
- Balanced Funds
- Sector/Specialized
- Index (S&P 500, Russell 2000, etc.)

Fixed Income
- Investment Grade
- High Yield
- Tax-Exempt (municipal bonds)
- Short-Term Treasury
- Short-Term Tax-Exempt (muni)
- Short-Term Corporate
- Intermediate-Term (treasury, muni, corporate)
- Long-Term (treasury, muni, corporate)

Money Market
- US Government/Treasury
- Tax-Exempt (muni notes, near-term bonds)

Structure of the Fund Company

A mutual fund operation is divided among several important players: board of directors, investment adviser, custodian, transfer agent, sponsor.

Board of Directors

A mutual fund has a board of directors that oversees operations of the fund or family of funds. The board's responsibilities include the following:
- Establish investment policy
- Select and oversee the investment adviser, transfer agent, custodian
- Establish dividends and capital gains policy
- Approve 12b-1 plans

Remember, the board of directors does not manage the portfolio; they manage the company. The shareholders of the fund elect and re-elect the board members. Shareholders also vote their shares to approve the investment adviser's contract and 12b-1 fees. Those with enough moxie to open the proxy do, anyway.

Investment Adviser

Yes, we're still talking about investment advisers, the folks who need the Series 65/66. Each fund has an investment adviser, whose job is to manage the fund's investments according to its stated objectives. Shareholders and the board vote to hire/retain investment advisers, who are paid a percentage of the fund's net assets. That's why they try so hard. The more valuable the fund, the more they get paid.

Their fee is typically the largest expense to a mutual fund. Investment advisers have to advise the fund (select the investments) in keeping with federal securities and tax law. They must also base their investment decisions on careful research of economic/financial trends.

Custodian

The fund also keeps its assets in a safe place at the custodian bank. Under very strict rules, some funds do this themselves, but most still let a bank take custody, since banks have vaults and security guards and stuff. The custodian receives the dividends and interest payments made by the stocks and bonds in the fund's portfolio. The custodian is also responsible for the payable/receivable functions involved when the portfolio buys and sells securities.

Transfer Agent

The transfer agent is incredibly busy. This is the bank or other company that issues new shares to buyers and cancels the shares that sellers redeem. Most of these "shares" are simply electronic files (book entry), but it still takes a lot of work to "issue" and "redeem" them. While the custodian receives dividends and interest payments from the portfolio securities, it is the transfer agent that distributes income to the investors. The transfer agent acts as a customer service rep for the fund and often sends out those semi-annual reports that investors have to receive. Finally, the transfer agent handles name changes. So if Joann Williams gets married and becomes Joann Williams-Davis, or if Calvin Broadus starts a music career and becomes Snoop Doggy Dogg, the transfer agent can change the names on the mutual fund shares accordingly.

Distributors

As we saw, some funds are sponsored by underwriters, who bear the costs of distributing the fund up front and then get compensated by the sales charge that they either earn themselves or split with the broker-dealers who make the sales. Underwriters (AKA "wholesalers," "distributors," or "sponsors") also prepare sales literature for the fund, since they're the ones who will be selling the shares, either directly to the public or through a network of broker-dealers.

If a fund wants to distribute itself, it can charge 12b-1 fees to cover the costs connected to landing new customers: printing and mailing the prospectus to new customers, paying sales reps, and buying advertising. In other words, mutual funds charge their customers for marketing costs. They either charge sales loads on the front or back end, or they charge little quarterly deductions called "12b-1 fees."

In fact, many charge *both*. As long as it keeps the 12b-1 fees to .25% of average net assets, the fund can call itself "no load."

There are many conveniences and services offered to owners of mutual funds:

- Investment decisions made by a professional portfolio manager
- Ease of diversification
- Ability to invest fixed amounts in full and fractional shares
- Ability to liquidate a portion of the investment without losing diversification
- Fund shares provide collateral for a loan (after 30 days)
- Simplified tax information (1099s make tax prep easier)
- Simplified record keeping (rather than getting 50 annual reports from 50 companies, you get two semi-annual reports from one mutual fund)
- Ease of purchase and redemption of securities
- Automatic reinvestments of capital gains and income distributions at NAV
- Safekeeping of portfolio securities
- Ease of account inquiry
- Mutual fund shareholders also have the right to:
  - Vote their shares by proxy on:
    - Board of director positions
    - Investment adviser's contract
    - Changes in investment objectives/policy
    - Changes in policy involving real estate or commodities transactions, borrowing/lending money, underwriting other issuer's securities
  - Receive a semi-annual report and an audited annual report (both have an income statement and a balance sheet)

The disadvantages of investing in mutual funds would be that the individual gives up the ability to pick individual securities and that funds have expenses including 12b-1 fees and/or sales charges.

Prospectus

The prospectus is how the mutual fund provides full disclosure to prospective investors. See the connection? We send a prospect-us to a prospect-ive investor. First thing you'll find in the prospectus is a statement about risk/reward. This is generally the first page of information where they describe the investment objectives of the growth, income, bond, or whatever fund. In case the first few paragraphs don't sufficiently scare the bejeezus out of you, they often end up making statements that are as clear as the warnings from the Surgeon General. The prospectus I'm looking at (you should be looking at a few, too) says:

```
Your investment in the fund is not a bank deposit and
is not insured or guaranteed by the FDIC or any other
government agency, entity, or person.
```

And, in case that didn't hit home, they follow up with a bold-letter warning:

```
You may lose money by investing in the fund. The like-
lihood of loss is greater if you invest for a shorter
period of time.
```

In the prospectus, we'll find the fund's 1-year, 5-year, and 10-year returns. If the fund hasn't been around for 5 or 10 years, they report their returns over the life of the fund. The investment adviser(s) is/are named and discussed. The portfolio's allocation is laid out as a pie chart showing which percentage is in, say, retail or pharmaceutical companies, or how much of the bond fund is generally devoted to BBB- versus AAA-rated issuers. The top 10 stock holdings are usually shown for equity funds; we don't get the actual holdings of the portfolio, because those can change every day, but we do get a pretty good idea of how this portfolio is laid out. The prospectus is really the "summary prospectus." Few folks actually read it, although everybody should, especially everybody sitting for a regulatory exam like the 6, 7, 63, or 65/66.

Yes—that includes *you*.

If someone is really curious, he can request the Statement of Additional Information (SAI), which provides pretty much what it sounds like. These are filed with the SEC and are available at the SEC's and the fund company's websites. Remember that corporations have to provide a prospectus when they do their IPO. Well, mutual fund companies are in a continuous state of IPO, which is why they have to provide full disclosure to investors in a prospectus. And, on the back of that prospectus, the prospect can also find a link to the SAI and even the fund's semiannual and annual reports to shareholders.

ETF/Exchange-Traded Funds

Most investors probably associate the phrase "ETF" with index funds, which is a good place to start. Examples of exchange-traded index funds include the Spiders™ or

Diamonds™ that track the major S&P indexes and the Dow Jones Industrial Average. There were already traditional open-end versions of those index funds, but those have to be redeemed, and all investors received the same price on an open-end fund—the closing NAV. With the ETF, investors buy and sell shares back and forth just as they trade shares of Microsoft, GE, and Starbucks throughout the day. As we mentioned, since they trade like shares of stock, they can be sold short to protect against market or systematic risk.

Hedge Funds

Since the mutual fund is open to the average Joe and Joann, they can't focus on extremely risky investment strategies. It would be sort of rude to take the average Joe and Joann's retirement nest egg and lose it all on a couple of ill-placed foreign currency bets or poorly timed short sales. But, when the investors are all rich folks and institutions, the regulators can relax a little bit.

This is where hedge funds come in. In general, hedge funds are only open to institutions and to individuals called "accredited investors." An accredited investor includes any individual with over $1 million in net worth or who makes > $200,000 per year. If it's a married couple, the assets held jointly count toward that $1 million figure, and the annual income needs to be > $300,000. Now, that's *exactly* the kind of number that could change without warning and make a book look dated. First, the exam doesn't let you off that easy, anyway—you don't get to spit back a bunch of memorized numbers. The exam makes you think and analyze in either a very stimulating or painful manner depending on your experience. So, please, don't make the mistake that many test-takers do and start obsessing over numbers such as retirement plan maximums or the annual gift tax exclusion—that stuff can change quickly without warning. The test writers know this. You think *they* want to constantly have to rewrite all their questions just because the SEC changed a rule?

Anyway, we still have to give you the numbers, because they are "testable." Just don't put the *focus* of your studies on all the numbers. Learn the concepts well enough to get test questions right and keep moving.

So, why does the hedge fund investor need to be rich? Because these hedge funds use some very high-risk strategies including short selling, currency bets, risky options plays, etc. If you're an average Joe and Joann, it generally wouldn't be cool to let you risk your money on such high-risk investing. On the other hand, if you're a rich individual or big institution, chances are your hedge fund investment is just a percentage of the capital you invest. So, if you lose $1 million, chances are you have several more where that one came from. Also, hedge funds generally tie up your money for two years or more—there is, basically, no way to sell or liquidate your investment, so this had better not be your only investment. People do have financial emergencies, so a hedge fund is only for money you can afford to risk and don't need to touch any time soon. It is a "highly illiquid and speculative" investment, in other words.

The hedge fund escapes having to register under the Investment Company Act of 1940 because they have 100 or fewer investors and do not offer their securities generally to the public, or because their investors are all "qualified" high-net-worth individuals or institutions. If the exam mentions a "3(c)(7) fund," it is talking about the particular section of the Investment Company Act of 1940 that says an investment company does not include an issuer whose investors are qualified purchasers and who is not making a general public offering.

So, the hedge fund itself escapes having to register, and since the hedge fund counts as just one client, the hedge fund manager can escape registering with the SEC as an investment adviser using the exemption for advisers not holding themselves out to the public and with fewer than 15 clients in the preceding 12 months.

What's the big deal about registration? Well, if the adviser doesn't have to register and neither does the hedge fund, the SEC has no authority to examine the books and records, and even the investors are often kept in the dark about what the fund owns. Now the hedge funds can keep their cards closer to their chests and take on much bigger risks than virtually all mutual funds would employ.

Now, just to keep everything nice and simple, although a non-accredited investor cannot invest directly in a hedge fund, there are mutual funds called "funds of hedge funds," which she can invest in. As the name implies, these mutual funds would have investments in several different hedge funds. In most cases, the investor would not be able to redeem her investment, since hedge funds are illiquid (they don't trade among investors). Also, these investments would involve high expenses, since there would be the usual expenses of the mutual fund, on top of the high expenses of the hedge funds the mutual fund invests in.

So, while some hedge funds have been known to make extremely high returns, even in bear markets, the regulators also want us to remember that they are expensive, very risky, and make it really tough for the investor to liquidate her position. The main testable points on hedge funds would seem to be:

- Open to sophisticated, accredited investors with high net worth
- Illiquid—usually can't be sold for two years
- Employ riskier, more diverse strategies
- Charge high management fees and usually 20% of all gains
- Non-accredited investors can buy mutual funds that invest in hedge funds

Glossary

A-shares: a class of mutual fund share charging a front-end sales charge that can usually be reduced through breakpoints, letters of intent, rights of accumulation, etc. A-shares charge lower annual operating expenses than B- or C-shares.

Accept: communicating to the offeror of securities that the buyer accepts the offer, whether orally or in writing.

Accredited investor: sophisticated investor meeting certain net worth or income requirements allowing the person to participate in certain securities offerings or advisory programs that ordinary investors may not.

Accumulation period: the period during which the annuitant is contributing to the annuity contract and/or holding accumulation units that (we hope) are growing tax-deferred.

Accumulation unit: what the annuitant buys during the accumulation period when allocating contributions among the various sub-accounts.

Adjudicatory hearing: a hearing before the administrator to determine if a denial, suspension, or revocation order should be issued.

Administrator: official or agency designated by the Governor or legislature to administer the securities laws and rules of the state.

Agent: individual other than a broker-dealer representing either a broker-dealer or issuer in effecting or attempting to effect transactions in securities.

Applicant: person who has applied for registration with the Administrator.

Annuity: a contract that promises to make payments to an annuitant for a specified time period, sometimes at a minimum specified rate (fixed annuity).

Arbitrage: exploiting a disparity in the price of two related securities. For example, if a stock were trading for $25.00 on one exchange but only $24.50 on another, an arbitrageur would begin buying it for $24.50 and selling it for $25.00 at the same time. Arbitrage is not a violation, just a high-risk trading strategy.

Arbitration: method of handling disputes among broker-dealers or customers and their agents/broker-dealers used by SROs such as CBOE, FINRA, NASD, NYSE, etc.

Assignment of contract: the transfer of an investment advisory contract by the adviser or a transfer of a controlling block of the adviser's outstanding voting securities by a security holder of the adviser. Not allowed without consent of the advisory client, who is the "other party to the contract."

B

B-share: a class of mutual fund share charging no front-end load but imposing a declining back-end load and higher annual expenses than A-shares.

Back-end load: the declining sales charge imposed on B-shares when the investor sells. Also referred to as CDSCs or "contingent deferred sales charges."

Backing away: a violation in which a market maker fails to honor a published quote.

Bearish: speculating that a stock, bond, or index value will drop. For example, speculators who sell stock short or buy puts on stock are bearish, profiting if the stock value falls.

Best efforts: type of underwriting in which the underwriters have no liability for unsold shares.

Bid: the price representing what a dealer will pay for a security to a willing seller.

Blind-pool offering: an offer of limited partnership interests in a program that is not stating all or most of the assets. Investors in a blind-pool raw land or oil exploration partnership are putting their "blind faith" in the promoter and/or the general partner. This term is not defined elsewhere in the book.

Breakpoint: a quantity-based discount offered on purchases of mutual fund A-shares.

Breakpoint selling: a violation in which the investor does not receive the quantity-based discount her purchase entitles her to, or is not informed of the quantity-based discount.

Broker-dealer: a person in the business of effecting transactions in securities for others or for its own account.

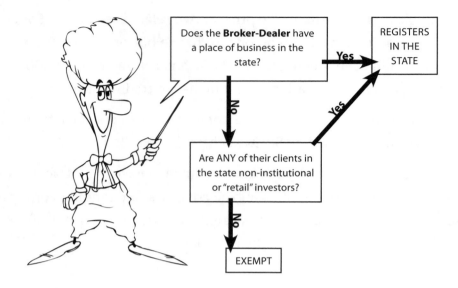

Bullish: confident that a security or index value is about to rise.

Bull market: a prolonged series of higher highs and higher lows for stock, bond, or index values.

C

Call: (1) an option to purchase something at a stated price, (2) early redemption of a bond or preferred stock.

Callable bond/preferred: a bond or preferred stock that can be repurchased/redeemed by the issuer on set dates at set prices.

Collateral: an asset pledged to a lender to secure a loan, e.g., pledging title to a house to the mortgage lender, or title to the securities purchased on margin to a broker-dealer.

Collateralized Mortgage Obligation: or CMO, a complex derivative product. CMOs are a type of mortgage-backed security with different classes of bondholders receiving different pass-through rates with varying maturities, called tranches.

Confirmation: a document confirming a transaction, which must be delivered to customers no later than settlement. For a new issue, the final prospectus must be delivered with or before confirmation. For a secondary market transaction, stocks, corporate bonds, and municipal bonds settle on the trade date (T) plus three business days (T + 3).

Consent to service of process: a form that gives the Administrator the power to accept "service of process" connected to a civil or administrative action against the person filing the consent.

Contempt: violating a court order/injunction/subpoena.

Contingent Deferred Sales Charge: associated with mutual fund B-shares. The buyer pays a declining sales charge only upon selling the shares, where a portion of the sales proceeds is deducted with the amount contingent upon the length of time the shares have been held.

Contumacy: disregarding an Administrator's order.

Convertible securities: bonds and preferred stocks that allow the holder to use the par value to purchase the issuer's underlying common stock at a set price, regardless of the stock's actual market price at the time.

Custody: having/maintaining possession or control of client securities and/or cash.

Custodian: a bank or broker-dealer that has possession and control of assets held in advisory accounts, retirement accounts, etc.

D

Debenture: a bond secured by no specific collateral.

Default: a bond issuer's inability to make interest or principal payments

Deferred annuity: an annuity contract in which the investor funds the contract now but delays making withdrawals, usually with a surrender period in which withdrawals are penalized by the annuity company.

Defraud: to deceive for financial gain.

Dilution: the effect on existing shareholders when convertible bonds are converted to shares of common stock, driving down earnings-per-share and the amount of dividends that can likely be paid per share.

Disgorgement: an order to return ill-gotten profits. For example, insider trading violations generally lead to a court order to return all the profits before they even start figuring all the penalties against the folks who cheated.

Discourage: what the Series 63 is trying to do to you.

Distributor: the sponsor/underwriter of a mutual fund, limited partnership investment, etc., with a financial interest in getting the thing marketed and sold.

Double taxation: paying tax on the same money twice. A small business owner with a C-corp pays corporate taxes on business profits, then when the dividends are distributed to the owners (including himself), he is taxed on that income once again. Mutual funds and REITS operate under the "conduit theory" to avoid double taxation on the 90% of net income distributed to the shareholders.

Discretion: having the authority to choose securities purchases and sales on behalf of a client. Must be in writing to choose the asset, activity, or amount. Written authorization is not required to choose time and/or price.

Discretionary income: what an individual or a business has left after covering all essentials. Discretionary income is spent on movies, fine linens, and books, all of which consumers can avoid during a recession.

Disposition: as in "disposition of a security," a fancy way of saying "to get rid of." A security that has been "disposed of in exchange for value" has been offered and sold, meaning it was subject to registration requirements and anti-fraud regulations.

Dividend: a share of profits paid to shareholders when and if declared by the board of directors.

E

Effect: to complete, as in "to *effect* a transaction in a security."

Enjoin: to issue an injunction that restrains someone's activities under threat of civil, criminal, and/or monetary penalties.

Excepted: outside the definition of, e.g., a bank is excepted from the definition of either "investment adviser" or "broker-dealer."

Exempt: not subject to registration requirements, e.g., a federal covered adviser is exempt from state registration requirements.

F

FNMA: federal national mortgage association. Public company with special relationship with US Government—still not a *direct* obligation. Issues mortgage-backed securities.

Federal covered adviser: an adviser registered exclusively with the SEC. A federal covered adviser is an adviser with at least $25,000,000 of assets under management, or anyone (even with an office in the state) who advises a registered investment company, or whose sole clients are investment companies or insurance companies. Note that federal covered advisers still pay fees, provide notice, and possibly file a consent to service of process with the state. But they're really under federal/SEC jurisdiction.

Federal covered security: a security not subject to the state's requirements for filing of advertising materials and registration. Exchange-listed securities, investment company securities, and securities sold to qualified purchasers.

Fiduciary: a person managing investments on behalf of another party, e.g., an investment adviser, trustee, or member of a pension fund's investment committee.

FHLMC: federal home loan mortgage corporation, like Fannie Mae (FNMA), only smaller. Issues mortgage-backed securities; not a direct obligation of US Government.

G

General account: the investments of an insurance company backing up fixed, guaranteed payments on life insurance policies and fixed annuities.

General obligation: a municipal bond issued by a city, state, school district, etc., backed by the issuer's full taxing authority or "full faith and credit."

Gift: transferring property to someone else and expecting nothing in return. Gifts over a certain amount are taxable to the person who makes the gift.

GNMA: government national mortgage association. GNMA pass-through securities are direct obligations of the US Government.

Government securities: direct obligations of the United States Government, e.g.,. T-bills, T-notes, T-bonds, and Treasury STRIPS.

Grantor: the person who creates and transfers assets to a trust.

Guarantee: a promise by someone other than the issuer to pay interest, principal, or dividends if the issuer of the security is unable to. Not a guarantee against loss.

H

Hypothecation: pledging securities as collateral to secure a margin loan

I

Immaterial: not important, irrelevant.

Impoundment of proceeds: establishing an escrow account where proceeds from the offering of securities are impounded/not released to the issuer by the Administrator until the specified amount of money has been raised. Note that if the amount of money raised is insufficient, the proceeds (plus a pro rata share of the interest) goes to the investors, not the issuer or underwriters.

Injunction: court order to prevent a person from committing further violations of securities law.

Insolvent: more liabilities than assets, unable to pay obligations as they become due, bad news for creditors.

Investment adviser: any person who receives compensation for providing advice on investing in securities, including those who hold themselves out as financial planners.

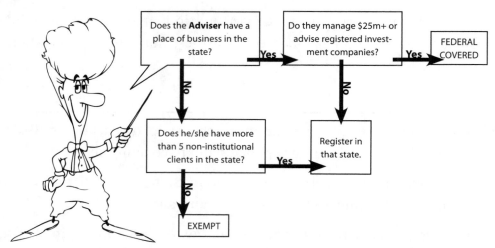

Investment adviser representative: individual who represents an investment advisory firm by managing money, making recommendations, selling the services of the firm, or supervising anyone doing any of those things.

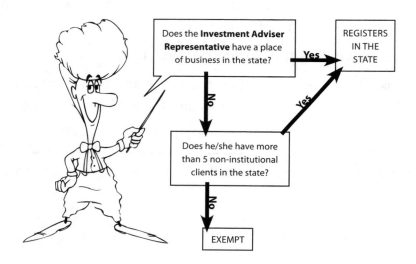

Issuer: anyone who issues or proposes to issue any security.

J

Joint account: investment account owned by more than one investor.

Joint Tenants In Common: joint account in which the death of one owner causes his/her stated share of the account to pass to his/her estate.

Joint Tenants With Rights Of Survivorship: joint account in which the death of one owner causes his share to pass equally to the other owner(s).

K

Keogh plan: qualified retirement plan for sole proprietors.

K-1: tax form filed by owners of partnership and S-corp interests.

L

Liabilities: obligations that must be paid in the short- or long-term including mortgage balances, accounts payable, and pension obligations.

Liability: as in "civil liability," having to make a harmed investor whole by returning the price paid for the security or advice, plus interest and court costs, but minus any income received (in the case of a security).

Limit order: an order to buy or sell a security at a stated price (or better).

M

Management fee: a percentage of assets charged by an investment adviser as compensation for managing a portfolio.

Market maker: a firm that provides a "market" in a security by continuously displaying both a bid and an asked price that allow willing buyers and sellers to trade a certain number of shares or bonds. NASDAQ functions only because there are market makers willing to buy and sell NASDAQ securities at stated prices.

Market manipulation: using rumors, scams, etc., to push the price of a security up or down. Includes words like: *pegging, capping, painting the tape, wash sales, matched purchases.*

Market order: an order to purchase or sell securities without stipulating any price conditions.

Market risk: the risk that the market price of a security will drop due to unpredictable events including war, famine, weather disasters, or general panic; also called "systematic risk."

Margin account: type of account in which investors borrow money through their broker-dealer to purchase securities by making a deposit rather than paying in full and pledging the securities as collateral for the loan.

Margin agreement: paperwork signed by a margin customer indicating that he understands the risks involved with margin but wants to do it anyway.

Material facts: information that an investor needs when trying to decide whether to purchase, sell, or hold a security.

Material inside information: non-public information that would reasonably affect the market price of a security and, therefore, may not be disseminated or acted upon.

Municipal bond: a bond issued by a state, city, school district, park district, or other taxing authority.

Money market: short-term debt securities with maturities of one year or less, usually 270 days or less.

N

National Securities Markets Improvement Act: NSMIA, legislation that separated federal covered securities and federal covered advisers from those subject to state registration requirements.

New Issue Market: another name for the primary market in which transactions are performed for the benefit of the issuer, e.g., IPOs and additional offerings of securities.

Nolo contendere: a Latin phrase you hope you've never had to use in the past when filling out a U-4 form. An individual who has pled *nolo contendere* (no contest) to felony charges or misdemeanors relevant to the securities industry can be statutorily disqualified and either lose his license or have his application denied.

Non-exempt: has no exemption; registration requirements <u>do</u> apply.

Non-issuer transaction: not for the benefit of an issuer of securities but a transaction between two investors, possibly a former CEO offering restricted shares to the public after leaving the company.

Non-punitive termination: leaving a place of employment because you want to—not because you got in trouble.

Non-qualified variable annuity: a variable annuity contract purchased with after-tax dollars.

Non-recourse loan: a loan made to a partnership for which the partners are not personally liable.

O

Odd lot: a small order for securities, e.g., an order for fewer than 100 shares of common or 10 shares of preferred stock.

Offer, Offer to sell: an attempt to dispose of a security for value, or the solicitation of an offer to buy a security.

OID: an original issue discount bond, including zero coupons such as Treasury STRIPS.

Order confirmation: document that confirms a purchase or sale of securities through a broker-dealer delivered to the customer in paper or electronic format no later than settlement/completion of a transaction.

Order ticket: paper or electronic form used by a registered representative to enter a customer's purchase or sale order for securities. Essential information includes: buy or sell, stock symbol, market/limit/stop order, agent's ID #, customer account #, trade and settlement date, whether solicited—unsolicited—discretionary.

OSJ: office of supervisory jurisdiction, the stated compliance office for various broker-dealer branch offices.

P

Painting the tape: a form of market manipulation.

Parity: when the market price for a convertible bond is exactly equal to the market value of the underlying shares of stock that the bond converts to.

Passive income: income that is not eligible for an IRA contribution, including rental income or limited partnership interests.

Penny stock: a thinly traded, low-priced stock that is not listed/traded on a major exchange.

Person: not dead, a minor, or mentally incompetent; a legal entity.

Preliminary prospectus: AKA "red herring." This is the prospectus before the final public offering price (POP) and the release date have been determined.

Private placement: unregistered securities sold through a transaction exempt from the Securities Act of 1933 and/or the Uniform Securities Act.

Prospectus: a disclosure document that provides relevant, important, *material* facts about a security to a buyer.

R

Render: to make and deliver, as in "to render" investment advice.

Rescission: the act of rescinding a previous transaction by which the seller repurchases the securities sold in violation of the securities act plus interest less any income the security might but almost certainly didn't pay to the buyer.

Risk-averse: an investor interested first of all in avoiding loss of principal whether actual or "just on paper."

S

Sale/sell: includes every contract of sale of, contract to sell, or disposition of, a security or interest in a security for value (verbatim from Uniform Securities Act).

Settlement: completion of a securities transaction, when the buyer of a security is officially recognized as the owner by the transfer agent.

Solicit: attempt to find investors or advisory clients through marketing, advertising, and sales efforts.

Solicitor: someone who tries to obtain advisory clients for an investment adviser. All states require solicitors to register as investment adviser representatives, except the states that don't.

Subpoena: a court or Administrative demand to appear at a hearing/trial or turn over documents *now*.

T

Tippee: the person who has received insider information.

Tipper: the guy who told him.

Treasury security: a security guaranteed by the United States Treasury, including T-bills, T-notes, and T-bonds.

Treasury stock: stock that was issued but later repurchased by the issuer to reduce the number of outstanding shares.

U

Unit Investment Trust: a type of investment company security, distinct from a face amount certificate or a management company. No board of directors.

UGMA account: an account established by an adult for the benefit of a minor child who will have title to the assets upon reaching the state's age of majority (adulthood).

UTMA account: an account established by an adult for the benefit of a minor child who will have title to the assets usually at age 25.

Uniform Prudent Investor Act: a model act that spells out fiduciary obligations for investment managers managing trust accounts.

Uniform Securities Act: a model act that keeps securities acts uniform.

V

Variable Annuity: an annuity contract in which the insurance company does not guarantee investment results, invests annuitants' net payments in the separate account, and passes off investment choices and risks to the annuitant, who is hoping to use the stock and bond markets to achieve better returns than those offered on a fixed annuity.

Variable Life Insurance: both a life insurance contract and a security in which cash value and death benefit are tied to results from investments chosen by the policy owner.

Venture capital: groups of rich people and institutions that invest in promising companies at various stages of development.

Viatical Settlement: a somewhat disturbing investment in which somebody buys somebody else's life insurance policy and cashes it in when the insured dies, the sooner the better.

W

Wash sale rule: IRS rule requiring an investor who sells a security at a capital loss to wait 30 days before and after the sale to repurchase the security or a security that is substantially identical (calls, convertible bonds, etc.).

Withdrawal: a non-punitive order filed by an agent, broker-dealer, adviser, etc., to officially withdraw registration; recognized by the Administrator.

Z

Zero coupon: a bond that does not pay interest, but, rather the bond's par value increases over time.

Zero interest: what most people have in taking the Series 63 exam.

Practice Final 1

1. **All of the following are considered dishonest or unethical except**
   A. an agent describes an investment company share as "no-load" even though the fund charges a 12b-1 fee equal to .25% of average net assets
   B. an agent describes an investment company share as "no-load" even though the fund charges a 12b-1 fee greater than .25% of average net assets
   C. an agent selling investment company shares with a front-end load fails to disclose breakpoints
   D. an agent selling investment company shares with a front-end load fails to disclose a Letter of Intent that reduces sales charges

2. **Which of the following is/are considered dishonest or unethical practices?**
   A. an agent discloses the current yield of a mutual fund without clearly explaining the difference between current yield and total return
   B. an agent states that an investment company's performance is similar to that of a savings account, CD, or other bank deposit account without disclosing that the shares of the investment company are not guaranteed or insured by the FDIC or any other governmental agency
   C. an agent states that a government bond mutual fund portfolio holds securities guaranteed against default by the U.S. Government without also disclosing other risks such as interest rate risk
   D. all choices listed

3. **Under the Uniform Securities Act, to say that a security is exempt means that:**
   A. transactions involving the security are not subject to the antifraud provisions of the Act
   B. an agent who sells the security does not have to be registered with the state
   C. a broker-dealer that underwrites a new issue of the securities does not need to be registered with the state
   D. the security does not need to be registered with the state to be sold there

4. **What is true of Investment Company shares?**

   A. delivering a prospectus to the prospect satisfies all disclosure requirements of an agent/broker-dealer

   B. no-load mutual fund shares often involve 12b-1 fees

   C. sales charges, but not operating expenses, must be disclosed in the mutual fund prospectus

   D. capital gains are commonly combined with income distributions in order to calculate the yield of an investment company share

5. **According to NASAA policy statements, all of the following concerning dissemination of information on products and services via the Internet are true except**

   A. information on products/services may be disseminated to residents of states where the firm and/or representative are unregistered

   B. transactions via the Internet are not allowed with residents of states where the firm and/or representative are unregistered

   C. the Interpretative Order concerning Internet communications applies equally to state-registered persons and persons not subject to the Administrator's jurisdiction as a result of NSMIA

   D. the broker-dealer or investment adviser must first authorize the dissemination of information on products/services and retains responsibility for the communications

6. **Which TWO of the following represent true statements?**

   I. Investment advisers may be compensated as a percentage of assets under continuous, supervisory management

   II. The Administrator has no power over federal covered advisers engaging in fraudulent, deceptive activities

   III. Federal covered advisers are subject to notice filing fees

   IV. Investment advisers are excluded from the definition of "broker-dealer"

   A. I, III

   B. I, IV

   C. II, IV

   D. II, III

7. **An investment adviser may typically borrow money or securities from all of the following except**

   A.   a broker-dealer

   B.   a financial institution engaged in the business of making loans

   C.   an affiliate of the adviser

   D.   a client

8. **Which of the following statements is true concerning investment advisers with custody of client securities and/or funds?**

   A.   they are regulated solely by banking regulators

   B.   advisers may only maintain custody of mutual fund shares

   C.   at least once per year the adviser must schedule an inspection by a CPA or public accountant, to commence within 48 hours

   D.   unless the Administrator specifically prohibits custody of client assets, the adviser may take custody of client assets if written notice is sent to the Administrator

9. **Which of the following represent true statements concerning broker-dealers operating on the premises of a bank, savings & loan, or other financial institution?**

   I.   Wherever practical, the broker-dealer services shall be conducted in a physical location distinct from the area in which the financial institution's retail deposits are taken

   II.   In all cases the broker-dealer must clearly distinguish its services from the financial institution's retail deposit-taking activities

   III. In those situations where physical space is limited, the broker-dealer may occupy the same physical space where retail deposits are taken, provided that the broker-dealer takes greater care to distinguish its services from those of the financial institution

   IV.   An arrangement whereby a broker-dealer operates on the premises of a financial institution taking retail deposits is referred to as a "networking arrangement"

   A.   I, II, III, IV

   B.   I, II

   C.   I, II, III

   D.   II, IV

10. **Which of the following persons would be defined as investment advisers subject to registration under the Uniform Securities Act?**
    A.   an advisory firm with no office in the state who has five non-accredited clients residing in the state
    B.   an advisory firm with no office in the state who advises for compensation 11 pension funds as to the value or advisability of investing in particular securities
    C.   an advisory firm with an office in the state who advises for compensation 11 pension funds as to the value or advisability of investing in particular securities
    D.   an advisory firm in the state whose sole clients are Investment Companies as defined under the Investment Company Act of 1940

11. **All of the following are persons except**
    A.   a joint-stock company
    B.   a federal covered investment adviser
    C.   a building & loan organization
    D.   a 7-year-old child

12. **Which of the following persons would be defined as an "agent" under the Uniform Securities Act?**
    A.   a broker-dealer with an office in the state whose clients include pension funds, mutual funds, and other institutional investors
    B.   a part-owner of a broker-dealer who performs no sales activities
    C.   a broker-dealer selling only non-exempt securities to clients not averse to the risks involved
    D.   an individual representing an issuer in the sale of the issuer's stock to employees for which a commission is received

13. Which two of the following would most likely be defined as investment advisers under the Uniform Securities Act?

I.   An economics professor with an active consulting business providing regular advice to pension funds as to which money managers to retain for the fund

II.   A bank

III. A building & loan institution

IV.   An accountant who frequently advises clients as to the advisability of investing in particular securities for compensation

A.   I, II

B.   I, IV

C.   II, III

D.   II, IV

14. Under the Uniform Securities Act, which of the following persons would be considered broker-dealers subject to registration requirements?

A.   an agent selling promissory notes maturing in more than 12 months

B.   a bank selling products insured by the FDIC

C.   a firm with no office in the state that effects transactions with 7 pension funds in the state

D.   a firm with no office in the state that effects 17 transactions with non-accredited investors who are residents of the state

15. Which two of the following are securities?

I.   Variable Annuity

II.   Fixed Annuity

III. Equity Straddle

IV.   Commodity Futures Contract

A.   II, IV

B.   II, III

C.   I, III

D.   I, IV

16. In which of the following instances has a sale of securities been effected?

A.   an investment representative offers variable annuities to several individuals

B.   an individual makes an actual gift of non-assessable stock

C.   a partnership makes an actual gift of assessable stock

D.   a fiduciary pledges shares of NASDAQ stock as collateral to secure a loan for a client

17. In which of the following cases has an investment representative sold a security?

   A. an agent of a broker-dealer donates convertible preferred stock to a tax-exempt foundation

   B. a broker-dealer sells common stock to an individual client

   C. an agent sells a client a fixed annuity

   D. an agent sells an interest in a profit participation plan

18. The Administrator may do all of the following except

   A. issue injunctions

   B. investigate outside the state

   C. enforce subpoenas from out-of-state Administrators

   D. proceed against violators even over 5th Amendment objections

19. The Administrator may do which of the following?

   A. publish violations without consent of the respondent(s)

   B. issue subpoenas

   C. seek judicial injunctions in the case of contumacy

   D. all choices listed

20. The Administrator would have authority in all of the following cases except

   A. offer to sell originated in the state

   B. offer to sell was directed into the state

   C. payment for securities was made from the state

   D. an offer to sell was accepted in the state

21. All of the following Administrative orders usually stem from unethical practices in the securities business except

   A. denial

   B. revocation

   C. suspension

   D. cancellation

22. **All of the following orders require prior notice, opportunity for hearing, and written finding of fact and conclusions of law except**
    A. denial
    B. revocation
    C. suspension
    D. summary suspension

23. **All of the following orders require prior notice and opportunity for hearing except**
    A. stop order
    B. denial
    C. cease and desist
    D. revocation

24. **All of the following will likely lead to denial, revocation, or suspension except**
    A. an individual completing Form U-4 answers "no" when asked if she has ever been convicted of wrongful taking of money because the conviction happened 12 years earlier
    B. an individual has been convicted of a non-securities-related felony 8 years ago
    C. an individual has been convicted of a non-securities-related misdemeanor 2 years ago
    D. the agent is insolvent

25. **All of the following can lead to denial of a registration except**
    A. the individual is insolvent
    B. the broker-dealer is enjoined by a court of law
    C. the individual lacks experience in the securities business
    D. the broker-dealer was subject to adjudication 7 years ago under federal securities law

26. **Which of the following is true concerning criminal penalties under the Uniform Securities Act?**
    A. there is no statute of limitations for securities fraud
    B. the statute of limitations for securities fraud is 2 years from discovery or 3 years from the alleged event
    C. ignorance of the law/rule has no bearing in criminal proceedings
    D. the maximum penalty is 3 years in jail, $5,000 fine, or both

27. **Which of the following companies will most likely use qualification to register their securities for sale in the state?**

   A.   XYZ Corporation, which plans to effect an IPO in all 50 states

   B.   ABC Corporation, which plans to effect an IPO in the state of Kentucky

   C.   GE, a listed company, plans to effect an additional offering of securities in all 50 states

   D.   MSFT, a NASDAQ company, plans a rights offering in all 50 states

28. **Which of the following is/are true statements concerning securities offerings in a state?**

   I.   The Administrator must be informed of all states where the security will be offered

   II.   The Administrator must be informed of the total amount of securities offered in all states

   III. The Administrator must be informed of the total amount of securities offered in the state

   IV.   Securities offered by qualification or coordination may be placed in escrow and proceeds impounded until the issuer receives the specified amount

   A.   I, II, III, IV

   B.   I, III, IV

   C.   I, III

   D.   II, IV

29. **If a company plans to register its securities by filing, all of the following may be required except**

   A.   a statement as to the company's eligibility for registration by filing

   B.   no failure to make a debt payment or preferred dividend payment in the preceding 36 months

   C.   securities trading at no less than $5 per share

   D.   company must have a net profit margin of not less than 5%

30. **All of the following methods of securities registration would lead to an effective date determined by the SEC except**

   A.   filing

   B.   notice filing

   C.   coordination

   D.   qualification

31. Which of the following securities would most likely be subject to registration requirements under Blue Sky law?

A.   stock listed on NYSE

B.   stock listed on AMEX

C.   NASDAQ stock

D.   non-NASDAQ OTC stock

32. All of the following are federal-covered securities except

A.   GE

B.   MSFT

C.   mutual fund shares

D.   OTC Bulletin Board stock

33. All of the following persons are investment adviser representatives except

A.   individual employed by a federal covered adviser who determines recommendations for clients

B.   individual selling the advisory services of a federal covered adviser

C.   individual performing clerical work for an investment adviser

D.   individual who helps determine recommendations to clients

34. A federal covered adviser may be required to do all of the following except

A.   pay fees to the state

B.   submit a consent to service of process

C.   provide notice to the state

D.   submit to regular inspections by the Administrator

35. An offer to buy that is unsolicited would include:

A.   a person purchasing securities after receiving a prospectus in the mail

B.   a person purchasing securities after reading a tombstone advertisement

C.   neither choice

D.   both choices

36. Under the Uniform Securities Act, an issuer of registered securities is required to file statements or reports with the Administrator as long as some of the securities remain:

A. unsold

B. outstanding

C. in the hands of insiders

D. diluted

37. All of the following are prohibited practices except

A. an investment representative recommends municipal bonds to a client based on the prima facie evidence that the woman wore expensive jewelry and drove a foreign sports car to their last meeting

B. an agent feels it is likely that a company like GRZ will be NYSE-listed and so she indicates to her clients and prospects that GRZ is a listed company

C. An investment adviser takes custody of client funds in the absence of a rule against custody, informing the Administrator in writing

D. An investment adviser representative tells a prospect that she has been approved by the Administrator to provide both technical and fundamental analysis on NYSE-listed securities

38. Commissions charged at Bobby Brown Broker-Dealers are normally $45 per trade. Recently, JoAnn Jackson was charged a commission of $75 for purchasing 1,000 shares of XYZL securities, which trade regularly on the OTC Bulletin Board. Which of the following statements are true of this situation?

I. This is a fraudulent activity, punishable by five years in jail and a $3,000 fine

II. The higher commission must have been disclosed to Ms. Jackson before effecting the transaction

III. Ms. Jackson must have given her consent to the higher commission rate before effecting the transaction

IV. Bulletin Board stocks should involve lower, not higher, commissions and/or markups

A. I, IV

B. II, III

C. II, III, IV

D. I, II

39. **Your client has become fearful that XYZ common stock could plummet over the next several days. You are convinced that XYZ is a solid company about to report higher earnings, so when the client tells you to sell out the position, you over-ride her decision, based on the suitability information obtained on the new account form, and decide not to sell the security. What is true of this situation?**

    A. this is an acceptable practice based on accurate use of suitability information

    B. this is a prohibited activity

    C. this is a fraudulent activity

    D. this is an example of trading on material inside information

40. **Under the Uniform Securities Act, which of the following would NOT have to be disclosed when filing a registration by qualification?**

    A. A statement analyzing the issuer's profit margin over the last three years compared to the profit margins of its primary competitors

    B. The capitalization and long-term debt of the issuer and any significant subsidiary

    C. The general character and location of the issuer's business and a statement of the general competitive conditions within the industry or business in which it operates

    D. The estimated cash proceeds to be received by the issuer from the offering

41. **All of the following activities by an investment adviser are prohibited except**

    A. entering into a contract that clearly states compensation shall be a percentage of assets taken as of a specific date

    B. asking clients to sign exculpatory provisions

    C. failing to include a non-assignability clause in a client contract

    D. disclosing the identity, affairs, or investment of a client to a third party without consent of client or court order

42. **Which of the following is a true statement concerning broker-dealers?**

    A. a broker-dealer is always a natural person

    B. all broker-dealers must post fidelity/surety bonds

    C. financial requirements must be paid in cash

    D. all broker-dealers must meet certain capital requirements and/or post fidelity/surety bonds

43. None of the following persons is an "agent" except

    A.   an individual representing the City of Chicago in selling Chicago Revenue Bonds

    B.   an individual representing a broker-dealer selling Chicago Revenue Bonds

    C.   an individual working for Microsoft selling Microsoft stock to members of the Board of Directors and receiving no commissions

    D.   an individual representing Microsoft in transactions with underwriters

44. Which of the following persons are not agents?

    A.   an individual selling exempt securities for a broker-dealer

    B.   an individual selling IBM stock to IBM employees for which a small commission is received

    C.   a partner or officer of a broker-dealer who effects sales

    D.   an individual representing the Government of Montreal, Canada, in selling Montreal revenue bonds

45. Which two of the following Administrative orders most likely indicate that a person has engaged in conduct inconsistent with just and equitable principles of trade in the securities business?

    I.   Denial

    II.   Cancellation

    III.   Withdrawal

    IV.   Revocation

    A.   I, II

    B.   II, III

    C.   I, IV

    D.   II, IV

46. Which of the following is a true statement concerning civil liabilities under the Uniform Securities Act?

    A.   after receiving a written offer from the seller, the buyer may not sue if no action is taken within 15 days

    B.   the Administrator's ruling on the matter is final and binding on the plaintiff

    C.   if the plaintiff dies, his/her children are prevented from pursuing the matter

    D.   the buyer is entitled to recover the price paid for the security/advice plus interest less any dividends/interest received

47. A customer was sold an unregistered, non-exempt security. Under the Uniform Securities Act:

I.   The customer is entitled to recover the amount paid for the advice and securities, plus court costs, reasonable attorney fees, and an unspecified amount for pain and suffering

II. The customer is entitled to recover the amount paid for the advice and securities, plus court costs, reasonable attorney fees, interest, minus any dividends/interest received from the securities

III. The customer may not sue if the advice was rendered by a federal covered adviser

IV. The customer may not sue if she has known of the illegal nature of the sale for 25 months

A. II, IV
B. I, IV
C. II, III
D. I, III

48. Karen Crenshaw discovers on April 10, 2007, that she was sold an unregistered, non-exempt security. It is now July 3, 2009, and therefore

A. Karen still has the remainder of five years to pursue the matter before the statute of limitations precludes civil action

B. Karen may not sue the advisory firm at this point

C. Karen still has three years to pursue the matter before the statue of limitations precludes civil action

D. Karen still has the remainder of two years to pursue the matter

49. All of the following are defined as securities under the Uniform Securities Act except

A. a certificate representing a 12% interest in a prize-winning racehorse
B. a certificate of participation in 1,000 head of cattle
C. a collateral trust certificate
D. a fixed annuity

50. The Sheriff of Macon County has seized the assets of Billy Ray Roberts. Billy Ray's assets to be auctioned off at the upcoming pig roast and asset liquidation party in Macon County include three Corvette convertibles, several dozen vintage collectible firearms, and a sizable portfolio of stocks and bonds. With whom must the securities be registered before liquidating proceedings commence?

A. Administrator

B. SEC

C. NYSE

D. no one, as this is an exempt transaction

51. What is true of a consent to service of process?

I. If a registered person violates any provisions of the Uniform Securities Act, actions against that person may commence by the service of process upon the Administrator

II. Only the most ethical professionals may obtain such consent to service of process

III. It may be used in lieu of a fidelity bond

IV. Filing the consent to service of process is equivalent to appointing the Administrator as the person's true and lawful attorney upon whom may be served all lawful process in any action against the person

A. I, IV

B. II, III

C. II only

D. III only

52. If a broker-dealer or investment adviser goes out of business, the Administrator will most likely issue which of the following orders?

A. revocation

B. withdrawal

C. suspension

D. cancellation

53. If an applicant files a withdrawal, the withdrawal becomes effective

I.   As soon as the Administrator orders

II. No later than 30 days after filing

III. Provided no revocations are pending

IV. Provided no suspensions are pending

A.   I, III

B.   II, III

C.   I, IV

D.   I, II, III, IV

54. Which of the following represents a violation of the Uniform Securities Act?

A.   an agent shares commissions with other registered agents at the firm

B.   accepting an unsolicited order for an unregistered, non-exempt security

C.   soliciting orders for unregistered, non-exempt securities

D.   an investment adviser takes custody of client funds in the absence of a rule prohibiting custody

55. An investment representative took a leave of absence from her broker-dealer employer in order to complete a 3-year MBA program. Now that the degree has been completed, the investment representative may

A.   return to work at the broker-dealer provided that her license was properly parked at the firm during her absence

B.   return to work at the broker-dealer provided that she earned her degree from an accredited university

C.   not return to work without posting a surety bond for $25,000

D.   not return to work as an investment representative before completing required licensing exams

56. Which of the following is a true statement?

    A.   a person who has operated as a broker-dealer for three years is automatically qualified to operate as an investment adviser

    B.   an individual who has five years' experience as an agent is automatically qualified to operate as an investment adviser

    C.   if the Administrator grants a broker-dealer a license, he/she has, in effect, also granted an investment advisory license to that firm

    D.   if the Administrator determines that a broker-dealership is not qualified to operate as an investment adviser—even though the firm has three years' experience as a broker-dealer—the Administrator may condition the applicant's registration as a broker-dealer upon their not transacting business in this state as an investment adviser

57. Which of the following is a true statement concerning a summary suspension of a registration?

    A.   the Administrator may not summarily suspend a registration until the applicant has had an opportunity for a hearing

    B.   an applicant whose registration has been summarily suspended must request a hearing within 15 days of receiving notification

    C.   when the Administrator summarily suspends a registration, the applicant must be notified promptly and informed that if a hearing is requested in writing, it shall be granted within 15 days after the receipt of the request

    D.   only a court of law can summarily suspend a registration

58. A retail customer was sold a security by an investment representative who told her that XLU, Inc., had reported increased earnings the past 8 consecutive fiscal quarters, when, in fact, XLU had reported net losses in 3 of the past 5 quarters. What is true of this situation?

    A.   it was a fraudulent sale and the customer may sue to recover the amount paid for the security, plus interest, less any income received from the security

    B.   it is not prohibited if the security is exempt

    C.   it is not prohibited if the transaction is exempt

    D.   it was fraudulent, but the customer may not sue if she no longer has the security in her possession

59. All of the following transactions are exempt except

A. an offer and sale of securities to 17 pension funds and 10 non-accredited investors in the state who buy for investment purposes and for which no commissions are paid by non-accredited buyers

B. a sheriff liquidates securities at a public auction

C. a receiver in bankruptcy liquidates an insolvent company's portfolio

D. an investment adviser sells listed securities to several high-net-worth individuals

60. Which of the following is a true statement concerning investment advisory firms established as partnerships?

A. if a partner with a minority interest withdraws from the partnership, assignment of contract has occurred in violation of the Uniform Securities Act

B. if a partner with a minority interest withdraws from the partnership, customers do not need to be informed

C. if a partner with a minority interest withdraws from the partnership, customers need to be informed

D. if a partner with a majority interest withdraws from the partnership, assignment of contract has not occurred

ANSWERS TO PRACTICE FINAL 1

1. **ANSWER:** A

   EXPLANATION: the 12b-1 fee can't exceed .25% (25 basis points) of "average net assets" if the fund wants to call itself "no-load." Features like LOIs and breakpoint schedules must be pointed out to the customer.

2. **ANSWER:** D

   EXPLANATION: yield is just income distributions divided by share price. Never include capital gains in that figure and be clear with your customer about the difference between income distributions (yield) and total return. Total return factors in income plus the increase/decrease in market value. So, a security that is paying a nice yield of 5% could have a total return of, say, negative 15%. Therefore, the full story needs to be told. Also, you can't compare an investment to a CD or bank account without also pointing out that, unlike with the bank product, a mutual fund, stock, or bond could easily become worthless. And, even though US Government bonds won't default, investors will see the market values drop when interest rates rise.

3. **ANSWER:** D

   EXPLANATION: an exemption only means that the security is not required to be registered. To imply that it means anything more than that is a violation.

4. **ANSWER:** B

   EXPLANATION: "no-load" funds usually do involve 12b-1 fees that cover the same distribution expenses (printing, advertising, mailing, selling) that sales loads cover. They can still call themselves "no-load" as long as the 12b-1 fee doesn't exceed .25% of average net assets.

5. **ANSWER:** C

   EXPLANATION: not surprising that the firm has to first authorize all communications their reps make about products/services provided by the firm. "C" is the answer because the order does not apply equally to federal covered advisers. The

Administrator has very little authority over federal covered advisers who are not defrauded investors.

6. **ANSWER:** A

   EXPLANATION: the Administrator has power over anyone who commits securities fraud in his/her state. Federal covered advisers do pay notice filing fees; if not, the states would drop that requirement like a rock.

7. **ANSWER:** D

   EXPLANATION: are there some clients from whom an adviser can borrow money? Yes. But, you have to choose the answer that works best.

8. **ANSWER:** D

   EXPLANATION: at least once per year there must be a <u>surprise</u> audit of the adviser's books and records by the CPA, not a scheduled inspection. If the adviser knows it's coming, it's not much of an audit, right? It's not that advisers can only hold custody of certain types of securities. The issue is that if they want to maintain custody of any client securities, they have all kinds of regulatory issues to deal with. By the way, it's the transfer agent for a mutual fund who typically holds custody of mutual fund shares. Mutual fund shares aren't usually covered by SIPC because broker-dealers don't hold custody of them either. If advisers or broker-dealers maintain custody, they do not suddenly become banks subject only to banking regulators. They would still be broker-dealers and advisers subject to SEC, state, and SRO (in the case of broker-dealers) regulation.

9. **ANSWER:** A

   EXPLANATION: memorize it and keep moving.

10. **ANSWER:** C

    EXPLANATION: if the firm has no office in the state, it can deal with 5 non-accredited/non-institutional investors and as many institutional (pension fund, mutual fund, insurance company, bank, trust company, etc.) investors as they want. Once you see they have an office in the state, though, you know they're always going to be defined as investment advisers, unless they are federal covered.

11. **ANSWER:** D

    EXPLANATION: they're a "person" as long as they're not a minor, dead, or declared mentally incompetent by a court of law—as opposed to a former spouse.

12. **ANSWER:** D

    EXPLANATION: if the individual representing the issuer receives commissions or is hired specifically to do this work, he/she is defined as an agent of the issuer and must register. If he/she does NOT receive commissions and is not hired primarily to do this activity, he/she is NOT defined as an agent and does NOT have to register. Choices "A" and "C" can be eliminated as soon as you see the word "broker-dealer."

13. **ANSWER:** B

    EXPLANATION: often teachers and accountants are NOT defined as advisers, but that's only if the advice is incidental to their services. In choice "I" and "IV" both professionals are clearly providing advice, and even if you disagree, what choice do you have with the four cards you've been dealt?

14. **ANSWER:** D

    EXPLANATION: choices "A" and "B" can be eliminated since B/D's are never agents or issuers. They're all separate players, like the pitcher, catcher, and first baseman.

15. **ANSWER:** C

    EXPLANATION: fixed annuities are insurance products, not securities. Commodities futures are also not securities. An "equity straddle" is a derivative in which an investor purchases a call and a put with the same strike price and same expiration month, hoping to profit if the stock moves up or down by more than the total premiums paid.

16. **ANSWER:** C

    EXPLANATION: eliminate choice "A" because an "offer" is not a sale; it's merely an attempt to sell or the "solicitation of any offer to buy." A "purported gift of assessable stock" is considered both an offer AND a sale. A gift of non-assessable stock is neither.

17. **ANSWER:** D

    EXPLANATION: you can eliminate choice "B" right off, since broker-dealers are not agents and vice versa. You can eliminate choice "A" when you see the words, "donate to a tax-exempt foundation." And, you can eliminate choice "C" because a FIXED annuity is NOT a security. And, the Uniform Securities Act specifically mentions "participation in any profit-sharing agreement" in its list of "securities."

18. **ANSWER:** A

EXPLANATION: only a court can issue an injunction.

19. **ANSWER:** D

EXPLANATION: the Administrator can't issue an injunction, but if somebody is ignoring his authority (contumacy), he can seek an injunction. Denial, suspension, and revocation orders are all public record; the Administrator loves to publish these things on their website, in printed bulletins, etc.

20. **ANSWER:** C

EXPLANATION: think D-O-A. The Administrator of a state has authority when the offer is D-directed into the state, O-originates in the state, or A-is accepted in the state. The state where payment is made is not relevant.

21. **ANSWER:** D

EXPLANATION: "cancellation" just means the person can not be located, no longer exists, or has been declared mentally incompetent by a court of law. If the person stopped sending in their renewal forms with the required fees, the state could cancel the registration, too. But, they only deny, suspend, or revoke when it's in the public interest, it provides the public some form of protection, and the person did something really sneaky, stupid, or otherwise not a good idea.

22. **ANSWER:** D

EXPLANATION: what's going on is so out-of-control that the registration will go into limbo until the hearing has been held and the matter has been finally decided. A "summary suspension of a registration pending final determination." The other three actions require what the stem of the question is stating.

23. **ANSWER:** C

EXPLANATION: it's like the principal of a school telling a suspected bully he has to go sit in the office a while because it looks like he might be thinking of hitting another kid later on in the day. Cease and desist. We'll sort it out later, but for now cease and desist. The other orders require prior notice and an opportunity for a hearing.

24. **ANSWER:** C

EXPLANATION: if the misdemeanor is not considered "securities-related," the individual does not even have to disclose it, but if it's a felony of any kind, no way. And, if the misdemeanor involved things such as forgery, theft, embezzlement, etc., that would be a "securities-related misdemeanor" that must be disclosed on Form U-4. If the agent is insolvent, that could be a reason to take him out of the business.

25. **ANSWER:** C

EXPLANATION: if they didn't let beginners get started, how would anyone ever gain experience?

26. **ANSWER:** D

EXPLANATION: three years, five grand. "A" is false because there IS a statue of limitations—five years. "B" is false because that's the statute of limitations for civil liability, not criminal. And "C" is false because if the ignorant person can conclusively prove just how ignorant he/she was of the rule or order he/she violated, that person cannot be sentenced to jail. Although they can be fined and made to wear a big, scarlet "I" on their lapels for a period of time prescribed by the Administrator.

27. **ANSWER:** B

EXPLANATION: you can see that XYZ, GE, and MSFT are all going inter-state, which is the jurisdiction of the SEC. So they have to register with the SEC. ABC will only deal with one state in their intra-state offering. So, they'll use qualification.

28. **ANSWER:** B

EXPLANATION: what's the deal with "impounding proceeds?" Well, there's actually an adopted policy statement called "Impoundment of Proceeds" under NASAA's library. Not sure how far they'll go into that material, but you should know that some securities offerings have to be done through an escrow account where the proceeds are impounded (not released) until the issuer has raised what they said they were trying to raise. If they say they're raising $10 million and have only raised $1 million, the state isn't going to let them take the cash and walk away. The proceeds would be returned to the buyers, plus interest earned in escrow, and the whole offering would be canceled.

Remember, the states don't like fly-by-night operations raising a little bit of money, grabbing the proceeds, and maybe fleeing the state.

29. **ANSWER:** D

   EXPLANATION: choice D is not a requirement. It's not really worth commenting beyond that.

30. **ANSWER:** D

   EXPLANATION: qualification puts the issuer solely on the Administrator's turf. The other three are really dealing with the SEC and sort of keeping the Administrator informed, too. So those effective dates are always concurrent with federal…unless there are problems, like stop orders.

31. **ANSWER:** D

   EXPLANATION: the other three are listed and/or NASDAQ, which gives them the "manual" or "blue chip exemption" and makes them "federal covered" securities.

32. **ANSWER:** D

   EXPLANATION: GE is listed; MSFT is NASDAQ, and both are federal covered because of their "blue chip" exemption. That just means they deal with the SEC, which is plenty to deal with, by golly. Investment company shares (mutual funds, UITs, variable contracts) are federal covered and they may be required to do a "notice filing," but that's not a registration—just a filing of notice. If an OTC stock is "Non-NASDAQ," it gets no break from registration requirements.

33. **ANSWER:** C

   EXPLANATION: if the employee is doing "clerical/ministerial" work, that individual is excluded from the definition. But if they're selling the services of the firm or doing anything that smacks of analysis/money management—or supervising those folks who do that egghead stuff—these employees are all investment adviser representatives, even though they wish they weren't.

34. **ANSWER:** D

   EXPLANATION: choice "D" is going too far—it suggests that the federal covered adviser is under the jurisdiction of the Administrator, which it isn't. The adviser firm lets the state know they're in the state. They pay a fee, because that always makes the states real happy. And they provide a consent to service of process because the Administrator has authority to enforce antifraud regulations on ANYONE.

35. **ANSWER:** B

EXPLANATON: if you send an investor a prospectus, you are making an offer to sell the security. A tombstone advertisement has a caveat at the top clarifying that this announcement is neither an offer to sell nor a solicitation of any offer to buy a security.

36. **ANSWER:** A

EXPLANATION: the Administrator can require quarterly progress reports from the issuer until all the securities have been sold.

37. **ANSWER:** C

EXPLANATION: choice "C" describes exactly how an adviser should proceed when taking custody. No rule against it? Go ahead and take custody, as long as you inform the Administrator in writing. Choice "A" doesn't sound like an acceptable procedure, does it? The client could have rented the jewelry and the sports car, hoping to get preferential treatment from the firm. You need more tangible financial information than "she looked real rich" before recommending municipal securities.

38. **ANSWER:** B

EXPLANATION: do you see anything "fraudulent" here? Did anybody lie about anything? Markups on the illiquid stocks are higher (not lower) to compensate for the risk of holding them in the dealer's inventory.

39. **ANSWER:** B

EXPLANATION: an agent can not deliberately refuse to sell a stock that the customer wants to sell. You can talk and cajole to the point of exhaustion, but if the customer wants to sell her stock, you have to sell it. Suitability information helps you recommend securities, but you aren't a fiduciary running a trust account, right? There's no deceit (fraud) or material inside information here, so "C" and "D" can be eliminated.

40. **ANSWER:** A

EXPLANATION: the use of the proceeds must always be disclosed, and if the issuer ends up doing something else with the proceeds—like purchase a Cadillac

Escalade—they will regret it. Choice A does not jump out at you—that's why test-taking skills are so important

41. **ANSWER:** A

    EXPLANATION: a "percentage of assets" is the right way to charge for advisory services. An "exculpatory provision" would be an adviser's ill-advised attempt to get the client to hold him "without fault" no matter what. Bad idea. Advisory contracts cannot be assigned without client consent, and the contract must state that fact.

42. **ANSWER:** D

    EXPLANATION: the financial requirements can be paid in cash or securities, usually Treasury securities. Not ALL broker-dealers post fidelity/surety bonds. They either meet minimum net capital requirements, or they post a bond to cover the requirement and/or the shortfall.

43. **ANSWER:** B

    EXPLANATION: if the individual represents a broker-dealer, he's an agent.

44. **ANSWER:** D

    EXPLANATION: choices A-C were probably tempting, but if you looked at them hard enough, you saw that those folks were, in fact, agents. In choice "A" the individual represents a broker-dealer. In choice "B" the individual got a commission. In choice "C" the individual was effecting sales. Is there any way you could argue that those folks ARE NOT agents? No, so "D" has to be the answer. In choice "D" the individual represents an exempt issuer in the sale of exempt securities.

45. **ANSWER:** C

    EXPLANATION: cancellation means the applicant no longer exists physically or mentally. Nothing punitive about cancellation. Withdrawal means the applicant has changed her mind. Denial, suspension, and revocation orders usually result from something unethical being done.

46. **ANSWER:** D

    EXPLANATION: cause of action goes on even after the death of the plaintiff or the defendant. Plaintiff = the one who's upset. Defendant = the one accused of upsetting the plaintiff. So the kids could still pursue the matter. The Administrator does not decide civil matters—that's up to the courts. And the buyer has 30—not 15—days before it's too late to sue.

47. **ANSWER:** A

EXPLANATION: no "pain and suffering" is available. They get their money back plus interest, minus any dividends/interest received from the security.

48. **ANSWER:** B

EXPLANATION: the statute of limitations has kicked in: it's been more than 2 years from discovery. Sorry, Karen.

49. **ANSWER:** D

EXPLANATION: don't miss the lay-ups and/or slam-dunks. Fixed payments do NOT equal securities, so it's the "fixed annuity" you're looking for.

50. **ANSWER:** D

EXPLANATION: if a fiduciary is liquidating assets and some of the assets are securities, that's an exempt transaction.

51. **ANSWER:** A

EXPLANATION: you don't "achieve" a consent to service of process—you just provide one. And when you do, an aggrieved party can serve papers on the Administrator, which is just as good as serving them on you.

52. **ANSWER:** D

EXPLANATION: we've already gone over this fascinating point.

53. **ANSWER:** D

EXPLANATION: if there are no Administrative actions pending (like deny/revoke/suspend), then the withdrawal is effective no later than 30 days after filing, or as soon as the Administrator says so. Of course, if they find out over the next year that the person withdrawing was doing some bad stuff, they can see the withdrawal and raise it to a much more painful suspension or revocation.

54. **ANSWER:** C

EXPLANATION: "A" is okay. "D" is okay, as long as the Administrator is informed—if the question doesn't explicitly say the Administrator is NOT informed, don't assume he/she wasn't.

55. **ANSWER:** D

EXPLANATION: the securities regulators are about as fond of parking as the police hassling all drivers outside O'Hare Airport these days. You can't park it here, pal. Sorry about dat.

56. **ANSWER:** D

EXPLANATION: just something lifted directly from the Uniform Securities Act. Get yourself a copy at the NASAA website under "exams" and "FAQs."

57. **ANSWER:** C

EXPLANATION: another good one to memorize, lifted from the Uniform Securities Act.

58. **ANSWER:** A

EXPLANATION: if a customer buys a security that was not properly registered for sale in the state, or if the seller offers/sells the security in a fraudulent manner, the customer may recover the amount paid for the security and/or advice, plus reasonable attorneys' fees and court costs, plus interest, minus any income received from the security.

59. **ANSWER:** D

EXPLANATION: don't confuse a "federal covered security" with an "exempt transaction." A federal covered security simply has different registration requirements than those not federally covered. Review the list of exempt transactions, which includes sales by fiduciaries (sheriff, Marshal, Administrator, receiver), private placements (choice "A"), and several more.

60. **ANSWER:** C

EXPLANATION: two things going on with advisory firms structured as partnerships. If any member dies, withdraws or is admitted, customers must be informed. On a separate matter, if the change in ownership represents only a change in the minority owners, no assignment of contract has occurred. What's if it's a majority? Then, new contracts must be signed.

Practice Final 2

1. **Which of the following statements relating to the National Securities Markets Improvement Act (NSMIA) of 1996 is/are correct?**

    I.   seeks to promote efficiency and capital formation in the financial markets

    II. amended Section 18 of the Securities Act of 1933, creating a class of securities called "covered securities"

    III. seeks to provide more effective and less burdensome regulation

    A. I, III
    B. II
    C. III
    D. I, II, III

2. **Under the National Securities Markets Improvement Act of 1996 (NSMIA), all of the following are federal covered securities except**

    A. common stock listed on the American Stock Exchange
    B. common stock listed on the NASDAQ Capital Market System
    C. commercial paper of $150,000 denomination rated in the second highest credit tier
    D. a security sold to a qualified purchaser

3. **Under the National Securities Markets Improvement Act of 1996, all of the following are federal covered securities except**

    A. preferred stock issued by a corporation whose common stock is listed on NYSE
    B. preferred stock issued by a corporation whose common stock will trade on the NYSE after the primary offering period
    C. Real Estate Investment Trusts
    D. security issued to individuals participating in a variable life insurance contract

4.   Under the National Securities Markets Improvement Act of 1996, the SEC, in addition to protecting investors, is also responsible for

A.   promoting efficiency in securities markets

B.   promoting competition in the securities markets

C.   promoting capital formation

D.   all of the above

5.   A federal covered investment adviser is:

A.   an investment adviser registered with the SEC under the Investment Advisers Act of 1940

B.   excluded from the definition of "investment adviser" under the Investment Advisers Act of 1940

C.   both A and B

D.   neither A nor B

6.   The National Securities Markets Improvement Act of 1996 stipulates that, in addition to exchange-listed and NASDAQ securities, securities sold to qualified purchasers are federal covered. Qualified purchasers include

I.   Family-owned business with $5 million or more in investments

II.   Any person with $25 million or more in investments

III.   Any natural person with $5 million or more in investments

IV.   Any natural person who, jointly with his/her spouse, owns $5 million or more in investments

A.   I, III only

B.   III only

C.   I, II, III, IV

D.   II, IV only

7. **SEC Release IA-1092 declares that many industry professionals need to be registered as investment advisers, even though such professionals often do not think of their activities as falling under the definition of "investment adviser." The so-called "three-pronged" test used to determine if a person is, in fact, an investment adviser includes all of the following EXCEPT the person:**

   A. provides advice or analysis on securities either by making direct or indirect recommendations to clients or by providing research or opinions on securities or securities markets.

   B. receives compensation in any form for the advice provided.

   C. engages in a regular business of providing advice on securities.

   D. is registered under the Investment Advisers Act of 1940

8. **All of the following investment advisers would register with the state(s) in which they maintain a place of business except:**

   A. an adviser with $20 million of assets under management

   B. an adviser that does not provide supervisory services

   C. an adviser to a registered investment company

   D. a solicitor for other advisers who provides no advice to clients

9. **All of the following statements are true concerning federal covered advisers EXCEPT:**

   A. federal covered advisers may still be required to pay fees to the state(s) where they maintain a place of business or service 6 or more clients

   B. an investment adviser eligible for an exemption by rules or orders under the Investment Advisers Act of 1940 is federal covered

   C. federal covered advisers file form ADV with the SEC and are not required to provide copies to the states

   D. an adviser providing services in 30 or more states is federal covered

10. **Johanna Jackson and Associates would like to register as an investment adviser in State X. Which of the following represent requirements for registration of the firm?**

    I.   Filing a complete Form ADV with the state(s) in which the firm wants to offer services.

    II. Providing any state-specific forms required.

    III. Filing a Form U-4 application for each investment adviser representative who will provide services on behalf of the investment adviser.

    IV. Remitting all required fees for the investment adviser and the investment adviser representative.

    A. I only
    B. II only
    C. I, II, IV only
    D. I, II, III, IV

11. **A notice filing for a federal covered adviser is usually made by:**

    A. filing a complete copy of its Form ADV as filed with the SEC
    B. filing a Form U-4 application for each investment adviser representative who will provide services on behalf of the investment adviser
    C. payment of any required notice filing fees
    D. all choices listed

12. **An investment adviser does not wish to be deemed to have custody. However, last week a client inadvertently sent securities to the investment adviser and also a check made out to a third party. All of the following statements are true except:**

    A. the adviser must return the securities to the client within 3 business days to avoid being deemed to have had custody
    B. the adviser must forward the third-party check to the appropriate party within 24 hours
    C. to avoid being deemed to have had custody of the securities, the investment adviser may forward the securities to the qualified custodian
    D. even though the check is forwarded and the securities returned within specified time frames, additional records must be maintained by the adviser

13. **Joshua sells the services of a federal covered adviser with its principal office in State A. Once or twice per month Joshua meets with clients in State B. Therefore**

    A.   Joshua is not required to register in State B if he sees no more than 5 clients there in any 12-month period

    B.   Joshua must register in State B because he has a place of business in the state

    C.   Joshua is not required to register in State B because he works for a federal covered adviser

    D.   Joshua must register in State B because he has clients who are residents of the state

14. **Jones and Barker, a registered investment adviser, buys securities for the advisory omnibus trading account before allocating shares to the various client accounts. Which of the following represent(s) true statements concerning this practice?**

    A.   Jones and Barker must take great pains not to allocate the shares based on subsequent market movements

    B.   Jones and Barker may allocate those stocks with subsequent favorable price movements to accounts that pay performance fees and allocate those stocks with subsequent unfavorable price movements to accounts that pay a % of assets-only

    C.   both A and B

    D.   neither A nor B

15. **When crafting advertisements for her advisory firm, Linda Perkins should avoid making performance claims that could be deemed misleading. All of the following could be considered misleading performance claims except**

    A.   creating distorted performance results by constructing composites that include only selected profitable accounts, or are for selected profitable periods

    B.   failing to deduct the adviser's fees from performance calculations, without disclosure

    C.   stating performance figures without maintaining records to verify the figures.

    D.   the period measured is one calendar year or longer

16. **Which of the following represent violations for broker-dealers?**

    A.   executing an initial transaction in a margin account and then promptly obtaining the customer's signed margin agreement

    B.   executing a discretionary transaction and marking the trade ticket "unsolicited"

    C.   recommending a U.S. Government money market mutual fund to an investor who has not provided all requested suitability information

    D.   paying a bonus to the highest-producing registered representative at the firm

17. **Which of the following situations represent(s) an investment adviser's failure to implement a comprehensive system of internal controls and supervisory procedures?**
    A. an investment adviser's operating procedures allow a portfolio manager to value the securities recommended, or override values provided by a custodian, for purposes of reporting to clients and calculating advisory fees without any independent review
    B. an investment adviser does not have an oversight process to determine whether risks taken in managing client portfolios are consistent with each client's stated investment objectives and/or to measure and evaluate each client's risk tolerance
    C. both A and B
    D. neither A nor B

18. **All of the following activities are prohibited except**
    A. an agent requests that clients write checks for mutual fund investments in the name of the agent, who forwards payment to the mutual fund distributor within 24 hours
    B. an agent services accounts for only 5 retail clients in a state without being registered there
    C. an agent forwards written customer complaints received at the end of each financial quarter to the branch manager
    D. an agent purchases some of the same stocks recommended to customers

19. **Donna is insurance and securities licensed in State A and State B. Her coworker Jill is insurance licensed in State A and State B and securities licensed in State A. Jill and Donna both work for the same broker-dealer and plan to share commissions on variable annuity sales to clients in either state. Therefore:**
    A. as long as a principal approves the arrangement, the arrangement is acceptable
    B. since variable annuities are primarily insurance products, this arrangement is acceptable
    C. this is an unacceptable sharing arrangement
    D. this is an acceptable sharing arrangement

20. **Which of the following statements is/are true concerning the registration of investment advisers with offices in more than one state?**
    A. an investment adviser may operate in only one state, or it must register with the SEC
    B. no State may enforce any law or regulation that would require an investment adviser to maintain a higher minimum net capital or to post any bond in addition to any that is required under the laws of the State in which it maintains its principal place of business, if the investment adviser is registered or licensed as such in the State in which it maintains its principal place of business; and is in compliance with the applicable net capital or bonding requirements of the State in which it maintains its principal place of business
    C. both A and B
    D. neither A nor B

21. **Which of the following investments are most likely suitable for JoAnn, a 72-year-old investor living on a state teacher's pension?**
    I. Variable annuity
    II. Treasury Bond
    III. Treasury Note
    IV. Aggressive Growth Fund

    A. II, IV only
    B. III only
    C. I, II, III only
    D. II, III

22. **Jill, an investment representative for Broker-Dealer XYZ, is meeting with a 73-year-old client who is a retired school teacher. The client has been investing with Jill for 3 years now and the two have developed a good business relationship over that time. This morning Jill hands her client a prospectus for a variable annuity and tells her that the variable annuity is an ideal investment because it offers excellent liquidity and provides a stream of income to cover medical expenses that can and do often arise for retired investors. Which of the following statements best explains this situation?**
    A. senior citizens should never buy variable annuities; only fixed annuities are appropriate
    B. as long as the prospectus is provided, Jill is making a suitable recommendation
    C. variable annuities are typically not suitable investments for senior investors, who may need to withdraw funds to cover medical expenses when those withdrawals will be reduced by surrender charges
    D. as long as Jill's principal has approved the recommendation, Jill is making a suitable presentation to her client

23. Melanie Moore is a sales agent for Winthrop Securities, a broker-dealer registered in the state. Melanie is trying to decide which securities investments to recommend to her clients. Which of the following statements best addresses Melanie's decision?

A. Melanie should recommend the lowest-risk investments to most of her clients, specifically direct obligations of the U.S. Government

B. Melanie should recommend the mutual fund that performed the best last year to most of her clients

C. Melanie should recommend variable annuities—which pay the highest commission—to most of her clients, especially those past the age of 65

D. Melanie should generally not recommend variable annuities to her senior investors due to the high commissions paid and the high surrender charges

24. An issuer of securities may need to register all of the following investments with the state securities Administrator EXCEPT:

A. interest in a profit-sharing arrangement

B. ATM contract

C. NASDAQ stock

D. non-NASDAQ OTC stock

25. Which of the following offers of securities is most likely acceptable?

A. earn double-digit returns on this unregistered promissory note

B. invest in Treasury bonds, which bear no default risk but do carry certain risks such as inflation and interest-rate risk

C. earn double-digit returns on this registered promissory note

D. if you have a low risk tolerance, you should consider risk-free guaranteed high-yield instruments

26. **Charlie Rosen has been in the oil & gas exploration industry for three decades, starting out as a geophysicist and now focusing primarily on capital formation for new ventures. Recently, Charlie sold interests in a natural gas field located in Kansas to 25 investors located in the states of Kansas, Arkansas, and Oklahoma. In his offering documents, Charlie disclosed that profits from the gas field would be distributed monthly and would be treated as a royalty distribution from profits. As it turns out, the gas field has yielded no natural gas in its first year of exploration. Charlie mails a report to the investors and attaches a check of $1,500 each, which he characterizes as profits from production. Which of the following statements best addresses this situation?**

    A.   oil and gas interests are generally not suitable investments

    B.   as long as the investors receive profit distributions, it is immaterial whether the distributions are, in fact, paid from profits

    C.   by distributing the check and characterizing it as a profit distribution, Charlie has misled investors and may be investigated for fraud

    D.   since the investors were located in more than one state, there was no need to register the securities

27. **An investment adviser explains to several clients that a particular government bond mutual fund is suitable as a long-term investment but not a short-term investment due to a contingent deferred sales charge starting at 7%. The adviser has discretion over the client accounts but has gone out of his way to disclose the contingent deferred sales charge. This week, five investors call to liquidate their holdings in the fund, and the investment adviser refuses to comply with the requests. Which of the following represents a true statement?**

    A.   as an investment adviser with discretion, the adviser may refuse to sell/liquidate the holdings

    B.   as long as the contingent deferred sales charge was disclosed, the adviser, as a fiduciary, may refuse these transactions, which are clearly not in the best interest of the clients

    C.   the adviser may attempt to dissuade the investors, but, failing to convince them, should comply with the requests to liquidate the holdings

    D.   the adviser, as a fiduciary, must refuse these transactions, which are clearly not in the best interest of the clients

28. **What is true of a broker-dealer's authority over outside activities of their agents?**
    A.   the firm has no such authority
    B.   the firm must be informed only if compensation exceeds $100 annually
    C.   the firm must be notified of, and may reject, an agent's decision to work outside the firm for compensation
    D.   the firm must be notified of, but may not reject, an agent's decision to work outside the firm for compensation

29. **A registered representative notices that several emails to a client have been rejected due to a filter the client has set up on his email program. The representative makes several phone calls and finally leaves a voice mail asking the client to call, but the client does not. The client is a growth investor, and this morning the registered representative sees an opportunity in a growth stock he and the client have been discussing. In order to get through the client's email filter, the registered representative changes the name of the broker-dealer to the bank the client uses, which was provided on the new account form. In this situation the agent has**
    A.   acted appropriately
    B.   acted appropriately by making several telephone calls before altering the name of the firm
    C.   acted improperly
    D.   acted improperly by calling the client

30. **The Administrator may deny a security's registration for which of the following reasons?**
    I.   The issuer's operations are illegal where performed
    II.   The company has not been paying dividends
    III. A court in another state has issued a restraining order preventing the offer in that state only

    A.   I only
    B.   I, III only
    C.   I, II, III
    D.   II only

31. An agent may offer or sell a security in a state if the security is

    A.   federal covered

    B.   exempt from registration

    C.   registered under the Uniform Securities Act

    D.   all of the above

32. All of the following statements concerning securities registrations are true except

    A.   the registration statement must specify the amount of securities, states in which the offering is to be made, and any adverse order or judgment by a regulatory authority

    B.   the Administrator may rule that the securities registered by coordination or qualification may only be sold on a specified form of subscription

    C.   the Administrator may not deny the registration due to excessive underwriter compensation

    D.   the Administrator may by rule permit omission of any item of information or document from any registration statement

33. Securities of all the following issuers are exempt under the Uniform Securities Act except

    A.   state banks

    B.   national banks

    C.   savings institutions

    D.   bank holding companies

34. Which of the following transactions is/are exempt from the state's filing requirements and anti-fraud rules?

    A.   isolated non-issuer transactions in outstanding securities

    B.   transactions between an issuer and an institutional investor

    C.   both A and B

    D.   neither A nor B

35. A "non-issuer transaction" is best represented by which of the following?

    A.   additional offering of stock three years following the IPO

    B.   secondary offering

    C.   an offer that provides capital to an expanding corporation

    D.   an offer that provides capital to an issuer and certain large shareholders

36. Registration by coordination is possible under which of the following?

A.   Securities Act of 1933

B.   National Securities Markets Improvement Act

C.   Securities Exchange Act of 1934

D.   Trust Indenture Act of 1939

37. When an investment adviser acts as a broker to the seller and adviser to the buyer, this is

A.   an agency cross transaction, subject to certain required disclosures

B.   a prohibited practice known as "selling away"

C.   a prohibited practice known as "pegging"

D.   an exempt transaction

38. Which of the following determines the fairness of a markup on a "principal transaction" executed by a broker-dealer?

A.   highest asked price

B.   highest bid price

C.   lowest bid price

D.   lowest asked price

39. A customer has $5,000 to invest but will not provide an investment representative with information on her previous investment experience. Therefore the representative

A.   may recommend only growth stocks

B.   may recommend a U.S. Government Money Market Fund

C.   may recommend only municipal bonds issued within the state of residence

D.   must refrain from recommending any security

40. Unless renewed, registrations for persons registered under the Uniform Securities Act

A.   expire December 31st

B.   are revoked

C.   expire one year from the date of the person's registration

D.   none of the above

41. **A non-discretionary customer of a broker-dealer tells her registered representative to sell 200 shares of ABC if the stock continues to drop. When the stock drops, the representative sells 100 shares, choosing to wait to sell the rest at a more favorable price. This activity**

    A.   is fraudulent on the part of the registered representative

    B.   is fraudulent on the part of the broker-dealer

    C.   is an example of a violation of rules on discretionary orders

    D.   represents a normal, permissible activity in the brokerage business

42. **An out-of-state adviser will not have to register in the state if it does not direct business communications to**

    I.   More than 7 non-institutional clients

    II.   More than 5 non-institutional clients

    III.   Within 9 consecutive months

    IV.   Within 12 consecutive months

    A.   I, III

    B.   I, IV

    C.   II, IV

    D.   II, III

43. **All of the following statements concerning broker-dealers are true except**

    A.   a broker-dealer is defined as a person in the business of effecting transactions in securities for the accounts of others or its own account

    B.   a broker-dealer can not be a natural person

    C.   a broker-dealer is a legal person

    D.   broker-dealer properly registered in Maine may effect securities transactions with 15 banks and/or pension funds located in Virginia without having to register in Virginia

44. **An agent may make recommendations based on**

    A.   rumors

    B.   carefully researched inside information

    C.   information obtained while working in a fiduciary capacity

    D.   none of the above

45. **Which of the following are defined as "offers" under the Uniform Securities Act?**

  A.   the delivery of a prospectus

  B.   calling a customer and informing him that you may only sell XYZ on an unsolicited basis, should he be interested in the stock

  C.   an agent fails to sell a security

  D.   all of the above

46. **Which of the following represent exempt transactions?**

  I.   U.S. Government securities

  II.   Private placements

  III. Offerings of pre-organization certificates to 10 buyers in the state

  IV.   Municipal bonds

  A.   II, III only

  B.   I, IV only

  C.   I, II, III, IV

  D.   IV only

47. **Which of the following would require a specific response from the Administrator?**

  A.   registration by coordination

  B.   notice filing

  C.   registration by filing

  D.   registration by qualification

48. **If a broker-dealer's license is revoked, what is true of the licenses of agents working at the firm?**

  A.   they are no longer in effect

  B.   the state will appoint a local broker-dealer to oversee the agents

  C.   the agents' licenses are held in escrow

  D.   the agents' licenses may continue to sell on an unsolicited basis only

49. **An investment adviser is considered to have custody of client funds in all of the following situations except**

  A.   the firm forwards a client's check to a 3rd party within 24 hours of receipt

  B.   the firm has the ability to deduct fees from the client's bank or brokerage account

  C.   the firm is holding the clients' securities for only three weeks

  D.   the firm is holding the clients' cash and securities for only three days

50. **Which of the following must register as an investment adviser in the state?**

   A.   Joe Williams, an agent for XYZ Securities, has an active financial planning business that he conducts outside the scope of his employment at XYZ

   B.   A lawyer occasionally discusses the value of her clients' securities when putting together trusts

   C.   An accountant regularly advises clients to make IRA and 401K contributions while preparing their taxes

   D.   Jennifer Williamson is an investment adviser representative for a federal covered adviser located in the state

51. **After an agent passes both her license exams she may begin selling securities**

   A.   immediately

   B.   with approval from a principal at the firm

   C.   when she has been granted a license by the Administrator

   D.   when she receives SEC approval

52. **Jerome Lansky has passed both his Series 6 and Series 63 exam and is awaiting the issuance of his license by the securities Administrator of the state. At this point Jerome may**

   A.   accept unsolicited orders only

   B.   offer and sell securities

   C.   sell only exempt securities

   D.   do none of the above

53. **Which of the following would be considered the least important information to a prospective investor in an offer of securities?**

   A.   the issuer currently has an employee benefit plan

   B.   the issuer's products require heavy investments in research and development

   C.   the issuer competes with several larger, better capitalized entities

   D.   the issuer's products are the subject of investigation by several state attorneys general

54. **If a security is exempt from registration requirements, it is also exempt from**

   A.   the state's anti-fraud provisions

   B.   civil liabilities provisions

   C.   the filing of sales literature and advertising

   D.   all of the above

55. All of the following securities are exempt from state registration requirements except

    A.   stock listed on the American Stock Exchange (AMEX)

    B.   bond issued by a company with stock listed on the NYSE

    C.   a NASDAQ stock

    D.   bank holding company preferred stock

56. Which of the following would most likely cause a private placement to lose its exemption?

    A.   the securities are offered to more than 10 institutional buyers

    B.   a commission is paid to the agents who sell the offering

    C.   buyers are required to meet certain net worth requirement

    D.   buyers are asked to sign a statement expressing their good faith intent to hold the security at least one calendar year

57. Which of the following must register as an investment adviser in the state?

    A.   an attorney who writes a legal opinion for a municipal bond issue

    B.   an individual representing a federal covered adviser

    C.   a broker-dealer whose advice is incidental to the course of their business and charges no special compensation

    D.   an adviser in the state whose only clients are banks and savings institutions

58. All of the following represent market manipulation except

    A.   two active securities traders agree to buy and sell 100 shares of XYZ between themselves in 10 separate transactions throughout the day

    B.   two active securities traders agree to place large purchase orders on ABC, a thinly-traded Bulletin Board stock, at the same time several times throughout the day

    C.   a specialist buys and sells securities for his own account throughout the day

    D.   pegging

59. When a security is sold under an exemption from registration under the Uniform Securities Act, the burden of proof for the exemption is imposed on:

    A.   the Administrator

    B.   the person claiming the exemption

    C.   any person bringing a lawsuit against the seller

    D.   the purchaser

60. Which of the following represent(s) accurate statements concerning provisions of the Uniform Securities Act?

I. An exempt security is not subject to anti-fraud statutes

II. A fixed annuity is subject to anti-fraud statutes

III. Both exempt and non-exempt securities are subject to anti-fraud statutes

IV. If the security is exempt, the agent representing the broker-dealer does not need to register

A. I, II only

B. II, III only

C. III only

D. I, IV only

ANSWERS TO PRACTICE FINAL 2

1.   **ANSWER:** D

     EXPLANATION: you may have noticed that many of our practice questions are simply presenting three or four new concepts to learn. Our questions are not designed to be tricky or misleading, except for the tricky, misleading ones.

2.   **ANSWER:** C

     EXPLANATION: a federal covered security would include the stock that trades on NYSE, AMEX, NASDAQ, or any other exchange that the SEC decides has listing standards equal or higher to those three. And, any security senior to common stock (preferred, bonds) would be federal covered if the common stock is federal covered. While the commercial paper would be exempt, as long as the maturity is 270 days or less, that's not quite the same thing as "federal covered."

3.   **ANSWER:** C

     EXPLANATION: the other three choices are clearly federal covered securities. The stock is either listed on NYSE, AMEX, or NASDAQ, or will trade there when the IPO is completed. And, the preferred stock and bonds of those issuers would also be federal covered. Also, mutual funds and variable contracts are federal covered securities.

4.   **ANSWER:** D

     EXPLANATION: just three things to keep in mind, along with all the other stuff.

5.   **ANSWER:** C

     EXPLANATION: just another way to define a "federal covered adviser." I don't want to delve into how something can be "covered by exclusion." You're welcome.

6.   **ANSWER:** C

     EXPLANATION: memorize these examples of qualified purchasers, and remember the significance of a "qualified purchaser." They are sophisticated purchasers who can get in on private placements, hedge funds, and other things generally not open to the average Joe and JoAnn.

7. **ANSWER:** D

    EXPLANATION: choice D is trying to say the regulators would not make somebody register if he isn't already registered. Wait—the whole point of the release is to make people register.

8. **ANSWER:** C

    EXPLANATION: if the IA advises registered investment companies, he/she/they are federal covered. I'm not saying that the other choices would always register with the states—I'm saying they don't provide any definitive reason to deem them as "federal covered."

9. **ANSWER:** C

    EXPLANATION: a federal covered adviser still provides notice to the states where they have an office/do business. On their Form ADV, they check off the states who need to receive a copy of the form. Those states might also require notice filing fees, a consent to service of process, and U-4's for each IAR working at the firm. But, it's not like they have to register with the states or anything. Just a filing of notice, a "notice filing."

10. **ANSWER:** D

    EXPLANATION: four important things to know about registering an investment advisory business.

11. **ANSWER:** D

    EXPLANATION: a textbook definition of a notice filing for a federal covered IA.

12. **ANSWER:** C

    EXPLANATION: a third-party check should be forwarded to the third party it's made out to. But, send the securities back to the client; otherwise, the IA had custody of them.

13. **ANSWER:** B

    EXPLANATION: a "place of business" is any place where business is conducted. Joshua is conducting business in State B, so he has to register there. The question does not clarify whether the clients are residents of State B. Remember that the de minimis exemption only works if the adviser or adviser rep does not have a place of business in the state.

14. **ANSWER:** A

EXPLANATION: in other words, the IA had better not say, "Hmm, now that the stock has jumped considerably, how could we best benefit ourselves?"

15. **ANSWER:** D

EXPLANATION: IAs need to be really careful when they advertise their performance. The period covered should be at least one year. It needs to be clear if advisory fees are being deducted from the results. And you have to show the whole picture—rather than touting the one profitable stock pick you managed to snag after picking the other 999 losers.

16. **ANSWER:** B

EXPLANATION: trade tickets should be market as solicited, unsolicited, or discretionary. To mark the ticket "unsolicited" indicates that the customer called in the order when, in fact, the firm used its discretion. The margin agreement has to be signed promptly after the first transaction in the account.

17. **ANSWER:** C

EXPLANATION: many, many questions will be answered correctly simply because you're a good reader and a good test-taker. If that didn't work here, look at what's going on a little closer. An IA is figuring out his performance fees in choice "A." If the custodian says the portfolio is worth $1 million, is it okay to let the dude calculating his performance fees decide the portfolio is really worth more than that, especially with no independent review? If you excluded the other choice, that's not a good sign. You simply have to be a better test-taker than that, and I mean no offense. I'm just saying that you'll pass the 63 by using reasoning skills and going with likely answers. If you read that one as somehow being unimportant, well, please call us or send an email.

18. **ANSWER:** D

EXPLANATION: never act as a custodian for customer funds, and never deposit customer funds in your own account (commingling). Broker-dealer agents don't enjoy the de minimis exemption that advisers and IARs enjoy. Written complaints must be forwarded to the supervisor/principal promptly. A financial quarter is roughly 91 days long, so the complaints would be a bit old by the time they reached the supervisor's desk, right?

19. **ANSWER:** C

EXPLANATION: variable annuities are both insurance products and securities, so they would both need to be securities licensed in both states.

20. **ANSWER:** B

EXPLANATION: something more to memorize for the test. And, it basically makes sense. If the IA is properly registered in, say, Michigan and complies with all of Michigan's net worth/bonding requirements, the other states where it does business can't raise the bar on them. Of course, if the firm were not in compliance with Michigan's requirements, that would be different.

21. **ANSWER:** D

EXPLANATION: no need for the aggressive growth opportunity—any mutual fund prospectus would tell you that a long time horizon and a high risk tolerance are required for those. How about some nice, guaranteed interest payments from Uncle Sam?

22. **ANSWER:** C

EXPLANATION: most annuities have surrender periods in which the investor would be nailed for 7% on down for any early withdrawals. Also note that a principal's signature is a not a magic cure-all. Just means that he, too, can get in trouble. And handing a prospectus to a client doesn't relieve you of helping to determine suitability. You have to deliver a prospectus. And, you have to recommend suitable investments.

23. **ANSWER:** D

EXPLANATION: if everybody invested in safe, guaranteed securities, how would we grow our capital for retirement? In the money market? Earn 3% interest minus .75% expense ratios? Also, last year's hot fund is seldom this year's hottest fund. You could lose a ton of money investing in last year's hottest funds, and, please, do not attempt to prove me wrong.

24. **ANSWER:** C

EXPLANATION: only the NASDAQ stock is federal covered.

25. **ANSWER:** B

EXPLANATION: risk-free simply can't go together with "high yield." Double-digit is pretty vague, since the difference between 10% and 99% would be rather significant. Don't offer unregistered notes, and I don't see why a promissory note should have to pay huge amounts of interest . . . unless the whole thing is a scam where you never intend to pay anybody back, thereby making triple-digit returns of 100% for yourself.

26. **ANSWER:** C

    EXPLANATION: by now, this should simply look like the right answer to you. If you chose the one that said, basically, "Hey, look, as long as you pay 'em, who cares?" that's a good indicator that compliance is not going to be a major component of your career path. Oil and gas programs are perfectly suitable for a select group of investors—those who can laugh off big six-figure losses and are looking for tax shelter.

27. **ANSWER:** C

    EXPLANATION: I don't know WHY a mutual fund needs a 7% contingent deferred sales charge, but the IA did explain this should be a long-term holding, as anyone holding long-term bonds needs to understand. Now, it's still the clients' money, so if they want to liquidate and pay the back-end sales charges, try to talk them out of it. But, ultimately, it's their money. The regulators can protect the clients from smarmy professionals, but they can't protect the investors from their own stupidity.

28. **ANSWER:** C

    EXPLANATION: broker-dealers must not only be notified when an agent thinks he's going to work outside the firm for compensation, but also they have the authority to restrict or put the brakes on such activity.

29. **ANSWER:** C

    EXPLANATION: to get around the client's email filter, I'll pretend I'm the bank. Hmm, that's okay, right? As long as the client ends up buying a good stock, right?

30. **ANSWER:** B

    EXPLANATION: lots of great companies do not pay dividends. They can do share buybacks, instead, which tends to raise the EPS and, therefore, the share price of the stock. Or, they can use their profits in many other constructive ways. The state just wants to make sure nothing funky is going on—are a couple of underwriters going to make a huge amount of money selling overpriced securities to unsuspecting investors? If so, no go.

31. **ANSWER:** D

   EXPLANATION: the security is either registered or not required to register. If it's required to be registered (non-exempt), and you offer/sell it even though it is unregistered, you have just offered/sold and unregistered, non-exempt security. Try not to do that if you can help it.

32. **ANSWER:** C

   EXPLANATION: the state usually wants to see the underwriting agreement between the issuer and underwriters, plus the agreement among the underwriters. If it looks like the securities offering is mostly designed to make a few broker-dealers rich and leave investors with overpriced securities, it doesn't pass the smell test.

33. **ANSWER:** D

   EXPLANATION: bank securities are regulated by bank regulators. A bank holding company registers just like any other corporation.

34. **ANSWER:** D

   EXPLANATION: read carefully. If it's a security, it's subject to anti-fraud rules.

35. **ANSWER:** B

   EXPLANATION: the word "secondary" means that the proceeds go to someone other than the issuer. The word "primary" means that the issuer receives the proceeds, the "capital."

36. **ANSWER:** A

   EXPLANATION: the issuer registers with the SEC under the Securities Act of 1933, then coordinates the registration with the state regulators.

37. **ANSWER:** A

   EXPLANATION: why would there be required disclosures? Because the customer might wonder if this is a good recommendation or maybe the IA just wants to make a commission for also brokering the trade. Whenever there is motivation for the adviser to get the customer to accept the advice, we have a potential conflict of interest that must be disclosed.

38. **ANSWER:** D

   EXPLANATION: the "inside" or "inter-dealer market" is the highest bid and lowest asked/offer price. The amount that a firm charges a customer above the lowest asked price is considered the amount the security was "marked up." If the markup is excessive, the broker-dealer is subject to disciplinary action. Similarly, when the firm buys securities from a customer, the amount of the markdown is the amount the customer received below the highest bid price.

39. **ANSWER:** B

EXPLANATION: a truly stupid question. You wouldn't even "recommend" a US Government money market fund—the un-invested cash would simply be "swept" into it. This way, it's a security for purposes of SIPC protection, and the investor makes insulting little rates of interest on the safest securities known to humankind until she decides to buy stocks, bonds, growth funds, value funds, etc.

40. **ANSWER:** A

EXPLANATION: registrations for persons (agent, broker-dealer, IA, IAR) expire at the end of each calendar year and must be renewed by paying a fee. Registrations for securities are effective for one year from the effective date.

41. **ANSWER:** C

EXPLANATION: you have to have discretion before choosing ANY of the "three A's." The "three A's" are Asset/Activity/Amount. This registered representative chose the Amount (of shares) when he didn't have discretion.

42. **ANSWER:** C

EXPLANATION: some things are simply memorization points. This is one of those.

43. **ANSWER:** B

EXPLANATION: use process of elimination. I'm not trying to say that you absolutely must know a broker-dealer could be a natural person (human being). I'm just making you use process of elimination. Also, the number 15 was not significant. You were just supposed to read that choice and decide if it was a true statement or not. Weed out the wrong answers—the one you can't eliminate is the answer. Keep moving. This nightmare will be over soon.

44. **ANSWER:** D

EXPLANATION: a good test-taker would have snagged this one. If you missed this question, that makes me very nervous.

45. **ANSWER:** D

EXPLANATION: every attempt to dispose of a security for value, or every attempt to talk someone into offering to buy a security would be an offer. Which means the security needs to be registered and the one making the offer needs to mind his p's and q's.

46. **ANSWER:** A

EXPLANATION: just a weasely question reminding you that there is a difference between a security and a transaction.

47. **ANSWER:** D

EXPLANATION: see, you never know how the question will be phrased, but if you reason through it, you say, "Well, which one gives the Administrator the most authority?" And, which word sounds like it does—qualification.

48. **ANSWER:** A

EXPLANATION: you're only an agent when you represent a broker-dealer registered under the Act. If the broker-dealer's license is suspended/revoked, it's time for you to find a new employer. Your license doesn't get suspended—that's a punishment that could lead to suspension/revocation in every other state. It's just time to U-5 out and U-4 into a new firm.

49. **ANSWER:** A

EXPLANATION: if it's a third-party check, the IA can't cash it. So, they don't have custody of the money as long as the check is forwarded within 24 hours. But, if they can deduct their fees out of the bank account, well, we sure hope they don't deduct a bit more than they should.

50. **ANSWER:** A

EXPLANATION: see how the question used the word "advises" in a misleading way?

51. **ANSWER:** C

EXPLANATION: the words "SEC" and "approval" don't go together.

52. **ANSWER:** D

EXPLANATION: don't offer or sell securities without a license, period.

53. **ANSWER:** A

EXPLANATION: why would investors care about employee benefits? Information on the company's products and competitors is always material.

54. **ANSWER:** C

EXPLANATION: that is all that the word "exempt" means. You don't have to register; you don't have to file sales literature, advertising, etc. But, the offer of securities is still subject to anti-fraud rules, meaning that people could still be sued and prosecuted, even though the security and the offering escaped registration requirements. Remember, if it is a "security," it is subject to anti-fraud rules. Fraudulent sales activities lead to civil liabilities and sometimes criminal prosecutions.

55. **ANSWER:** D

EXPLANATION: bank stock is exempt. Bank holding company securities are not excused from registration (non-exempt).

56. **ANSWER:** B

EXPLANATION: the number 10 is for the non-institutional buyers. If you're paying people commissions to find the non-institutional buyers, you'll lose your exemption.

57. **ANSWER:** D

EXPLANATION: read carefully. The fact that the adviser's clients are institutional only matters when they are out-of-state.

58. **ANSWER:** C

EXPLANATION: that's what a specialist does.

59. **ANSWER:** B

EXPLANATION: the Administrator does not have to prove why the security must be registered. Securities must be registered unless they are shown to be exempt by the one claiming the exemption.

60. **ANSWER:** C

EXPLANATION: if it's a security it is subject to anti-fraud rules. A fixed annuity is not a security. For purposes of agent registration, only ask if the security is exempt when the individual represents the issuer of that security

Index